Working with people in crisis
theory and practice

Working with people in crisis
theory and practice

Samuel L. Dixon, Ph.D.

College of Social Work, The Ohio State University,
Columbus, Ohio

Illustrated

The C. V. Mosby Company

ST. LOUIS · TORONTO · LONDON   1979

To our children
Samuel, Pamela, and Mark

Printed in the United States of America

The C. V. Mosby Company
11830 Westline Industrial Drive, St. Louis, Missouri 63141

Library of Congress Cataloging in Publication Data

Dixon, Samuel L   1934-
  Working with people in crisis.

  Bibliography: p.
  Includes index.
  1.   Crisis intervention (Psychiatry).   I.   Title.
RC480.6.D58   616.8'9   78-31227
ISBN 0-8016-1320-5

C/M/M   9 8 7 6 5 4 3 2 1   03/B/299

PREFACE

The demand for crisis intervention is growing exponentially as shown in the many crisis centers, suicide prevention centers, and telephone help lines that are springing up as well as the crisis units in community mental health clinics and social agencies. All of these centers need trained crisis counselors. In response to this growing demand, many articles (and a few books) on specific techniques for working with people in crisis have been written. However, there is still no comprehensive model of crisis intervention. What is needed is a basic guide to a fundamental body of knowledge and techniques of interventions to apply in helping people in crisis.

This book is designed to fill that gap. The purpose of this book is to provide both students and beginning practitioners with a unified conceptual framework of knowledge and methods of interventions basic to increasing effectiveness in working with people in crisis. The book relates crisis theory to the whole of human behavior, most notably by looking at the emotional and behavioral manifestations that are universally found in people in crisis.

The book is divided into two parts. Part I provides the conceptual framework and theoretical base. Although empathy alone is helpful in crisis intervention, it is even more effective when combined with relevant knowledge of human behavior. Part I covers fundamental knowledge that will help the intervenor to reduce the crippling effects of the client's excessive emotionality. Chapter 1 presents a definition of crisis and differentiates a crisis from an everyday problem. Chapter 2 discusses characteristics of human behavior on which intervention can be based. Rather than briefly discussing several theories of human behavior, this book considers only those human characteristics universally manifested by those in crisis. To be familiar with them is essential for anyone working with people in crisis. Understanding these common crisis manifestations transcends theoretical biases. Chapter 3 looks at interpersonal communication with an eye toward the interview, which is covered in more depth in Chapter 4. The discussion of communication and the initial interview is designed to give the therapist more conscious control over interviewing skills. It facilitates a better understanding of the interaction between therapist and client.

Part II focuses on the application of intervention skills and techniques. Using theoretical formulations as guidelines, Chapters 5 and 6 are designed to help readers develop their own intervention skills. Ample illustrations of common crisis situations are included, and methods of intervention are suggested. Chapter 7 discusses family and life crisis situations, specifically adolescence, middle age, and old age. At the end of each chapter, suggested readings refer the reader to more detailed sources on particular topics.

This book is written for those who work with people in crisis, specifically students in any of the human services and beginning practitioners working in crisis intervention centers, suicide prevention centers, and mental health clinics. Its content and organization are based on my years of experience in working with people in crisis, teaching graduate students, and presenting workshops and seminars for people with varied educational backgrounds. Because of the variation in education and training of those working with people in crisis, fairly detailed knowledge of human behavior relevant to this process is presented. For some it may serve as a review, for others it may be new. Helping professionals should have a thorough understanding of human behavior before beginning to work with people in crisis.

The case illustrations included in this book are from many different records and settings. Names have been changed and situations disguised. If they seem recognizable, it is because of the universality of human experiences and reactions.

Many have contributed to the completion of this book. I would like to express my appreciation to just a few who have been of very special aid: Mrs. Frances S. Margolin, whose assistance was greatly appreciated; Dr. Rocco D'Angelo and Dr. Richard Medhurst, whose support and encouragement will always be cherished; Dr. Robert C. Trojanowicz, Michigan State University and co-author of our book *Criminal Justice and the*

Community; and Dr. Gordon Hopper and Dr. Dominic Pellegrino, Iowa State University.

Finally, I wish to thank my family, especially my wife Clara, for her understanding and support during the completion of this book.

Samuel L. Dixon

Note to instructors

Students learning to work effectively with people in crisis need to gain the skill and confidence that come from trying out the theory by applying it in practice situations. Role playing is a technique that allows students to practice their skills in class and receive feedback from instructor and fellow students. Students can play the roles of clients and workers in a variety of crisis situations, or actors and actresses may join the class to play out crises in which students can intervene. Scenarios can be drawn from case write-ups or from students' practice or practicum experience.

CONTENTS

Part I

CONCEPTUAL FRAMEWORK AND THEORETICAL BASE

CHAPTER 1

Concept of crisis

■ Joanne, a 29-year-old woman who had been divorced twice, came to a crisis center after the sudden and unexpected death of her third husband. She felt she could no longer go on living. Although her first two marriages had ended in divorce, this third marriage, which lasted 2 years before her husband died, was one of unusual happiness. She credited a sense of personal salvation to this relationship. With her husband dead, Joanne was now extremely depressed. Before she came to the crisis center, she had left the house only to go to the cemetery. Although she tried to forestall her progressive depression, she finally became deeply despairing and prepared to take her own life. Recognizing that her deceased husband would not want her to be that "weak," Joanne sought help at the crisis center. Following several sessions with the crisis therapist, her depression lifted and she returned to work and continued the normal grieving process without the extreme debilitation she had been feeling. About 2 months later her father died, also suddenly and unexpectedly. Again she handled the situation alone as long as she could before returning to the crisis center. This time it was not the loss that overtaxed her strength but the additional demands that her grieving mother now placed on her. A second therapist reached out to the mother and lightened the load on Joanne so that she could continue to function at her usual satisfactory level. In addition the mother was helped through this stressful period, and a crisis was averted.

■ Martha, a 25-year-old married woman well along in her first pregnancy, came to a crisis center pleading for relief from tormenting fears. She was afraid that she was going to die and that her unborn child would be born deformed or handicapped. These suspicions made her afraid that she was going to lose her mind. The terrifying feelings had started immediately after she learned she was pregnant.

■ Richard, a 37-year-old executive, called a crisis center because he felt overwhelmed by feelings of rage, frustration, disappointment, and resentment. His emotions were keeping him from carrying out his normal responsibilities. These feelings had begun shortly after he was passed over for a higher position that he felt he deserved because of his experience and ability. The job was given to a less experienced and capable man. Richard expressed feelings of personal failure and dejection. He said that he was so hurt by this rejection that he could not bear the pain. It was a violent attack on his self-esteem and pride.

Joanne, Martha, and Richard each went through a crisis—an increasingly common occurrence. Probably no subject of study is more applicable today than the study of crisis. The combination of human nature and the hazardous, uncertain, and anxiety-ridden world we live in increases the likelihood that everyone will face some situation that is potentially crisis producing. However, crisis is not new; it has always been a part of human existence.

In fact, human beings are born in a state of crisis—the birth trauma. From the very moment of birth, many of our efforts are intended to avoid crisis. Because neither human nature nor the external environment allows the needs, desires, and goals of any one person to be achieved unequivocally, people inevitably experience stress and strain (Erikson, 1959). But we are also endowed with the capacity to adapt to our environment so that we pursue goals that fit our society, goals that are socially determined. To this end we develop habitual patterns of adaptation as we grow up and are socialized into our culture. Habitual patterns of adaptation as used here means the human being's actions and reactions. It refers to a person's customary ways of functioning, including goals and values. It includes the ways in which people maintain control of themselves in relation to the environment. In sum, it is synonymous with personality.

We go along in our lives, taking for granted our ability to respond to the world and to solve problems, until something happens to interfere. Upsetting events—natural catastrophies, illnesses, separations, deaths, personal losses—have always been part of living. But there used to be other people (extended family, close friends) to step in and help an individual with a problem. People have traditionally intervened to help each other during times of crisis.

The systematic approach by professionals to helping people in crisis is relatively new. Its origin is credited to Lindemann (1944) and Caplan (1964). (The works of these men are so well known that they need not be reviewed here.) Since these two pioneers wrote the initial descriptions of the process, crisis intervention has grown enormously as a treatment modality. Its growth is attributed to several factors. First, there has been an increase in public acceptance of the idea of turning to professionals for help. At the same time there seem to be more potentially crisis-producing events than ever. Conflicts in the schools over desegregation, changing social roles, inflation, and increased crimes against individuals all can lead to a personal crisis. And we are placing greater emphasis on individuation, on the individual's "right" to achieve a personal goal. We are increasingly competitive; we face more open conflict than ever before, and hence greater tension and stress. At the same time we are more mobile. Few of us live in large, supportive, extended families; many of us are geographically separated from family and close, lifelong friends to whom we can turn for emotional support and actual help.

A second reason for the popularity of crisis intervention therapy was proposed by Lindemann and Caplan: we have come to see that intervention at the point of crisis can prevent later serious mental breakdown or the development of maladaptive patterns of behavior.

Third, crisis intervention techniques, skillfully applied, have been found to be effective with people in crisis regardless of their background or previous history. This claim has not always been accepted by mental health professionals whose traditional interest was in psychopathology. Crisis theory was based on the study of the behavior of people with no known history of psychological malady, that is, the study of adaptive and maladaptive reactions of "normal" people to accidental or natural catastrophes (Lindemann, 1944). Therefore many professionals assumed that crisis theory was not applicable to people with a history of psychopathology. Although they were working with people whose behaviors were characteristic of those in crisis, their original assumptions and definitions prevented them from applying crisis techniques with their clients. No doubt they were handling crises that they referred to as "emergencies." The relatively recent acceptance of crisis theory as a bona fide treatment modality has expanded the whole concept of mental health. Services are now available to more people than ever before.

CRISIS THEORY

Crisis theory is based on a holistic concept of personality, where personality is seen as always evolving through experience. The accumulated life experiences, from birth through adulthood, result in an organized psychic system. Each individual's psychic system is dynamic; it is influenced by biological, psychological, and sociological experiences and events. The psychic system could also be called the *ego*, the *self*, or simply a set of learned patterns of thinking and behaving that are the result of the socialization process. This concept implies the influence and inseparable relationship between the human being and the environment.

To understand this better, let us briefly look at the development of the psychic system (see also Chapter 2). Human infants are born helpless but with a set of biological reflexes that help them survive by communicating their needs to a parent or other caretaker. Most infants also have capacities that ultimately will let them function independently. The child's ability to function independently grows according to his or her individual maturational and developmental schedule. But not only do human infants need another person to take care of basic survival needs, they also need someone to stimulate their innate capacities for independent social functioning. Furthermore, the direction of individual development is also determined by the social environment. In sum, the human being is biologically endowed to function independently, but the specific way any individual does function is determined by psychosocial experiences within the specific environment.

The human capacities of adaptation—perception, memory, intelligence, mobility, emotions, consciousness, and purpose—enable individuals to retain and recall experiences so that they can organize their emotions and intellect into specific and habitual patterns of social functioning. In this regard each person brings to each new situation a set of responses, needs, feelings, attitudes, values, and expectations, all the result of unique life experiences that are both personal and interpersonal. The psychic system, values, and goals of every person are different from those of every other person because life experiences, social environments, and ways of learning are different. Thus each person's perceptions, psychic reality, and reactions to various stimuli and events also differ. Any two people, even identical twins, will experience the same situation differently.

Satisfying needs

The foundation stimulus of all human behavior is survival (Hartmann, 1958). If life is endangered, all other needs pale in comparison, and the degree of satisfaction of survival needs influences the degree to which a person is able to concentrate on psychosocially determined needs. In other words, the degree to which people can concentrate on higher processes is determined in part by whether they must worry about survival. If survival is threatened, even a well-adjusted person experiences a crisis, and *the threat does not have to be real in fact but only perceived as real.*

When survival is not threatened or in question, psychosocially determined needs are more important. They can, and often do, assume value as high as survival. The cases of Joanne, Martha, and Richard illustrate how important psychological needs can become.

When the human being's survival needs are adequately satisfied, the process of qualitative psychic development can take place. Consequently parents and significant others are very important in the functioning of the child's psychic system. As infants mature, they learn quickly that parents are the source of satisfaction of their survival needs; dependence on parents produces a life-or-death attachment. As infants grow, they begin to recognize that to maintain parental love, affection, and protection parents must be pleased. Thus the child's psychosocial needs such as love, respect, recognition, and security assume primary importance when the child is confident that survival needs will be satisfied. In effect, survival needs become secondary until the child perceives them to be threatened. Another need that develops as survival and love needs are met is the need for achievement or self-fulfillment. This develops with age and experience. By the time people reach adulthood, they have accumulated a unique psychic system that reflects all self-perceptions and perceptions of the environment.

This idiosyncratic process creates the variations we see in how people behave. Most important, each individual evolves a system that functions in habitual ways to meet personal needs and goals, to meet the demands and limitations of the social environment, and to resolve everyday problems. In general this personal system keeps people in relative equilibrium and enables them to restore equilibrium when it is upset.

Because there are always many internal and external stimuli in people's lives, temporary disequilibrium or upset is common, so common that it can be regarded as part of the human condition. To react to conflicting stimuli, an individual simply uses habitual patterns of adaptation to restore equilibrium, then sets about resolving the next conflict or meeting the next need. Each person learns techniques to cope with stress that allow him or her to carry out daily responsibilities while attempting to maintain internal constancy.

The process of maintaining psychic equilibrium is called homeostasis, a process that is so much a part of life that it is probably taken for granted. Many people are unaware of the ways in which they attempt to maintain homeostasis. But just ask yourself: What do you do most often when you are angry? When you are depressed? How do you get over upsetting feelings? Whatever you do is the way you restore and maintain equilibrium.

Restoring equilibrium while satisfying a multitude of needs and reacting to conflicting stimuli is the basis of all social functioning. The degree to which a person is successful in this process is a very important measure of social functioning, since emotional upset interferes with effectiveness. Because there are so many different things to react to, most people develop patterns that let them react to a whole class of things in similar ways. These familiar patterns help keep emotional upset to manageable proportions. When a person cannot keep emotional upset manageable, when none of the usual ways of responding works, two conditions can result: (1) a crisis that is successfully resolved or (2) an unresolved crisis that leads to the development of new, maladaptive patterns.

To sum up, a human being's emotional state is constantly changing. In graphic terms we can think of a perfect emotional life with no stress as a straight line. As shown in Fig. 1, we would expect that most people would waver above and below the baseline most of the time. We can call this state *average expectable behavior* (term adapted from Hartmann [1958], Concept of Average Expectable Environment). The term *average expectable behavior* is a more accurate term than *normal,* as many deviations from average are "normal." Note that the length of time that a person is at a steady state, exactly on the baseline, is very short.

Some people's behavior deviates from average expectable behavior to

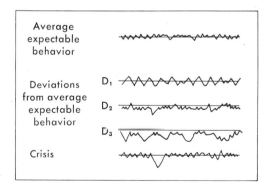

Fig. 1. Degrees of social functioning.

such an extent that they would be traditionally thought to show clinical syndromes. D_1 corresponds to the clinical syndrome or diagnostic categories commonly called psychoneuroses (neuroses), D_2 to personality disorders, and D_3 to psychoses. Historically these terms have been used to describe the varying degrees of psychopathology, sometimes called mental illness and often referred to in psychology books as abnormal psychology. The common basis of psychopathology is faulty personality development. In simple terms this means that the socialization process (i. e., the satisfaction of needs for love, security, acceptance, recognition, and guidance in a social environment responsible for the nature of interpersonal relationships and opportunities for self-fulfillment) was not conducive to the development of a psychic system that enables the individual to function adequately in a variable social environment; that is, to satisfy personal needs and goals within the limitations, expectations, and demands of the social environment. Consequently, patterns of thinking, feeling, and behaving characteristic of the clinical syndromes are developed as a compromise effort to meet personal and common human needs, to adapt to the social environment (regardless of how maladaptive), and most important, to prevent total personality disintegration. It should be remembered that although patterns of human behavior can be identified and classified, behavior is best represented by the concept of a continuum. This means that all human beings experience the same feelings and behavior; the difference is in quantity, not in kind. In other words, everyone at some time or another will experience feelings or behavior characteristic of the clinical syndromes. However, to temporarily experience such behavior is not the same as being psychoneurotic, having a personality disorder, or being psychotic. To do so means that the person's habitual patterns of behavior are characterized by the clinical syndrome it represents. Of the clinical syndromes, the psychoneuroses are the least severe. They are characterized by such habitual, not transitory, patterns of behavior as anxiety, phobias, various obsessive-compulsive behaviors, depression, dissociation, and conversion. The latter is the process by which the mind makes a part of the body or body system dysfunctional in absence of organic cause. The functionally impaired body part or system represents symbolically the intrapsychic conflict. For example, to keep from testifying in a court of law against a friend under the threat of contempt, a person could functionally lose his or her voice. To be a conversion, no organic cause exists, which makes it different from the so-called psychosomatic conditions. The personality disorders are the bridge between psychoneuroses and psychoses. They are characterized by habitual acting out or impulsive, irresponsible, or antisocial behavior. The psychoses are the most severe. They are characterized by a break with reality and an almost subtotal psychic or personality disintegration, usually manifested by delusions and hallucinations. While actively psychotic such individuals generally require hospitalization. The term *mental illness* is more appropriately used for those experiencing psychoses than other clinical syndromes. It should be clear that a clinical syndrome's degree of interference with living varies from person to person depending on the nature of the social environment and the existence of certain events. The latter is the reason why many of the clinical syndromes are called *reactions* (e. g., anxiety reactions, depressive reactions). Some social environments prevent potential psychotic breakdowns, and conversely others contribute to psychotic breakdowns.

With this understanding of the clinical syndromes, let us return to Fig. 1. We can see that their variation in deviations from the solid line are greater and last longer than deviations in average expectable behavior.

In contrast, the crisis behavior line does not vary much from that of average expectable behavior until the occurrence of the event precipitating the crisis. At this point the emotional state drops way below the baseline. But once the crisis has passed, the graph returns to the average expectable behavior level.

WHAT IS A CRISIS?

Although the word *crisis* is extensively used, it is often misunderstood. Most people associate crisis with a temporary state of upset that exists while a problem is being solved. You hear people say such things as, "I had a crisis this morning" or "Bob is really upset." But as we have seen, being upset is an integral part of daily living. We deal with everyday stress with habitual patterns of adaptation and restore ourselves to maintain with some variability our usual level of social functioning. A true crisis occurs only when individuals find that they are unable to solve a problem by their usual problem-solving methods. As a consequence, personal upset increases until it is impossible to function as efficiently as before the problem occurred. We can define a crisis as a *functionally debilitating mental state resulting from the individual's reaction to some event perceived to be so dangerous that it leaves him or her feeling helpless and unable to cope effectively by usual methods.* Let us look at the four major elements of this definition.

Functionally debilitating mental state

The excessiveness of the response separates the individual in crisis from the temporarily upset person involved in solving a problem. For example, if a mechanical system malfunctioned during a space flight, the astronauts would probably become upset; that is, they would feel fear or anxiety, perspire profusely, have increased heart palpitations, and so forth. However, if the astronauts were still able to take the necessary measures to correct the situation and to make reasonable decisions in an effort to solve the problem, they would not be in crisis. On the other hand, if their emotional reaction was so excessive that they could not remember what to do and could not make reasonable decisions, they would be in crisis.

In other words, a person in crisis is unable to reason effectively. Thinking capacity is overwhelmed by the emotional response. On the other side of the coin, the occurrence of some events in life are so provocative that the appropriate emotional response can be of crisis proportions and not be abnormal, depending on the duration. For instance, the death of a loved one is so crucial that the person who does not feel extreme grief for a time can be in more serious trouble than someone with an excessive response.

Precipitating event

Each human being's capacity to tolerate stress and the pressures of life is finite and idiosyncratic. Under certain conditions or situations, everyone has a breaking point at which habitual patterns of adaptation and problem-solving methods are no longer effective in maintaining the usual degree of social functioning. A precipitating event in a crisis situation is always related to a perceived threat to survival or bodily integrity or to one or more psychosocial needs that have assumed a primary value. Consequently the idiosyncratic meaning of the precipitating event can only be found in the person's own reality, which houses his or her personal feelings, goals, expectations, and values, all determined by specific life experiences.

In some form a specific event almost always precipitates a crisis, even if the individual cannot readily identify the event. The cognitive processes of a person in crisis may be impaired to the point that the person is not aware of or cannot remember the precipitating event. Furthermore, the precipitating event could have occurred several weeks before the person becomes functionally impaired. For instance, Joanne's husband had died some time before she finally sought help. It is not unusual for a person who is already feeling overwhelmed to be unable to sort out the first link in this chainlike process. The search for a precipitating event, when it is not obvious, is a very important therapeutic process. Sometimes you may need to look at the events of several preceding weeks, although the precipitating event can usually be found to have occurred within 2 weeks of the crisis. As Bloom (1965) concludes:

The single most contributory variable involved in the crisis judgment in the present sample appears to be the experience of a precipitating event. On this basis, one could simply define the crisis state as inevitably following certain specified events.

If the functional debilitation is *not* related to a specific event, the excessive emotional response is probably a part of some clinical disorder (see Fig. 1).

However, there is some controversy in the literature on crisis intervention regarding whether a known precipitating event is necessary for the existence of a bona fide crisis. Bloom (1965) found that professional clinical judges reached greater agreement in defining a crisis when there was a known precipitating event than when it was unknown. Farberow (1967) believes that if all the components of a crisis are present except the known precipitating event, the person is probably experiencing psychiatric disorder. (But individuals with psychiatric disorders also develop crises.)

The idea of a precipitating event is central in the development of the theory of crisis, beginning with Lindemann (1944), who studied people's reactions to a catastrophic event (the Coconut Grove nightclub fire in Boston)—a known precipitating event. His work led to the recognition that any event that threatens human survival or significant needs or values can precipitate a state of crisis in any person, regardless of the person's psychological history. The theory has led to the idea that a crisis is a turning point that represents both a danger and an opportunity (Morley, 1970). The danger is that the person who does not resolve the crisis will develop a clinical psychological syndrome; the opportunity is for emotional growth as a result of successful learning from the experience.

Perceived meaning

Again, a crisis is a subjective state; it is the personal meaning attributed to the precipitating event that causes the person's excessive emotional state. While pregnancy precipitated a crisis for Martha, it does not for most women. In simple terms, a crisis is not caused by an event itself but is a reaction to an event. The point is that crisis conditions are subjectively and individually determined. Hence a crisis can only be understood from the frame of reference of the individual experiencing it.

Ineffective problem-solving methods

When habitual patterns of adaptation and coping mechanisms are no longer effective, the condition is a crisis. Although a crisis is an emotional condition, it reduces the individual's cognitive functioning (Taplin, 1971). This point is central to the treatment of a person in crisis; it will be elaborated in Part II.

IDENTIFYING A PERSON IN CRISIS

There are several characteristics to look for in identifying a person in crisis. First, there is generally some event perceived to have precipitated the crisis. It may be a real or subjectively perceived threat to survival or to bodily integrity. It can be the loss of something perceived to be essential for emotional survival, integrity, or nurturance. Examples include marital or family separation, divorce, death of a loved one, or loss of a beloved home. It may be a loss or threatened loss of self-esteem, identity, self-concept, status, or position. The birth of a child, healthy or defective, or a change in occupation can precipitate a crisis, as can a loss or perceived loss of a material possession or economic and social achievement, for

All crises identified in 266 admissions to day hospital

Nature of crisis	Number	Percent
Interpersonal difficulty in family	249	51
Antisocial behavior	30	6
Work problem	110	22
Financial problem	35	7
Physical illness	22	4
Bereavement	27	6
Accident	4	1
Pregnancy	8	2
Other	5	1
TOTAL	490	100

Nature of problems cited by 85 emergency services in United States

Nature of problem	Incidence
Family conflict including marital discord and impending divorce	51
Excessive use of alcohol	27
Problems relating to job or income	19
Bereavement or grief reaction	16
Exacerbation of chronic mental illness	12
Problems of adolescence	6
Problems of old age	5
School problems	4
Medical illness	4
Separation from familiar environment	3
Homosexual panic	3
Legal charges	2
Postpartum depression	2
Postoperative reaction	2

---

example, a major drop in the value of a common stock holding. Certain critical points in the life cycle can precipitate a crisis, such as the beginning of adolescence or birth of a first grandchild. Again, understanding the precipitating event is the key to understanding the person in crisis. The boxes on pp. 13 and 14 show Morrice's (1976) compilation of common precipitating events from 266 consecutive admissions to the Ross Clinic in Aberdeen, Scotland, and from 85 emergency services in the United States.

A second characteristic of a person in crisis is an unusual degree of personality disorganization and impaired social functioning resulting from excessive emotionality. Because the individual's habitual patterns of adaptation are not effective, they are abandoned. The ability to think and reason logically is impaired, and so the individual may turn from external reality toward the self. Because the individual feels confused and unable to cope with the situation at this time, he or she is most accessible to help. He or she is generally not defensive, self-protective, or mistrustful. This period of heightened disorganization usually lasts only a short while. It is the point for immediate and rapid intervention.

A third characteristic of a person in crisis is debilitating emotions (e.g., anxiety, depression, guilt, shame). Associated with these feelings may be physical symptoms or complaints. Manifestations of these emotions are discussed in Chapter 2.

A fourth characteristic of a crisis is that it often can be resolved within 4 to 6 weeks (with the possible exception of a bereavement crisis, which can take as long as a year to resolve). In summary, a crisis can be identified by four basic characteristics: (1) the existence of a subjectively defined precipitating event; (2) unusual personality disorganization and impaired social functioning; (3) debilitating emotional response; and (4) resolution of the problem within 4 to 6 weeks.

CAUSES OF CRISIS

Crisis theory assumes that social functioning is a continuous effort to maintain and restore equilibrium as one is exposed to potentially upsetting problems of living and pursuing goals. Each person maintains psychic equilibrium through individual adaptive patterns and coping mechanisms. Since everyone is exposed to potentially crisis-producing events, an important question is why a certain event causes a crisis for some people and not for others. We know that the same event that causes a crisis for one person may be perceived as a challenge to another. *The cause of a crisis is the significance of the event to the person involved.* Hence the basis for understanding and helping a person in crisis is through his or her subjective frame of reference: psychic reality. It is Martha's personal interpretation of pregnancy that represents a danger. It is Richard's reaction to being passed over that renders his habitual patterns of adaptation ineffective, creating the feeling of helplessness.

The next question is what causes the person in crisis to interpret the event as he or she does. The precipitating event is always associated with some kind of internal experience. It may not be the strength of the personality that determines whether a person develops a crisis. Rather, the determining factor may be whether an event is significant enough to the individual and occurs at a time when he or she is vulnerable. Another factor is the strength of the individual's defenses against the particular feelings brought on by the precipitating event. Most human reactions to crisis-producing events involve anxiety or depression or their derivatives. (Suicide and homicide are derivations of anxiety or depression.) Understanding these two universal emotions can be the key to understanding the meaning of the precipitating event for the person in crisis. They are discussed in depth in Chapter 2.

CRISIS THERAPY VERSUS TRADITIONAL PSYCHOTHERAPY

At this point another distinction needs to be made: the distinction between crisis therapy and traditional psychotherapy. (No significant qualitative difference is intended by the use of the words *crisis therapy* and *psychotherapy*. Crisis therapy is also psychotherapy.)

As Jacobson (1970) states:

The [crisis] therapist must be clear that he is dealing with a self-contained modality with its own particular characteristics. This modality in no way substitutes for other forms of psychotherapy, whether of immediate length or long-term, nor does it eliminate the need in some cases for full or partial hospitalization. It is one string in the therapeutic bow; but a string with its own particular and unique qualities.

There are several differences between crisis therapy and other therapies. First, crisis theory does not assume psychopathology or an underlying intrapsychic conflict, although persons with these problems can experience crisis. The spectrum of "normal" human behavior is broad enough to allow individuals with all sorts of other difficulties to benefit at times from short-term crisis therapy.

The purpose of crisis therapy is to return the person to his or her previous level of social functioning. For example, Marianne, a young divorcee who had been progressing well in psychotherapy, experienced a crisis when her 10-year-old son Dan demanded to leave her to live with his father and started to make the arrangements. Marianne presented the classic symptoms of a person in crisis; the crisis had to be resolved before she could return to her previous level of functioning and make further progress in her psychotherapy.

A related question is whether crisis therapy treats a person's underlying conflicts. Although everyone has these conflicts (Erikson, 1959; Hartmann, 1958), they are not significant except as they may relate specifically to the treatment process. An individual may have reactivated an underlying conflict in his or her effort to resolve the current crisis. If the problem does not respond to crisis intervention and continues to influence the person's social functioning, more traditional psychotherapy is probably indicated.

The second distinction between crisis therapy and traditional psychotherapy is the existence of a real precipitating event that unites the individual's internal and external worlds. Crisis theory assumes that the individual has no uncommon weakness in his or her general ability to adapt to life. Rather, it is the reaction to an event that causes a *temporary* social dysfunctioning, the outcome of which is significant to future social functioning.

A third distinction between crisis therapy and traditional psychotherapy is that the former is practiced in a variety of places and settings, for example, emergency rooms of hospitals, the client's home, or on the street, as well as offices of mental health clinics and counseling and crisis centers. Regardless of the setting, the practice of crisis therapy is basically the same.

A final distinction is the temporal nature of a crisis. By definition, most crises can be resolved in less than 7 weeks. Problems requiring traditional intervention for the most part require considerably longer to resolve and to achieve a given level of improvement.

GOALS OF CRISIS THERAPY

In general the goals of crisis therapy are the resolution of the individual's crisis, a change in perception of danger, and the restoration of social functioning to at least the precrisis level. As Paul (1966) states:

> In reversing the decompensation and restoring emotional equilibrium, we aim to strengthen the client's resources, to give him not only symptom relief, but also symptom control, social control, and some degree of insight.

For the individual who understands the theory of crisis, these are reasonably achievable goals compared with other psychotherapeutic efforts. The person in crisis is more amenable to help than at any other time in life. The feelings of helplessness make the person receptive to help; they increase the desire to learn to cope with a new situation. At the same time the situation is delicate and requires special skills, skills that traditional therapies may not require. Perhaps the first is the ability to intervene at a time when not much information can easily be acquired. The therapist also needs to be able to quickly establish a tentative formulation of the client's condition. The therapist must often be able to define the precipitating event and its meaning for the client. Third, the therapist is often much more active and involved than traditional therapists. Fourth, the therapist must be able to elicit powerful and painful feelings such as the reactions a client has to impending death. Closely related is the capacity of the therapist to tolerate painful emotions in others, to tolerate human suffering. Sixth, the therapist must be willing to assume responsibility for others. Finally, the therapist must have confidence in his or her ability to help a person in crisis. Goldstein (1962) found that the therapist's self-confidence has a significant impact on the client's improvement. In effect the crisis therapist must have the ability to quickly evaluate, teach, and facilitate problem resolutions. A sound theoretical understanding of how people behave is essential if you are to be effective with people in crisis. Some basic ways in which people behave are discussed in Chapter 2.

SUMMARY

This chapter emphasizes the universality of human crises and presents a conceptual frame of reference for understanding people in crisis. At this point you should understand the basic premise of crisis theory, what a crisis is, and how it differs from common problems of living. Of particular importance, you should be able to identify the characteristics of a person in crisis and should understand why one person develops a crisis and another does not. The differences between crisis intervention and traditional psychotherapy are also discussed. Finally, you should understand the demands placed on a crisis therapist.

REFERENCES

Aguilera, D. C., & Messick, J. M. *Crisis intervention: theory and methodology* (3rd ed.). St. Louis: C. V. Mosby, 1978.

Beers, T. M., Jr., & Foreman, M. E. Intervention patterns in crisis interviews. *Journal of Counseling Psychology*. 1976, 3(2), 87-91.

Bloom, B. L. Definitional aspects of the crisis concept. In H. J. Parad (Ed.), *Crisis intervention: selected readings*. New York: Family Service Association of America, 1965, pp. 303-311.

Caplan, G. *Principles of preventive psychiatry*. New York: Basic Books, 1964.

Caplan, G. *An approach to community mental health*. New York: Grune & Stratton, 1961.

Darbonne, A. Crisis: a review of theory, practice and research. In J. Fisher (Ed.), *Interpersonal helping: emerging approaches for social work practice*. Springfield, Ill.: Charles C Thomas, 1973, pp. 237-247.

Erikson, E. H. Growth and crises of the health personality. In Identity and the life cycle: selected papers. *Psychological Issues*, 1959, 1(1), 50-100. (Monograph)

Farberow, N. L. Crisis, disaster and suicide: theory and therapy. In E. S. Shneidman (Ed.), *Essays in self-destruction*. New York: Science House, 1967.

Fischer, J. (Ed.). *Interpersonal helping: emerging approaches for social work practice*. Springfield, Ill.: Charles C Thomas, 1973.

Forer, B. The therapeutic value of crisis. *Psychological Reports,* August 1963, *13*(1), 275-281.

Golan, N. Crisis theory. In F. J. Turner (Ed.), *Social work treatment: interlocking theoretical approaches.* New York: The Free Press, 1974, pp. 420-456.

Golan, N. When is a client in crisis? *Social Casework,* July 1969, *50*(7), 389-394.

Goldstein, A. P. *Therapist-patient expectations in psychotherapy.* New York: Macmillan, 1962.

Hartmann, H. Ego psychology and the problem of adaptation. *Journal of the American Psychoanalytic Association,* 1958. (Monograph Series, No. 1)

Jacobson, G. F. Crisis intervention from the viewpoint of the mental health professional. *Pastoral Psychology,* April 1970, *21*(203), 21-28.

Jacobson, G. F. Some psychoanalytic considerations regarding crisis therapy. *Psychoanalytic Review,* 1967, *54*(4), 93-98.

Jacobson, G. F. Crisis theory and treatment strategy: Some socioculture and psychodynamic considerations. *Journal of Nervous and Mental Disease,* 1965, *141*(2), 209-218.

Jacobson, G. F., Strickler, M., & Morley, W. Generic and individual approaches to crisis intervention. *American Journal of Public Health and the Nation's Health,* February 1968, *58*(1), 338-343.

Kalis, B. L., Harris, R. M., Prestwood, A. R., & Freeman, E. H. Precipitating stress as a focus in psychotherapy. *Archives of General Psychiatry,* September 1961, *5*(3), 27-34.

Lindemann, E. Symptomatology and management of acute grief. In H. J. Parad (Ed.), *Crisis intervention: selected readings.* New York: Family Service Association of America, 1965, pp. 7-21. (Reprinted from *American Journal of Psychiatry,* 1944, *101*.)

Maloney, E. The subjective and objective definition of crisis. *Perspective in Psychiatric Care,* 1971, *9*, 257-268.

Mackey, R. A. Crisis theory: its development and relevance to social casework practice. *The Family Coordinator,* July 1968, *17*(3), 165-173.

Morley, W. E. Theory of crisis intervention. *Pastoral Psychology,* April 1970, *21*(203), 14-20.

Morrice, J. K. W., Crisis intervention: studies in community care. Oxford, England: Pergamon Press, 1976.

Parad, H. J. (Ed.). *Crisis intervention: selected readings.* New York: Family Service Association of America, 1965.

Pasewark, R. A., & Albers, D. A. Crisis intervention theory in search of a program. *Social Work,* March 1972, *17*(2), 70-79.

Paul, L. Crisis intervention. *Mental Hygiene,* January 1966, *50*(1), 141-145.

Rusk, T. N. Opportunity and technique in crisis psychiatry. *Comprehensive Psychiatry,* May 1971, *12*(3), 249-263.

Taplin, J. R. Crisis theory: critique and reformulation. *Community Mental Health Journal,* March 1971, *7*(1), 13-23.

SUGGESTED READINGS

Caplan, G. *Principles of preventive psychiatry*. New York: Basic Books, 1964.

Caplan, G. Emotional crisis. *Encyclopedia of Mental Health*, 1963, 2, 521-532.

Golan, N. When is a client in crisis? *Social Casework*, July 1969, 50(7), 389-394.

Lindemann, E. Symptomatology and management of acute grief. In H. J. Parad (Ed.), *Crisis intervention: selected readings*. New York: Family Service Association of America, 1965, pp. 7-21. (Reprinted from *American Journal of Psychiatry*, 1944, 101(2), 141-148.)

Lindemann, E. The meaning of crisis in individual and family. *Teacher College Record*, 1956, 57, 310.

Parad, H. J. Crisis intervention. In *Encyclopedia of Social Work* (Vol. 1). New York: National Association of Social Workers, 1971, pp. 196-202.

Rapoport, L. The state of crisis: some theoretical considerations. In H. J. Parad (Ed.), *Crisis intervention: selected readings*. New York: Family Service Association of America, 1965, pp. 22-31.

CHAPTER 2

Basic knowledge of human behavior

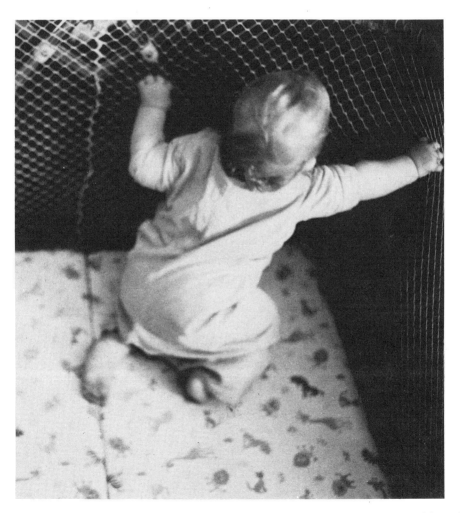

■ Doug, a 44-year-old man, requested an immediate appointment at the crisis center to discuss his concerns about things that had been happening to him. When he came in a few hours later, he stated that he had not been able to bounce back from failing his doctoral comprehensive examinations. Doug said that failing the exams, though not uncommon, was more important to him than to other students because of his age and responsibilities in life. He had switched from a field in which he had been quite successful to a totally new and unrelated field that required a doctorate. Now he was ashamed to tell his wife, who had returned to work after 15 years so he could pursue his goals, that he had flunked the test. He did not think that he could get his old position back because it had been more than 2 years since he had left it. Doug expressed intense feelings of self-depreciation and unworthiness. He felt that he had not only failed himself, but much worse, he had failed his wife and family. He did not know what he was going to do and felt like taking his life. Having come from a religious family, he recognized that the thought of taking his own life meant that he was at the final point of despair, and so he sought help immediately.

■ A middle-aged woman named Rosemary called the crisis center for an immediate appointment. She was in a state of panic because she had found a note from her husband Frank in which he spoke of suicide. Her husband was in love with another woman, whom he said he wanted to marry, but Rosemary had refused to give him a divorce. Rosemary and Frank had been married for 21 years, and she felt that his affair with the young woman was a passing fancy. He had been a loyal husband and a good father for all those years. On that basis she felt that he was having some "mental problems" and that he would snap out of it. However, since the affair had been going on for several months, the night before she found the note Rosemary had informed Frank that she was going to tell his mother about his behavior.

From our understanding of the concept of crisis, we can see that both Doug and Rosemary were in crisis. Their feelings of helplessness, overwhelming emotionality, and diminished cognitive functioning were typical, so they turned to someone else for help. In the first case the crisis was resolved. Doug regained cognitive control of himself so that he was able to work out a plan with his professors to take the comprehensive examinations a second time. In the second case Frank eventually committed suicide. Why were Doug and Rosemary (and Frank) in crisis? What caused their specific reactions to their precipitating events when others face the same kinds of problems with much less trouble? Why did they behave the way they did? We can find the answers in basic human behavior patterns. This chapter provides a basis for understanding human behavior that will help the therapist assess and evaluate his or her clients' social functioning and that can guide the therapeutic intervention.

While crisis theory does not require specific adherence to any one of the traditional theories of human behavior, a systematic theoretical approach to understanding social functioning is essential for maximum effectiveness and success. Intervention that is not based on some theory is a trial-and-error process; it leaves success too much to chance. A basic knowledge of theory gives the therapist greater control over the intervention situation. Some intellectual control is needed to reduce the unwanted emotional involvement that working with people in crisis entails. Some cognitive control helps the therapist develop confidence in his or her professional skills and abilities, which in turn helps the client (Goldstein, 1962). The therapist who feels confident is likely to project an image of strength and ability to deal with difficult problems.

Perhaps most important, theory allows the therapist to make predictions and thus to assess and evaluate the client's condition as a road map for intervention.

UNDERSTANDING HUMAN BEHAVIOR

There are many ways to conceptualize human behavior. Although each person who experiences a crisis is a unique individual, a broad perspective and relatively comprehensive study of human behavior is more useful in the long run than a single-subject study. Regardless of their individuality, all people in crisis have certain common characteristics. The therapist needs a comprehensive understanding of human behavior from which to begin.

We can start with some basic assumptions about human behavior:

1. All human behavior has a cause, and the causes always involve many complex interpersonal interactions between the individual and other people and the environment.
2. Human behavior is purposeful. People try to satisfy needs, to adapt to the social environment, and to defend against any stimulus that threatens their emotional equilibrium.
3. All human beings experience the same feelings and behaviors. The basic differences between people are not differences of kind but differences of degree.
4. The individual and his or her social environment are a united interactional field.
5. Stress and conflict are an inevitable part of life. To live happily and

productively, human beings must learn patterns of behavior that let them maintain and restore a sense of equilibrium.

6. The way a person functions psychosocially is the accumulative result of his or her life experiences and socialization process.
7. Effective social functioning is related to the nature of biological endowment, the social environment, and specific phases of the life cycle.
8. An individual's social functioning can range from highly effective to ineffective.
9. Social dysfunction can be ameliorated by assessing and evaluating contributing factors in the individual and the environment and intervening therapeutically.

Since we are concerned with a relatively comprehensive perspective of human behavior, let us begin with the human being's beginning, with biological behavior and its contribution to psychic development and social functioning.

Biological determinants of human behavior

Although the human infant is born helpless, most are also born with specific capacities that will eventually enable them to function independently and ensure their own survival over time. Two factors affect that outcome: heredity and the sum of experiences and environment. While the individual's heredity is determined by the time of birth, the environment is not. The rest of this chapter explores how biological, psychological, and social experiences result in a specific psychic system and habitual patterns of social functioning.

Family as basis for molding personality

Human babies are born with the capacity to communicate their needs to their primary caretakers and to adapt to the social environment. These capacities allow the otherwise helpless infant to survive. Although the infant's basic potentials are innate, the way they develop is determined by the individual's specific social experiences. If the baby's capacity to learn is to function, the baby must be stimulated and have social experiences conducive to that end. In contrast to other animals, human beings can use their experiences not only to survive and to adapt but also as creative tools.

The human infant is also born with a need for affection. This need for nurture, coupled with the biological drive for survival, leads to interaction between the baby and the caretaker. This interaction is the infant's first social experience.

The next social experiences most infants have are within the family. The family, a system of interacting personalities, the basic purpose of which is the satisfaction of the needs of its members within the parameter of a specific social situation, is the agency that begins the socialization process. No adequate replacement has been found for the family in molding the child's personality and preparing the child for independent social functioning. Specifically, family experiences determine the way the infant thinks and learns, the infant's way of loving and being loved, self-concept and identity, and feelings of self-worth, security, self-confidence, responsibility, and trust. Let us look a little closer at this process.

Even before birth, the human child lives in a psychosocial climate affected by the personalities of the parents. The parents' own childhoods and life experiences determine how they relate to their children. Their feelings about pregnancy, the quality and nature of their marriage, and the mother's physical and emotional health during pregnancy all determine the kind of environment the infant is born into.

Birth interrupts the comfort of the fetal state and thrusts the child into a new world that brings pain and discomfort. The level of activity after birth varies from infant to infant. Some infants are more sensitive and less tolerant of aversive stimuli; others are more cuddly and responsive. The baby's biological behavior evokes responses in his or her parents, who give this behavior a personal interpretation and meaning. This interaction is the beginning of the cumulative social interaction between parent and child. Again it is the parents who give the infant's biological behavior its psychosocial meaning. This meaning influences the way the parents relate to the child; some parents interpret it as the child's feelings for them. For example, one father said, "I knew my child did not love me from the beginning because he stiffened up everytime I picked him up." At this point the infant's behavior was purely a biological reflex, perhaps in response to the feeling of being moved. But the father's personality and feelings led him to interpret the child's behavior and *respond to his own interpretation*. This in turn would communicate something to the infant.

At this point in the infant's life the most important thing is the absence of pain; that is, the infant needs sleep, nourishment, and pleasurable sensations such as stroking. Research has shown that the infant's need for stroking and tactile stimulation beyond tension reduction is as vitally important for adequate psychosocial development as food is to the body. Spitz (1945) found that some children's will to live was greatly affected by the lack of interpersonal and affectional experiences. When the infant experiences pain, the reaction is automatic; the infant cries and contorts face and body as if life were in danger. This reaction is purely in the service of survival; it is so urgent because the infant's psychic system is not developed enough to let him identify the source of the pain. This confusion is the prototype of the feelings of anxiety. The same phenomenon occurs in anxiety in adults. Adults while experiencing anxiety react with physiological responses as if life were in danger. More will be said about this under the topic of anxiety.

As time passes, the infant internalizes experiences and learns that the source of feeding and pleasure and the elimination of pain and discomfort is parents or caretaker. This recognition activates a bond of love that will have infinite influence on the child's psychic development throughout life. It is one of the major considerations in understanding depression, as we shall see later. After needs have been satisfied repeatedly, the child develops confidence that they will be satisfied. The child soon learns that crying brings a parent, giving purpose to his or her behavior. For all practical purposes, mental functioning starts when the child can recognize a purpose for behavior, perhaps when he or she stops crying at the sight of parents before needs have been satisfied.

As the infant develops the certainty that biological needs will be satisfied in an environment of love and security, attention and learning can be directed toward higher psychosocially determined needs and adaptation to the social environment. If, on the other hand, the satisfaction of biological needs is threatened or inadequate, the basis for adequate social functioning is proportionately reduced and behavior continues to be biologically motivated.

As biological needs are satisfied and recede into the background on the basis of confidence created by repeated satisfaction, psychosocially determined needs assume the same urgency that biological needs once did. Now the need for love, affection, achievement, and so on, can produce disequilibrium. Now the stimulus for behavior is not just the satisfaction of biological needs but the satisfaction of psychosocial needs, a vital source of pleasure.

The problem of psychic development is not made easier by the assigned value of psychosocially determined needs. The process is further complicated by the demands and prohibitions of the social environment (i.e., parents, social institutions, peers), which establishes not only what needs are valuable but also how they must or can be satisfied. Consequently the child must learn about his or her environment. At the same time, children must reconcile their own needs and desires with the nature of the environment in which they find themselves. Fortunately the human being has the capacity and potential to adapt to the environment. The way each individual adapts is determined by the specific nature of the social environment, beginning with the parents. They set the stage for love, values, goals, and the pursuit of happiness. Recall in the case of Rosemary and Frank that the event that led to Frank's suicide note was Rosemary's threat to tell his mother about his behavior. Not only is a child dependent on parents for survival, but the bond of love or lack of it established early in life affects the individual throughout life. When the child reaches adulthood, love for another adult becomes as instrumental in psychic functioning as primary love.

In effect, human love represents a continuum that remains all of one's life. There are four important characteristics of human love. First, it is individually and idiosyncratically defined. Consider for a moment the battered wife who says she stays with her husband who beats her because she loves him. Second, the need for love is based on feelings of self-worth and being valued. Third, many human activities (e.g., work, creativity) can be substitutes for love, either enhancing it or destroying it. Consider the husband who claims that he works 14 hours each day because he loves his family. This is fine if the family also perceives it as love. Fourth, love is not given unconditionally. As the child grows, this is learned quickly. The child must do certain things or refrain from doing certain things. He or she must please parents. These demands do no harm if the parents love the child, if they are consistent in their responses, and clear and unambiguous in their expectations and communication. If the parents are happy with each other and their lives, if they understand, then it is not difficult for a child to please parents. However, family emotional and interactional relationships are complicated. In sum, love is individually and subjectively defined. This is why it is so difficult to describe what love is generally. Perhaps the most useful measure is the definition given by Freida Fromm-Reichman (1950.) She says that mature love is being as concerned about the welfare of the loved one as you are about your own. Now let us discuss further parental influence on personality development.

Parents are two different individuals who enter a relationship, with distinct pasts that in turn affect their motivation for selecting each other.

These motivations may or may not be compatible with each other. In addition parents bring to their relationship their own individual personalities, including their ideas of motherhood and fatherhood. The roles of mother and father are greatly influenced by their relationship and their experiences with their own parents.

As children mature they begin to manifest their own will and independent functioning. At this time the socialization process really begins, particulary if the child is restricted and prohibited from satisfying curiosity and meeting needs immediately and expediently. At some point the child's will clashes with the social environment (i.e., parents). The child's first conflict situation is whether he or she should please self or please parents. To the child it matters not whether the parents are acting in his or her own best interest. The child is driven by the desire for pleasure, which is influenced and limited by the threat of losing parental love or suffering some form of punishment if it is unacceptable to them. At this point the child has several options: (1) attempt to satisfy needs impulsively and expediently, thereby risking rejection and punishment by parents; (2) abandon the need or desire and pretend that it did not exist or that it really was not wanted in the first place; (3) find a substitute satisfaction or disguise the original need; (4) satisfy this need in a manner that is pleasing to the parents, thereby retaining their affection and avoiding their punishment and disapproval. Much of psychic development involves reconciling internal needs with external opportunities, demands, limitations, and prohibitions. How persons learn to resolve these conflicts to satisfy needs, values, and goals is part of the socialization process. Through this process the child evolves a specific psychic system.

PSYCHIC SYSTEM

The psychic system is a dynamic organization of mental faculties, the accumulation of all the individual's life experiences, including psychosocial, from birth to its completion near the end of adolescence (many theorists believe that the psychic system is completed by age 6). It is responsible for the individual's social functioning and specific ways of thinking, perceiving, feeling, and behaving. It is responsible for the individual's sensitivities. It ensures survival within the environment. Perception, memory, intelligence, language, and mobility are capacities of the psychic system. As a consequence of internalizing parental standards, values, expectations, and concepts of right and wrong, the child develops a conscience that helps regulate behavior according to past experiences. The child also seeks pleasure. All of these are forces in the personality, and their purpose is to make the individual a fully functioning, self-actualizing person. However, to achieve these purposes, these forces must be coordinated and regulated. The ego, or the self-system, has this unifying purpose. Through the years of socialization and learning, the individual learns to maintain equilibrium while satisfying needs, pursuing goals, and meeting the demands of the social environment. However, one generally has little control over outside events. Thus each individual develops habitual patterns or methods of coping with conflicting demands and upsetting events while remaining organized. These patterns are carried out routinely until some event overtakes the psychic system and attacks it at a vulnerable position.

Two important factors that stimulate or impel psychic functioning and human behavior are self-concept and needs. It is the satisfaction of these two that determines psychic equilibrium and the adequacy of social functioning. When either is threatened, some degree of disequilibrium results. We saw this in the cases presented at the beginning of the chapter. Doug's self-concept was threatened by his failure; Rosemary's needs for love and security were threatened by Frank's affair with a younger woman. To understand better, let us look at these two psychic forces in more depth.

Self-concept

Self-concept is how the individual sees himself or herself. It is who each individual believes himself or herself to be, identity, what one stands for, one's beliefs, occupation, the roles one assumes, and on and on. Self-concept is an emotional condition that we inferred from behavior. It is the value judgment that a person places on himself or herself, mainly as a result of early perceptions of parental feelings about the individual and the tremendous human need to be loved and accepted, first by parents and later by significant others. Of course the child's perception of what the parents feel about him or her may not be what the parents really feel; however, what is important is what is in the mind of the individual, his or her psychic reality. During early development the child internalizes the parents' feelings, behavioral expectations, and demands into his or her own psychic system. The parents evaluate the child's behavior as good or bad, acceptable or unacceptable. Most children cannot separate their actions from their selves. They feel that who they are is determined by what they do. When they do something "good" that pleases their parents, they feel good about themselves. When the child does something unacceptable, the action is translated into, "I am no good" or "I am bad." The child internalizes external experiences as part of self-concept. A very important part of maturity is the separation of the internalized parental perception of what and who the individual is and the establishment of one's own self-concept and identity. This separation is not easy to accomplish because parents have such an early and long-term influence on psychic development. Consider the following example of parental influence on self-concept and behavior.

Anne, a 27-year-old married mother of three children, complained that she no longer felt worthwhile or of value just being a housewife; she said she wanted to get a job. She expressed these feelings to her mother, who made her feel guilty about them because her children still needed her. Anne's husband was in favor of and supported her desire to get a job. Anne revealed her conflict when she said, "I could never please my mother." As a part of Anne's socialization process, she had internalized her mother's values of motherhood. This would have been all right had they been Anne's values also. However, as Anne's feelings about being a housewife changed, she also wanted to change her self-concept and feelings about herself. At age 27, still needing her mother's approval, she felt considerable tension over pleasing her mother or pleasing herself. She felt that if she took a job, she risked losing the love and acceptance of her mother. The conflict would probably have occurred even if her mother had not directly interfered, because her mother's values and perception of her had been internalized. For Anne to resolve this conflict, she needed help in overcoming the feelings of the internalized mother.

While there are other explanations for the origin of self-concept, it is clearly an important variable in human behavior, one no therapist can afford to ignore. It originates in the process of identification in which children want to be like parents. This process facilitates adaptation to society and ensures its continuity. A good or adequate self-concept generally means good or adequate social functioning. When self-concept is poor, social functioning is poor or ineffective. A threat or attack on an individual's self-concept can precipitate a crisis, as we saw in Doug's failing his doctoral comprehensive examinations.

Human needs

Needs are also very important impelling forces that initiate and maintain human behavior. Specifically, a need is experienced as tension that can be reduced by a specific source of satisfaction. The greater the need, the stronger the tension. The need-satisfaction sequence is as follows:

Need $\longrightarrow$	**Action** $\longrightarrow$	**Process** $\longrightarrow$	**Satisfaction**
Stimulus and tension	Behavior	Methods used to satisfy need	Tension reduction

The satisfaction of a need is pleasurable. But neither the individual nor society is so constituted that all human needs can be satisfied unequivocally. Consequently needs can be ranked in a hierarchy of relative potency. When one need is satisfied, another appears.

Hence human behavior is the satisfaction of one need after another. Some of the most powerful needs are for survival, sex, aggression, love, acceptance, self-esteem, recognition, achievement, value, and security. Human behavior can be understood in terms of a need disposition. Not only can common stimuli such as love or security serve as needs, uncommon stimuli can also be considered needs. For example, the need for punishment, the need for excitement, or the need to face danger can all lead people to act.

As long as needs are being satisfied, the individual can function adequately. If needs cannot be satisfied, frustration and social dysfunctioning can result. The degree of debilitation depends on the strength of the need, the significance of the need for the maintenance of adequate social functioning, the methods used to satisfy the need, and the availability of sources of alternate satisfaction. The length of time that a person can tolerate disequilibrium resulting from unsatisfied needs without breaking down is his or her frustration tolerance.

Each society not only sets forth which needs are acceptable but also establishes certain limits on the ways that they can be satisfied. Thus each individual must reconcile the existence and the satisfaction of needs with the structure of the social environment. This makes intrapsychic conflict inevitable. In such cases a person has four alternatives: (1) to satisfy the need directly and suffer the consequence; (2) to submit to the will of the opposing force and pretend that the need never existed; (3) to reduce the tension of the need by fantasy and wish fulfillment; or (4) to develop some compromise need as a substitute for the original need. The mind must develop ways to deal with powerful needs that cannot be directly satisfied. We will discuss three of these ways: motivation, the dynamic unconscious, and the methods of adaptation to conflict.

MOTIVATION

Understanding motivation is important to understanding human behavior. Motivation is both the reason for certain behavior and the force that impels a person to action. All human behavior, regardless of significance, is motivated and purposeful. Because needs are experienced as tension, the reduction of tension is motivation for the satisfaction of needs. This sounds simple, and it would be if people and societies were so constituted that all needs could be unequivocally satisfied. But such is not the case.

Motivation can exist on three levels: the conscious level, the preconscious level, and the unconscious level. One is aware of *conscious* motivation. For example, a crisis therapist might say that he or she wants to work with people in crisis in order to "help people." It follows therefore that for that therapist helping people satisfies a specific need(s). The therapist will continue to help people as long as the need exists and can be satisfied in that manner. Conscious motivation is generally realistic and truthful and should be accepted when the rational part of the psychic system is functioning without interference.

The *preconscious* level of motivation is that explanation or purpose that a person may have forgotten but that can be recalled fairly easily with some stimulation. The degree of preconscious motivation may vary, but for the most part it is generally close to that which is socially and personally acceptable. To use our crisis therapist as an example of preconscious motivation, he or she might recall that another reason for wanting to work with people in crisis was that it was the only job available at the time. Preconscious motivation is generally harmless and the product of forgetting and consciousness priorities.

Unconscious motivation is behavior that one is unaware of and cannot offer any rational explanation for when made aware of it. Unconsciously motivated behavior may be either constructive or destructive, but it is generally detrimental. When it is constructive, it is constructive in outcome only, since its success is so reinforcing that there is generally no need to question why. Unconscious motivation is detrimental when its consequences are destructive. For example, if the crisis therapist works so hard at helping people that his or her family is neglected, some question of unconscious motivation could be raised.

While unconscious motivation is important, one should not become preoccupied with hidden meanings. Simply remember that people do, say, or think many things without logical explanations. They appear at times to be motivated by unknown forces. This is especially true of the person in crisis. Nevertheless, whatever he or she does has some basis, some purpose, some meaning. In such cases it is often necessary for the person to discover his or her own motivation as part of the cognitive restoration process. Because all motivation has to be described by the individual or inferred by any outsider, the therapist must be aware of the influence of motivation in the causes of human behavior. For instance:

■ Ben called an agency in a state of crisis precipitated by his wife's leaving him. During the interview he revealed that his wife left him after he beat her because she did not want to become pregnant. He had beaten her before; each time she left, only to return the same day. This time she did not return, and Ben developed a state of panic. He rationalized away his beating of his wife as evidence of how much he loved her and could not stand to live without her. However, after four sessions he could accept the fact that his motivation for beating his wife was not that he loved her so much but that he wanted her to leave him so that he could justifiably return home to live with his mother. Follow-up 1 year later revealed that he was doing well living with his mother and had no desire to contact his wife, whom he had not seen since her leaving precipitated the crisis.

Ben's story not only shows how unconscious motivation can influence human behavior, but it also shows the importance of the next subject: the dynamic unconscious and human conflict.

DYNAMIC UNCONSCIOUS

The dynamic unconscious is behavior resulting from incompletely blocked unacceptable needs or drives. The strength of these needs or drives is so strong that counterforces cannot keep them completely blocked, and their derivatives are manifested in some form of behavior. The individual is unaware of the behavior and its meaning. An example of the dynamic unconscious is illustrated by the case of Phil:

■ Phil was told by his professor that a midterm examination was scheduled. On the day of the test Phil went through his usual procedure for getting to the university. However, after a period of time had elapsed he became aware that it was taking him longer than usual to get to the university. As he looked around to determine how far he had come, he observed that he was in unfamiliar surroundings. Looking further he became aware that he was in a different city, having completely bypassed the university. Hence he had missed the examination.

This kind of behavior occurs when people have strong unacceptable feelings that cannot be expressed directly. Had Phil been aware of his strong fear of failure, he would not have had to handle the examination in that manner. We will see later the influence of the dynamic unconscious in the case of Diana, who unconsciously behaved seductively. As we have seen, the influence of the dynamic unconscious in human behavior is generally counterproductive and often detrimental.

NATURE OF HUMAN CONFLICT AND METHODS OF ADAPTATION

The maladaptive management of an internal conflict precipitated by an external event can result in a crisis condition. Conflicts and their resolutions are parts of daily living. Learning to resolve conflicts as part of the socialization process results in the establishment of habitual patterns of adaptation necessary for adequate social functioning.

Conflict, by definition, is a clash between at least two opposing forces of equal strength. In essence, any obstruction to the satisfaction of a highly motivated need can produce conflict. Tension is the essence of true conflict. Recall that the ultimate goal of the human being is to maintain equilibrium. Tension, however, upsets equilibrium; it is painful. Consequently, whenever tension occurs some means must be found to get rid of it, restoring the individual to relative constancy. As Menninger (1963) states, "All human behavior represents the endeavor on the part of an organism to maintain a relatively constant inner and outer environment by promptly correcting all upsetting eventualities." The sources of conflict are innumerable.

Reference has already been made to the inevitability of conflict in the socialization process and personality development. It first occurs when the child matures to the point that individual needs, desires, or will clashes with those of the parents. It also should be kept in mind that the psychic system can control and manage conflict and still satisfy most needs within the limits of the social environment. It can also succumb to conflict and give way to impulsiveness and primitive satisfaction of needs if the need is strong enough and the opposition to its satisfaction is weaker. Evidence of this is seen in adults who fall back into various primitive behaviors such as temper tantrums, uncontrolled anger, fighting, and even murder to satisfy needs as a reaction to frustration or to release tension caused by unmet needs, deprivation, or threat to psychic values.

Intrapsychic conflict results from the discrepancy between internalized social standards and the desire to violate them or function differently. Conflict can arise when there is a desire to defy or deviate from one's upbringing, for example, intrapsychic conflict that can result from the Catholic Church's position on abortion versus the sociolegal position. It occurs also when it is felt that one has failed to meet personal standards. It can occur when there is a desire to satisfy forbidden needs and strong counterforces prevent such satisfaction. Consider Brian, a college student who grew up in a strict environment in which he developed a strong conscience that prohibited drinking alcohol or the kind of partying that is typical of university students. He is now confronted with the decision to violate his upbringing, thereby feeling that he will lose the love and respect of his parents while gaining the acceptance of his peers or lose the support of his peers while retaining good feelings about his behavior. Again, for this to be true intrapsychic conflict both goals must be equally desirable, and a decision either way results in dire consequences. Intrapsychic conflict always involves incompatible forces competing for satisfaction.

Another source of intrapsychic conflict is the human being's capacity to symbolize, to let objects and experiences come to represent other real objects or experiences that at one time were significant. For example, hearing a song that you associate with a particular person can bring to mind images and feelings you had about that person. Because a symbol is only representative of the actual experience or object and is not the real experience or object, there is always some degree of emotional distortion or exaggeration. The symbolized experience can never be reexperienced as it actually happened but only as it is remembered. The majority of intrapsychic conflicts significant to crisis therapy involve opposition between significantly powerful needs that are in conflict with one's conscience and interpersonal relationships. Such situations are illustrated by conflict over sexual mores, religion, or the desire to express undesirable behavior or satisfy personally unacceptable feelings or needs. Conflict always involves incompatible forces competing for satisfaction. Conflict per se is not bad, since successful resolution contributes to learning and growth. In fact, Erikson (1963) bases his theory of psychosocial development on a conflict model (e.g., trust versus mistrust, and so on).

The psychic system enables the individual to develop an array of coping mechanisms used to reduce or alleviate the tension resulting from either unresolved conflict or any other condition that makes it necessary for the individual to protect himself or herself against threats to the integrity of the self. These coping mechanisms not only reduce tension, which helps to maintain equilibrium, but they also aid adaptation. Everyone uses them to some extent. Hence a coping mechanism is any mental process or behavioral manifestation used to avoid or relieve painful affect and aid adaptation regardless of origin. Such mechanisms are also called *defense mechanisms, mental mechanisms,* or *dynamisms.* Coping mechanisms are prophylactic in nature; they do not resolve conflict or problems. Although they are used to some extent by everyone, they become detrimental when they prevent the individual from assuming responsibility for solving a problem or taking necessary action to change a situation when to do so is in the individual's best interest. Many of the coping mechanisms become a part of the individual's habitual patterns of adaptation and often facilitate problem-solving methods by preventing the psychic system from becoming overwhelmed with painful affect. Some people, for example, cope with depression by excessive sleeping. Others may cope by a special kind of physical exercise. Coping mechanisms are generally ineffective for the person in crisis for one or more of the following reasons: (1) they are used as a substitute for realistic problem-solving methods; (2) they are used to unduly falsify reality; (3) they are used excessively, preventing the individual from understanding and assuming responsibility for personal behavior; (4) they fail to prevent the individual from becoming overwhelmed with emotions. Part of the process of crisis evaluation is determining what habitual patterns of coping mechanisms the individual is using and why they are not effective. A discussion of some of the major and more generally accepted coping mechanisms will further the understanding of human behavior.

Repression. Repression is the process by which unacceptable or unmanageable experiences, feelings, ideas, acts, or needs are automatically and without conscious awareness made unconscious because conscious awareness would result in painful, unacceptable, or deleterious consequences. Repressed feelings are not permanently lost or forgotten. They are pushed deeply into the unconscious part of the mind. However, to keep them unconscious requires energy. Sometimes when events in daily life require additional energy the amount of energy available for repression is reduced, and the repressed feelings, needs, or drives tend to manifest themselves either indirectly or directly. That which is repressed ranges from current situations to significant early childhood feelings and conflicts. Repression functions similarly to forgetting, except that it occurs at a much deeper level and is much more significant to social functioning.

In effect repression is one way in which an individual can cope with conflict or any other source of pain that cannot be coped with consciously. It is like the words in the song "The Way We Were": "That which is too painful to remember, we simply choose to forget." That which is repressed is still laden with energy and presses for satisfaction. An unresolved conflict may remain throughout each phase of personality development but may be kept from interfering with social functioning through the process of repression. But remember, that which is repressed strives for satisfaction, and keeping it repressed requires counterenergy of the ego. As long as the counterenergy is greater than the strength of the repressed, equilibrium can be maintained.

However, ego energy needed to maintain repression is not always the same. It changes with difficulty of coping and adapting to daily events. Although an individual's psychosocial functioning varies from day to day, as long as the energy available to maintain repression is greater than the strength of the repressed material striving for expression or satisfaction, the repressed will not influence or interfere with current psychosocial functioning.

Several functions can reduce ego energy used to maintain repression, specifically alcohol or drugs, sleep manifested by dreams, intense changes in physiological development or function such as puberty, the absence of various kinds of emotional needs or deprivation, and as we have seen, events that threaten life or important values or needs. When repression fails, the significance of the old unresolved conflict forces the individual to ignore the current problem and to try once more to deal with the old conflict.

Dealing with pressure of the old conflict creates less feelings of helplessness and desperation than trying to deal with the current conflict or problems appearing to be insurmountable. This is supported by Rusk (1971, p. 250) when he talks about psychological regression:

The overwhelmed ego, inadequate to manage the stimulus, manifests increasing anxiety with increasing regression to earlier (infantile) previously satisfying (pleasurable and/or anxiety reducing) behavior less in touch with current reality, or more global ego, id, and superego regression to earlier but more manageable conflicts in which the anxiety level, although still present, is less overwhelming than in the current one.

It can be seen that whenever repression cannot be maintained, problems in psychosocial functioning can result. On the other hand, successful repression can aid and facilitate satisfactory social functioning and coping capacities.

Denial. Denial is a process by which an individual refuses to admit into conscious awareness some painful or unacceptable feeling or event that actually exists. Denial is similar to repression except that there is some implication of awareness in the necessity to deny. Denial operates more at a preconscious level than does repression. It can be used as a protection from a threatened loss of self-esteem and feelings of inadequacy or inferiority. A common example of the use of denial is the disbelief some people express when faced with the impending death of a loved one or close friend. A client may use denial when he says that his marriage is perfectly happy and he cannot understand why his wife wants to leave him. An elderly person may refuse to recognize deterioration of health by engaging in behavior that is detrimental.

Rationalization. Rationalization is the process by which excuses are used to make ones failures, disappointments, and painful feelings more acceptable. It can be used to justify behavior that would be harmful to self-esteem. It is used by everyone; everyone occasionally must account for personal defeats, misfortunes, or failures. Although it is frequently offered after the fact, it can be used to reduce the pain of anticipated negative consequences.

Intellectualization. In this process the individual turns unacceptable or painful feelings and needs into intellectual activities or discussions. The person may become preoccupied with some abstract subject such as philosophy, religion, or politics. Its primary purpose is to control painful feelings and emotions that would be intolerable otherwise. It is especially important for the crisis therapist, since it deprives the individual of needed emotional expression. Closely related to intellectualization is isolation. In that process feelings normally associated with painful events are separated and pushed into the unconscious. In essence it is a repression of emotions normally accompanying a specific situation or event. Rather than controlling such feelings by talking abstractly, the individual who uses isolation behaves as if he or she has no feelings. It is easy to misconstrue isolated feelings because so frequently the lack of emotion is considered a sign of strength. For example, when a parent has gone through the traumatic loss of a child and remains in control, showing no sign of emotionality, many people interpret that behavior as a sign of strength. Isolation is detrimental when it prevents humanly required affective expression.

Displacement. Displacement is the process by which feelings are shifted from their original source to another source or object because of a perceived danger in directing them toward the true source. The perceived danger may or may not be real. Both positive and negative emotions can be displaced. The only requirement is the perception that to direct them to where they belong is too dangerous. Scapegoating is an example of displacement. Another common example is the person who is angry at his boss but goes home and kicks his cat. The husband who has repressed hatred for his mother may be abusive to his wife as an unconscious substitute.

Reaction formation. This is the process by which manifest feelings and behavior are diametrically opposite of what is truly desired. Reaction formation is generally manifested by its excessive undesirable consequences. Maternal overprotection is an example. Another example is the wife who has repressed feelings of hate toward her husband and develops excessive concern for his welfare. Reaction formation can also take the opposite approach, in which behavior manifesting hate replaces strong feelings of love. The famous Johnny Cash song "A Boy Named Sue" illustrates this. Here the hard times given a boy named Sue makes him tough and he avoids any potentiality for being soft and unprepared for a hard life. Reaction formation for a fear of softness is excessive hardness or toughness.

Projection. In projection individuals attribute their own painful, unacceptable feelings to someone else or to another situation to protect self-esteem or avoid feelings of weakness. The purpose of projection is to protect oneself from experiencing unacceptable or painful emotions. It prevents persons from assuming responsibility for their own behavior, and so as long as it is used, change is difficult. It is the basis of suspiciousness and mistrust. A client who says that the therapist does not like him or her (assuming that that is not true) may be feeling that he or she does not like the therapist.

Compensation. Compensation is the process by which the individual attempts to make up for some real or imagined unacceptable feelings or shortcomings by some excessive activity designed for that purpose. Compensation is manifested by any exaggerated effort to attain success or distinction in an area of inadequacy or inferiority. Examples of compensation are numerous: the little person who exaggerates behavior to compensate for size, or the working parents who are oversolicitous toward the children because they feel guilty about neglecting them when doing what makes themselves happy. The need for compensation is subjectively determined, based on the absence of some value that is desirable.

Restitution. Closely related to compensation, restitution is the process by which a person amends and offers reparation to a person or group for wrongdoings, injuries, or damages for which he or she feels responsible. Restitution is used to alleviate guilt feelings and responsibility. For example, the father who feels guilty about punishing his child too severely may take her on a camping trip. Wrongdoings and guilt are the basis of the mechanisms of restitution.

Identification. Identification is a very important mechanism in psychic development and for ego reinforcement. It is the process by which individuals make characteristics or behavior of a loved or admired person an integral part of themselves. The attributes adopted may be feelings, behaviors, goals, ideas, or mannerisms. Identification is the process by which children learn to become like their parents. It is also the reason why famous persons are chosen to appear in commercials. Identification has great individual value because it makes persons feel better about themselves. It implies that identifying with the admired one will mean that the admired one will love you on the same basis that he loves himself and you can love yourself for being like the admired one. However, in the case of parents and children it does not always work that way, since the child sometimes identifies also with the negative or rejected part of the parent. That is, there can be negative identification also. It should be emphasized, though, that identification is very important to self-love. It is also important in the helping relationship, and the therapist should be aware of it. It is necessary for the establishment of rapport and empathy.

Introjection. Introjection as used here is a special form of identification in which the perceived feelings of parents and significant others are internalized and experienced as part of the self. It is instrumental in the process of depression. We can see how it is manifested in the grieving process following the death of a loved one, in which the survivor feels and reacts as if a part of the self has been lost, or in the case of Anne in which introjection was a part of development of the self. The manifestation of introjection is less obvious than some of the other mechanisms. Consequently its usefulness here is the recognition that it results from the lengthy closeness with parents, whose relationship and experiences become introjected into the ego or psychic system.

Sublimation. Sublimation is the process by which unacceptable needs, desires, or impulses are directed into socially approved activities.

The evidence of sublimation is generally the excessive zeal with which the individual is preoccupied with sublimated activity. It generally distracts the individual from being a well-rounded person. If the opportunity for sublimation fails, a crisis can develop. Athletics and professions, especially those requiring great amounts of education and training such as advanced degrees, medicine, and law, can be outlets for sublimated drives. When the outlet is blocked in some manner, a crisis may then ensue.

Regression. Regression is a major mechanism used by people in crisis. It is a process by which an individual returns to an earlier immature mode of feeling and behaving. Regression is illustrated by the child who has been toilet trained but begins to have frequent toilet accidents when the new baby is brought home. It is also illustrated by the middle-aged person who suddenly starts to act like an adolescent. We also see regression in the manifestations of anxiety and depression. Although regression generally occurs where one is unable to solve current problems, it can serve a constructive purpose. It is constructive during sleep and when it allows a person to return to a conflict situation stronger. It is deleterious when it is used as a permanent form of escape from problems in current reality.

Thus far the generally accepted coping mechanisms that relate most to people in crisis have been discussed. Others will be discussed as they arise in special situations. It is important to recognize that coping mechanisms are means by which people maintain equilibrium. They become a part of their habitual patterns of adaptation. Consequently, being able to identify them and understand how they work and function is essential for understanding the crisis process. When the initial stress of the precipitating event is too great for the usual coping mechanisms, initial tension is experienced and social functioning begins to deteriorate. Progressively, to halt the process the individual may move from his or her usual use of rationalization to a more serious mechanism such as projection. If this mechanism restores equilibrium, the individual need not go any further. If it does not, however, tension increases, requiring more elaborate measures. It is the failure of coping mechanisms that ultimately leads to a crisis state. How coping mechanisms function to maintain equilibrium and contribute to adaptation has been discussed. Attention can now be focused on what happens to the individual whose coping mechanisms and habitual patterns of adaptation are ineffective, leading to personality disorganization and a crisis state. The important question here is why an event causes a crisis in one person and not in another. We already know that it is not the event that causes the crisis, since the same event may be perceived as a challenge to one person and not to another. It is the meaning of that event to the individual, the personal interpretation of the danger to the individual. The emotional reaction to the perceived danger reduces the ability to cope with the problem. The more ineffective in dealing with the problem, the more emotional the individual becomes and the greater are the feelings of helplessness. Finally, the crisis state emerges.

If the danger of the event is subjectively determined, it is important to know what the precipitating event means to the person in crisis. Why is it personally interpreted as it is? The reason a person in crisis personally interprets the precipitating event as he or she does is revealed by the manifest reaction to the event. With the exception of suicide and homicide, almost all human reactions to events precipitating a crisis (i.e., catastrophes, illnesses, deaths, personal losses, values, and obstacles to happiness) are manifested by anxiety or depression or their derivatives. Even suicide and homicide are derivatives of anxiety and depression. Understanding the meaning, purpose, and function of these two universal emotions provides the key to understanding the person in crisis and the meaning to that person of the precipitating event. It also suggests the type of intervention needed.

ANXIETY

Anxiety is a powerful human emotion, dreadfully painful disequilibrium that everyone tries to avoid. Although the coping mechanisms we have discussed have some adaptive value, basically they are used to avoid or alleviate anxiety. When they fail, anxiety develops. When anxiety becomes so pervasive, so overwhelming that it is unmanageable, a crisis develops. If relief is not forthcoming relatively soon, the threat of personality disorganization exists. This is why people so often become desperate to find a way to alleviate a crisis. If they do so successfully, positive consequences result; if they do not, however, the best result that can be expected is some psychopathology or mental decompensation. As ineffective at resolving problems as most coping mechanisms are, they do to a great degree, when used successfully, reduce the effects of painful anxiety. The debilitating effect of a crisis condition is determined by the degree of anxiety present.

But what is this powerful emotion? First, it is an innate physiological response to danger in the interest of survival. To this end its purpose is to prepare the human being for fight or flight. It does this by increasing the activity level of the body systems. As we saw, the prototype of anxiety is the infant's crying and contortions. The repeated experiences of being cared for, coupled with normal development and maturation, relegate much of the purely instinctual survival anxiety to the past. It is always there, however, and comes to the surface if life is threatened. The remainder serves a psychological function. Psychosocial needs take on the same urgency as far as the purpose and function of anxiety are concerned. In other words, any perceived danger to significant psychosocial needs can reactivate anxiety in the same way that it does when survival is at stake. Thus anxiety serves both survival and psychological purposes.

With this in mind, anxiety is defined as tension and apprehension resulting from the subjective anticipation of danger from an unknown source. To be useful as a psychological concept, anxiety should be distinguished from fear. It is easy to confuse the two, since the physiological reactions are the same for both. The cause distinguishes one from the other. Fear is the apprehension resulting from a known source that is inherently dangerous. The response is appropriate. In fear the danger is real, objective, extrapsychic (e.g., a snake, a person with a gun). In anxiety the danger is subjectively determined; it is anticipated and unknown, internal and not readily determined. The source of anxiety is intrapsychic. Since the source of the danger is unknown, the individual has to engage in trial and error to try to escape from the danger, but what the individual seeks to escape from is the painful effect of the anxiety. However, as Schachtel (1959) states:

The threat of anxiety as a potentiality can be eliminated only by the actual encounter with the dreaded situation or activity, because until we actually meet the situation we do not know whether and how we will be able to live with it, master it, or perish in it, and thus we cannot transform the unknown and new into something knowable and known. Such encounter means leaving the embeddedness in the familiar and going forth to an unknown meeting with the world.

It is for these reasons that people most often want to reduce and alleviate anxiety. However, anxiety is a universally human emotion, and it is "normal" for people to experience it. Most of the time the individual can find an excuse or justification for normal anxiety: a test, a new job, an important report due, a new situation. Furthermore, coping mechanisms usually are effective in controlling and reducing normal anxiety so that the person continues to function well. Normal anxiety is proportionately manageable and serves as a constructive motivating force for the individual to be responsible in order to prevent greater anxiety. For example, to prevent greater anxiety from the threat of failing a test, the student studies. When anxiety goes beyond normal limits, it renders the individual dysfunctional, and the goal becomes getting rid of the anxiety rather than having it serve as a constructive motivating force. When anxiety becomes overwhelming, it is diffuse and vague. The individual complains of a feeling of nervousness and worry and feels afraid of something but is not exactly sure what it is.

Manifestations of anxiety

Overwhelming anxiety is a crisis state, and it is experienced and manifested in a variety of ways. The most common direct manifestations of anxiety are physiological and mental (psychomotor). Anxiety can affect almost every organ system in the human body. It makes a person feel as if there is something physically wrong. The most common physiological signs of anxiety are heart palpitation, flushing, tightness in the chest, inappropriate perspiration, increase in blood pressure, and rapid pulse. The individual may have tremors of various parts of the body such as the hands, or the entire body may shake. He or she may be restless or agitated, may pace the floor, or be unable to sit still. Sleeping disturbances, insomnia, excessive sleeping, and disturbing dreams are common. There may be a persistent cough, or clogging of the throat or a dry mouth. There may be a complaint of stomach pains, cramps, or burning sensations. The stomach discomfort may be referred to as a "nervous stomach." The person's appetite is generally poor, and he or she may complain of difficulty keeping food in the stomach, nausea, diarrhea or frequent urination, headaches, and backaches. There may be reduced interest in sex or even some sexual dysfunctioning. A disturbance in the menstrual cycle is not unusual. Hives or other changes in the skin can be caused by anxiety.

Anxiety greatly reduces mental functioning. It is in this area that the crisis therapist must assess and evaluate in order to determine the client's capacity for continued social functioning and the kind of treatment indicated. Anxiety may be manifested in the individual's communication and speech patterns. There may be slurring of words, rapid speech, or loud talking. Logical thinking capacity may be impaired, as may be judgment and decision making. Reality testing is most often affected. There may be poor or impaired concentration and attention span. There may be some confusion and poor memory. In essence, the emotionality affects normal mental capacity and leads to reduced social functioning.

Other indirect signs of anxiety include angry, hostile, or impulsive behavior. Various forms of acting out can be signs of anxiety, for example, behavior that is unusual for the individual such as sexual promiscuity, stealing, running away, excessive drinking, or drug use.

Meaning of anxiety for the person in crisis

Anxiety is one of the primary signs of a person in crisis. If an individual reacts to a precipitating event with anxiety, the basic meaning of the precipitating event to that individual is a perceived threat to survival, bodily integrity, or some psychosocially determined need perceived to have a life or death value (e.g., "I cannot live without her"). Anxiety resulting from a threat to survival or bodily integrity can be easily understood (e.g., illness, catastrophy, and other real threats to life). Anxiety resulting from the threat to a psychosocial need requires greater explanation. The basis of such anxiety is founded in the socialization process, specifically, in the human being's lengthy dependency on the mother or other caretaker for survival. When the child develops to the point that he or she can differentiate self from other objects and persons, he or she recognizes that mother is the major source of the satisfaction of survival needs and feelings of love, protection, and security. Early interactions with parents are especially important to emotional development. As confidence and contentment are developed through parents' repeated satisfaction of needs, and as the human being progresses through life, the importance of such needs are transferred to significant others (spouse, friend, loved one), symbols (money, home), situations (job, position), goals, and values. Their loss or threatened loss can create anxiety, and the reaction is similar to a threat to survival. In reality the feeling being experienced is, "This loss or threatened loss is so important to my survival, to my living, that I do not feel that I can function without it." "It is so significant to my emotional integrity and well-being that I cannot function. I feel helpless and confused. I do not know what I am going to do." "Without it something dreadful is going to happen to me." "I am no longer protected." "I cannot go on." Anxiety creates a general feeling of helplessness, unprotectedness, abandonment, or fear of physical or bodily harm.

DEPRESSION

Like anxiety, every human being periodically experiences some degree of depression. It may be called "feeling blue" or "feeling 'down' " or "in the dumps." However, our primary concern is understanding the degree of depression that is experienced in a crisis state, a debilitating depression. It should be pointed out, however, that the basic difference between "normal" depression referred to above, debilitating depression resulting from a crisis condition, and clinical depression is in degree and duration only. The psychodynamics are basically the same. In effect, clinical depression is an exaggeration of normal depression, which is why the individual's behavior and explanations are so unreasonable.

Depression, like anxiety, is a universally experienced emotion. However, depression and anxiety represent opposite ends of the affective continuum. Anxiety is a reaction to a perceived danger, real or imagined, in which survival is believed to be threatened. It is basically a physiological response that facilitates the individual's preparation for fight or flight, but in crisis its excessiveness is debilitating. Consequently anxiety is manifested by activity. In depression the opposite occurs. The individual is immobilized by turning energy (anger) inward. As Bibring (1953) states, "In extreme situations the wish to live is replaced by the wish to die." Depression as a mood disturbance is not in itself psychopathological. As previously stated, everyone becomes depressed at one time or another. Hence depression represents an affective continuum. For the person in crisis the depression reaches a debilitating degree. The extreme degree of depression reaches psychotic proportions manifested by delusions or hallucinations.

Manifestations of depression

Depression in a crisis state is a mood disturbance in which feelings of dejection, sadness, and despair are debilitating. Almost always, varying degrees of feelings of self-depreciation and unworthiness are expressed. The depressed person looks depressed and acts unhappy. Facial expression and posture reflect dejection and despair. The individual is generally pessimistic, feels helpless and very often hopeless. Sometimes suicidal intentions are present. There is generally a loss of interest in others, a tendency toward withdrawal, and preoccupation with self. Psychomotor retardation is manifested by lack of spontaneity and deliberate speech. Cognitive functioning and concentration are generally impaired. There are often physical complaints such as headaches or backaches. Constipation or gastrointestinal tract symptoms are often present; loss of appetite and insomnia are common. Guilt and self-blame are almost always involved, either directly or indirectly. There may be a preoccupation with thoughts of death or a wish to be dead. Sexual interest and affectionate feelings may decline. There may also be an excessive use of alcohol or various drugs.

Causes of depression

The causes of depression fall into two basic categories. The first is the loss or threatened loss of a love object or emotional support, self-esteem, status, position (e.g., economic failure), or role, and other ego values needed for psychic equilibrium. Feelings of being unloved and loneliness are the dominant features. The second cause of depression is failure to meet internalized standards, values, or goals. This category also includes violation of or a wish to violate moral values, right and wrong, good and bad, or the failure to achieve at a specific level. We saw such conditions in the cases of Rosemary and Doug.

Origin of depression

There are many explanations for the origin of depression. Freud said that it was similar to grief. The behavioral theorist says it is learned helplessness and loss of social reinforcement. The sociologist says that it results from loss of role status, and the existentialist says that it is the loss of meaning of existence. From this vantage point the basis of depression is twofold: (1) the seemingly innate need for human relatedness, affection, and psychosocially determined values to sustain psychic equilibrium; and (2) the nature and qualitative development of self-concept, self-esteem, and self-worth.

Earlier, reference was made to the internalization process, identification, and introjection. It is through these processes that the individual develops self-concept and self-values. Through socialization a set of functional self-values operates at all times to influence social functioning. When events occur that threaten self-concept or self-values, they are experienced as a personal loss to self, hence depression. When this happens, developmental feelings about the self, including those believed to be of the parents, are reactivated. Hence the individual evaluates self according to his or her interpretation of the meaning of the event causing the depression. For example, when Doug failed his doctoral comprehensive examinations he equated the external event with his worth. In effect he said, "Since I failed the examinations, I am personally no good, worthless." Such evaluations are the result of previous demands, standards, expectations, and evaluations by others, specifically parents. They are internalized and introjected into the individual psychic system, and functionally individuals respond to themselves in ways similar to the way their parents did or their perception of what would be the parents' response to their behavior, performance, or achievements. In sum, at the same time that it is believed that either directly or indirectly a human being is invariably involved in causing depression, another can help that individual through it. In other words, object relationships are both the cause and cure for depression. Depression is discussed further in Chapter 6.

Depression and anger

At the same time that the depressed person is angry, he or she generally feels the anger to be basically unacceptable in some form. Consequently he or she will have some feelings of guilt or unjustification for being angry. This is because the depressed person generally has difficulty expressing anger outwardly, perhaps because he or she feels that the person who is angry is a person who is not lovable. Consequently the individual, for fear of not being loved or not being nice, turns the anger inward rather than expressing it directly at the object or person causing the frustration or deprivation (e.g., a loved one or an enemy).

It follows therefore that generally the depressed person cannot express anger openly to an external source. If one could express anger, he or she would not become depressed. This does not mean, as so popularly stated, that the therapist should routinely force the depressed person to express the anger. It should be remembered that the depressed person feels guilty about the anger, and turning it inward is a form of self-punishment. The depressed person is already experiencing the "bad me" for the angry feelings, so to force the individual to express angry feelings before self-esteem has improved only reinforces the "bad" self-concept the person is currently experiencing. Sometimes permission to express anger to a person who is reluctant to do so may result in an excessive expression of anger. Therapeutic use of anger is discussed in Chapter 6. In the meantime it should suffice for therapists to recognize that sometimes the client will express anger toward them. Generally this is a subtle attack reflecting the client's expectation of the therapist's inability to help. This is often a reflection of the client's feeling of hopelessness; at other times it may be a test of the therapist's caring.

From this discussion of anxiety and depression, it is clear that the significance of the precipitating event to the person in crisis is reflected by whether the individual reacts with anxiety or depression. If the person reacts with anxiety, the precipitating event is perceived to be a threat to survival or welfare. If the person reacts with depression, the precipitating event represents a loss (e.g., love, self-esteem). Once the therapist determines whether the client is anxious or depressed, he or she can begin to ascertain why the precipitating event is perceived to have the significance it does. This can be determined by the client's communication, the subject of Chapter 3.

REFERENCES

Bibring, E. *The mechanism of depression*. In P. Greenacre (Ed.), *Affective disorders: psychoanalytic contributions to this study*. New York: International Universities Press, 1953.

Brenner, C. *An elementary textbook of psychoanalysis*. New York: International Universities Press, 1973.

Dixon S. L. *Dynamics of human behavior: an ego psychology perspective*. Unpublished manuscript.

Erikson, E. H. *Childhood and society*. New York: W. W. Norton, 1963.

Freud, A. *The ego and the mechanisms of defense*. (Rev. ed.). New York: International Universities Press, 1966. (Originally published, 1936.)

Goldstein, A. P. *Therapist-patient expectations in psychotherapy*. New York: Macmillan, 1962.

Laughlin, H. P. *The ego and its defenses*. New York: Appleton-Century-Crofts, 1970.

Laughlin, H. P., *The neuroses*. Reading, Mass.: Butterworths, 1967.

Menninger, K., with Martin, M., & Pruyser, P. *The vital balance: the life process in mental health and illness*, New York: Viking Press, 1963.

Reichmann-Fromm, F. *Principles of intensive psychotherapy*. Chicago: University of Chicago Press, 1950.

Rubinfine, D. Notes on a theory of depression. *The Psychoanalytic Quarterly*, 1968, *37*, 400-417.

Rusk, T. N. Opportunity and techniques in crisis psychiatry. *Comprehensive Psychiatry*, May 1971, *12*(3), 249-263.

Schachtel E. G. *Metamorphosis on the development of affect, perception, attention, and memory*. New York: Basic Books, 1959, p. 45.

Spitz, R. A. *Hospitalism: an inquiry into the genesis of psychiatric conditions in early childhood; the psychoanalytic study of the child.* New York: International Universities Press, 1945, *1*, 53-74.

SUGGESTED READINGS

Davitz, J. R. Fear, anxiety and the perception of others. *Journal of General Psychology,* 1959, *61*, 169-173.

Laughlin, H. P. *The ego and its defenses.* New York: Appleton-Century-Crofts, 1970.

May, R. *The meaning of anxiety.* New York: Ronald Press, 1950.

Mendels, J. *Concepts of depression.* New York: John Wiley & Sons, 1970.

CHAPTER 3

Communication process in crisis intervention

If crisis intervention is to have any value, the client must improve and change through the therapeutic relationship, that is, through his or her interpersonal interactions with the therapist. The ways the client and therapist communicate basically determine the nature of the therapeutic relationship, and on the other hand, the nature of the relationship affects the communication process. Hence the heart of learning how to work with people therapeutically is learning to communicate with them. Communication is the process through which clients convey their distress, the process through which the therapist implements his or her knowledge of human behavior. Most often the keys to therapeutic success or failure can be found in therapist-client communication. As a helping professional the therapist should control the communication situation (even though this relationship, as are all relationships, is mutually determined). Understanding the basics of interpersonal communication should increase the therapist's skills in helping people in crisis.

WHAT IS HUMAN COMMUNICATION?

Human beings are born with a capacity to communicate. We have inborn systems to transmit, receive, and process information, although the *ways* we do so are learned. Most of us learn to *encode* our meanings to transmit a message and to *decode* another person's messages to receive his or her meaning. (The words *encode* and *decode* are keys to understanding what communication is and how it functions.)

Let us now look at what communication is. For the purpose of this book, we can say that human communication is *the processes one individual uses to affect the behavior of another*. In our model a *sender* is one who wants to influence another by sending some stimulus. The *receiver* is the one whom the sender wants to influence. Regardless of the seeming insignificance of the message, the basic goal of the sender remains the same: to influence the receiver in some way. Thus each interpersonal communication "transaction" involves three elements: a sender, a message, and a receiver.

Communication is a social interaction between two or more people in a specific social context. Within the specific context the communication process starts with the sender, who first internally experiences some need to communicate. The sender wants to influence the receiver by sending a message; but to do so, he or she must use signals or symbols that both the sender and the intended receiver will understand. Words, gestures, or other symbols that the sender believes will transmit the message most effectively must be selected. These words and gestures become the symbolic representations of the sender's actual feelings and experiences. Again, the sender encodes the message.

It seems as though choosing effective communication signals would be easy, and it can be when the message is clear, forthright, and unambiguous. But it is a problem in most human communication. The exact meaning the sender really wants to communicate cannot be communicated as it was originally experienced inside the sender's head. Therefore the sender always takes the risk that the message might not be correctly understood, that his or her purpose might not be achieved, or that the message might be rejected. The difficulty can be created when the real meaning of the message transmitted is not even known to the sender, either because it has gotten lost in the encoding process or because some unconscious motivation interfered. In addition the individual's idiosyncratic psychic system, the ways he or she has learned to act toward other people, affects how messages are encoded and what is chosen to communicate. Thus when the client is the sender and the therapist is the receiver, the sender's real goal, to influence another person, must always be at the forefront of the therapist's mind.

Even before a thought, feeling, or impulse is transmitted as a message, it passes through a series of internal screens. Most persons give a great deal of thought to a message before they send it. They try to shape the message in whatever way is most likely to get the desired response. Even as young children we learn that our communication goals are not likely to be reached unless we transmit messages in intrapersonally and socially acceptable ways. These ways may not be the exact translations of our true feelings. The original message may be antisocial, hostile, self-centered, or otherwise socially unacceptable. Therefore we learn to encode, to translate the original message into symbols or behavior we believe to have the best chance to achieve the desired goals. If the sender believes that a message expressed in its original form will be rejected or work to his or her disadvantage, he or she will not express it directly or clearly but will disguise it to avoid rejection.

By the time people reach adulthood, they have developed internal screens that prevent them from transmitting emotionally unacceptable thoughts, feelings, and ideas. These screens may be used consciously, or the person may be unaware of them. Many messages never get encoded because of anticipated consequences. Certain words or feelings may be completely blocked and never encoded. Examples might include curse words or feelings of extreme jealousy.

FACTORS AFFECTING COMMUNICATION

Once a person decides that it is appropriate to express a feeling or idea, he or she must select and transmit symbols for that experience. One can choose words, language, affect, gestures, postures, and other behavioral manifestations as symbols. To understand the true meaning of the message, the receiver needs to know not only the meaning of the words but also their usage and form within the language. Because most of our daily communication is accomplished with relatively few familiar words, most people assume that the words and language they use mean the same thing to everyone. But they do not. Again, communication symbols are only substitutes for reality; they are not the reality itself. The specific ways a person communicates are determined by several significant factors.

First and foremost are the specific life experiences of the individual, the ways the individual has been socialized. Most newborn infants have the capacity to interact with their environment through biological reflex action. For instance, they cry when they are in pain. These biological reflex actions are given a meaning by the caretaker (e.g., the mother smoothes powder on the baby's chafed skin). Thus the infant begins to learn that reactions can be provoked from the external world. Eventually the baby learns to associate words and language with specific experiences and then with groups of experiences. "Milk" is not just the liquid in this cup; it is the liquid I drank yesterday and will drink tonight. Not only is language developed in this fashion, but people learn to meet needs and to negotiate the environment in this way.

Each human beings life is a continuity of experiences, and individual methods of communication reflect those experiences. Each word contains all the associations accumulated to date. Hence individuals from different cultures, subcultures, and even different neighborhoods will have different frames of reference and therefore different communication patterns. One important topic currently receiving a great deal of attention by linguists is minority communication patterns such as "black language," the idiosyncratic meanings of English used by many blacks. For example, many blacks use and understand the expression "sometimes it bes that way." To translate that statement into edited American English we would say, "That is the way life is sometimes; that is reality and is unchanging; so accept it and do not worry about it." That underlying meaning would not be known to someone who was not familiar with the American black subculture. The therapist who wishes to communicate with a member of a subculture must learn to "speak the language."

A second factor that determines the way a person communicates is the social context in which the communication interaction takes place. Most people usually communicate differently in a formal setting than in an informal one. For example, you use different language to express frustration in the office than on the tennis court.

A third factor that determines how a person communicates is the roles of those people communicating. For example, students generally communicate differently with their professors than with each other. Clients generally communicate differently with therapists than with peers. Roles and status are important in therapy situations because they can provoke feelings about authority and self-images.

This leads to the next factor that contributes to the way each person communicates: self-concept. *Self-concept* is how individuals see themselves and their own identities. It involves perception, real and imagined personability, abilities and weaknesses. Most individuals communicate most of the time in ways that are consistent with their self-concepts. Remember that communication involves both transmitting and receiving. People not only transmit information in ways that are consistent with their self-concept (be it positive or negative), but they also receive information that way. In fact, much communication is designed to enhance, maintain, or defend the person's self-concept as well as to reflect it. Thus a great deal of receptive communication is influenced by whether the receiver perceives the message as a threat to his or her own self-concept. However, most people are largely unaware of their feelings about themselves and therefore are unaware of a great deal of what they communicate. Whether recognized or not, self-concept is reflected by an individual's communication patterns. For example, negative self-concepts may be reflected when people do not take care of themselves or when they are unassertive or allow themselves to be exploited. Superior self-concepts can be reflected in habits of talking down to people or in using complex or complicated words and phrases to impress or dramatize.

Self-concept influences perception of others as well. The basis for perceiving others is directly related to how people perceive themselves.

A fifth factor that influences how a person communicates is educational. This factor can be very important when people who have different amounts or kinds of education are communicating, especially if the person with the greater education does not take this difference into consideration. It is important that the more educated person not look down on the other, but that he or she choose words and phrases that are common, clear, and easily understood. The skill of a therapist can be determined by how effective he or she translates theory and certain concepts into simple words that are understandable by all, regardless of educational level.

A sixth factor in determining how a person communicates with someone else is previous experience with the same person. People who communicate frequently learn each other's habitual patterns, feelings, and preferences. When people are familiar with each other, they can take shortcuts; they can make assumptions about the other's responses. For instance, you may hear a student say, "To get a good grade, you must say what Professor O'Connell wants to hear." The student is simply saying that he or she has already learned something about the professor. Many clients learn very quickly to say what the therapist wants to hear or to say what is socially expected.

RECEIVER

Thus far we have been discussing communication from the viewpoint of the sender, the person initiating the communication process. But the *consequence* of the communication process is determined by the receiver, by how the receiver interprets the sender's message, since that is what will determine his or her reaction. Once the sender transmits the message, he or she loses control over it. Communication is a process of cumulative social interaction. The receiver goes through a process similar to that of the sender. But what determines the way the receiver responds to the communication symbols, to the sender's words, language, tone of voice, nonverbal gestures? How does predisposition influence the way in which one reacts? The emotional disposition of the individual and the experiences associated with the symbols chosen by the sender determine the reaction. To understand this we need to recall our knowledge of human behavior and various concepts of emotions.

But first we should consider the communication system of the receiver. Reception is no less complicated than transmission. Each receiver also has a set of mental barriers and screens that control not only what is heard but how it is heard. People screen various stimuli in all communication situations, partially because there are too many stimuli (words, voice, movement, facial expression, hands) to attend to them all. They both consciously and unconsciously select certain stimuli to which they will respond while omitting others. Through this weeding-out process the whole meaning of the message can be changed. The receiver may be protected by being on guard against messages that make him or her feel anxious and uncomfortable or that disturb self-perception or self-esteem. For example, a woman who prides herself on being well liked as a defense against her own hostile feelings toward other people may be greatly upset by someone telling her that her friends do not like her when she talks too much. And she may choose to ignore that message, interpreting it as a sign of the sender's hostility or jealousy toward her. Most people have internal needs that result from the development of their own unique psychic systems and lead to particular sensitivity to certain stimuli.

Another factor that influences what people hear is self-interest. People generally hear those things that interest or stimulate them, that affect their own welfare, that meet their needs or expectations, either positive or negative. Some people are "set" to hear negative things about themselves, especially if they think negatively about themselves. On the other hand, they will ignore or misinterpret those positive messages that threaten their internal consistency. Just as the sender has motives for initiating the communication, the receiver has premessage motives and attitudes that facilitate reception of certain stimuli and avoidance of others.

Certain defense mechanisms (see Chapter 2) play a very important part in what one hears. For example, a person who is projecting may hear what he or she would have said rather than what actually was said. In reaction formation the opposite of what was actually said is heard; in the use of repression and denial the message is not heard at all. These defense mechanisms, so inherent in our mental processes, affect the degree of accuracy with which a message is received. They help to protect people from hearing things that would be inconvenient, harmful, or anxiety producing.

Another factor that influences what is received is expectation. People often hear what they expect to hear, whether it is said or not. Sometimes they do this because they have a stereotyped idea of a group to which the individual belongs. For instance, if a person wears a shaggy beard and long hair, he may be expected to express radical ideas, or a woman lawyer may be expected to be conservative. The tendency to attribute to individuals the characteristics of the group they are associated with is widespread, and often what is heard is what a person is expected to say rather than what is said. Professional therapists need to understand the various groups with whom they work and to look beyond the groups to individual people.

PROCESS OF RECEPTION

Any stimulus or message from a sender travels to a receiver, and the receiver uses some sense organs, usually the eyes and the ears, to take in the stimulus. The stimulus is transmitted to the brain, and the message is psychologically received. Then the process of decoding begins. The receiver interprets the message, making it consistent with his or her frame of reference. Again, each receiver has a unique frame of reference determined by his or her life experiences, self-concept, level of education, status in the relationship, and the social context. At times a message may remind a receiver (especially one under stress) of a previous similar situation that may not have any relevance. The receiver may compare the old and new situations and translate the current one according to previous meanings. In so doing he or she may distort the current messages by omitting some of the information and modifying certain ideas to make them acceptable or justifiable, thus responding to a different message than the sender intended. If the sender then responds to the distorted perceptions, that response may also be inappropriate.

SUCCESSFUL COMMUNICATION

The full meaning of the form and content of any communication interaction cannot be understood without considering both the sender and the receiver. When both the sender and the receiver feel that they have benefited, a communication exchange is successful. But it is not easy to achieve success. Let us look at why.

First, both the sender and the receiver have some goal in the communication exchange. The receiver's first response to the sender's first message begins a cumulative social interaction. Both the sender and receiver usually want to benefit from the exchange, which may lead to significant differences and disagreements.

Second, communication involves symbols, both verbal and nonverbal. While a fist to the eye is a pretty direct method of expression, even it is open to interpretation. And language is much less specific, much more open to the meaning each person brings to it. To better understand how language contributes to difficulties in communicating, we must look more closely at the nature of language itself.

Meaning of language

We use language to represent reality, but it can never be the reality itself. A language is a system of symbols that a social group uses to communicate. The members of the group agree on both specific symbols to represent specific ideas or objects, *words,* and rules by which to string those symbols together, *syntax.* Language is only a substitute for the reality that it attempts to represent, and reality is actually much more complex than the meaning language can convey. For example, we call a four-legged furry animal with a wagging tail and certain other characteristics simply a dog, and as long as everyone shares this understanding, communication can take place. The meaning of the word "dog" is arbitrarily assigned by the group of people who speak English. We could easily call this animal something else, perhaps chien, as the French do. The point is simply that the meaning of the word must be understood by everyone in the social group. Those who do not understand the common meaning cannot communicate.

However, the process of communication is not made simple by the sharing of a common language; there are not enough words in any language to give an exact representation of all shades of ideas, feelings, and experiences. Words call into play feelings and memories associated with previous experiences. To some people "dog" has a very specific meaning; to someone who has never owned a dog, the word conveys less information. Still other information is conveyed to someone who has been bitten by a dog. The meaning a word evokes for a receiver may be based both on experience with the symbol and with the referent itself.

In other words, using the same language is only half of the communication process. Experience gives language meaning. Each individual's perceptions, emotions, and thoughts come from experiences; language represents these experiences, and the experiences give meaning to the language. Thus communication is facilitated through common experiences. People in low socioeconomic groups and those in the middle socioeconomic groups may have difficulty understanding each other because of different life experiences and different goals and values. For instance, the word "hunger" will have a different meaning for someone who has actually faced not having enough to eat than for someone who gets "hungry" an hour before each meal. And those two people may have trouble communicating about the problem of a lost job if they do not understand their differences. It is important to remember that *experiences,* not class memberships, are the major differences between two individuals. Although a great deal is made over racial and cultural differences, it is personal *experiences* that should be the basis for understanding. Individual members of racial and ethnic minorities may have had the same experiences as the majority group. The romantic experiences of two white Anglo-Saxon teenagers, one healthy and one with cerebral palsy, may be more different than those of the healthy teenager and Chicano counterparts. Expectations and stereotyping should not be allowed to intrude into the communication process. Each exchange should start where the two participants actually are, not where each thinks the other is.

In most communication situations, the sender and the receiver assume that they are on the same frequency and that they both understand the words used. This is often a fallacy, and communication fails. How many times have you said, "I did not mean it that way" or "That was not what I said"? Thus for communication to be successful, both parties must choose their language carefully, taking into consideration all those factors we have discussed: the background of the other person, the status relationships, the specific situation, and educational background.

Language is problematic because it is composed of symbols that are emotionally laden, have multiple meanings, and represent memories of actual experiences and not the experiences themselves.

The weakness of language as a communication medium is not cause for alarm. Functionally language has a broader purpose than merely social interaction; it is a tool we use to describe, understand, and control the environment and extend it beyond our own physical capacities. We understand certain ideas only because we have language to describe them, not because we have personal experience with them.

Meaning of words

The basis of any language is an oral system; the basic unit is the spoken word. In everyday speech, most of us tend to use a relatively limited, familiar vocabulary that we take for granted. The words become so familiar that we may think that the words we use are real themselves, that they are not simply arbitrary sounds. But words *are* arbitrary; they are symbols representing experiences and feelings and are loaded with old emotions and experiences.

It is on this basis that words have a great capacity to evoke strong feelings. For example, words such as "macho," "equality," "libber," and "freedom" can provoke equally strong but widely varying meanings in different people and under different conditions. For example, the familiar word "independence" can be a very powerful emotional stimulus for adolescents attempting to emancipate themselves from their parents. Some words are so powerfully emotive that responses to people may be irrational. The words "busing" and "strike," for example, have become quite powerful. "Busing" only recently achieved this power, in spite of the fact that children have been riding buses to school for generations. But today, to many people, "busing" means poor education, mixing the races, wasting money, and fear.

Other taboo words have enormous emotional power and control over people's behavior and feelings. Magical and superstitious powers are attributed to certain words used in rituals and ceremonies. Words can make rational and logical people think and behave illogically. They can be used for deliberate deception or for arousing prejudices of all kinds.

For the therapist, words can reduce emotional upset and restore the client's cognitive control. Words can evoke strong emotions because a person has fused the word with what it represents in the mind. Words with double meanings or overly emotive words are more likely to have strongly personal interpretations, which decreases the chances that the sender's message will be understood. The therapist should remember this and carefully choose his or her words with the client's individual life experiences, educational level, and social context in mind. For example, a Caucasian could refer to "you people" or "your kind" with no harm in mind. But a minority client may interpret the phrase as being derogatory. The client may feel looked down on. Understanding how words can evoke powerful feelings is a critical skill for the therapist. In fact, for the nonmedical therapist words and language are his or her most important tools.

Denotative and connotative meanings of words

A second difficulty with words (in addition to their emotional power) is their multiple meanings. Words have two types of meanings: denotative and connotative. Denotative meanings are the literal meanings, the dictionary definition of a word that all the users of the language agree on. Some words have more than one denotative meaning. For instance, the word "class" can mean a group of items ranked together, possessing common characteristics or a group of people brought together for the purpose of education. A university student, asked to which class he or she belongs, may not be sure whether the question refers to educational level, economic status, or social background. And miscommunication can be the result.

The connotative meaning of a word involves all the word's associations, its emotional meanings. Again take "class" as an example. In addition to denoting a group, it can have the connotative meaning of "refinement": "She has class." The ordinary words "pig" and "turkey" have recently taken on negative connotative meaning. Connotations can be given to a word by a small subgroup of a population and offer another hurdle in the path of successful communication between therapist and client. For instance, if the therapist were not familiar with the current connotation of "turkey," he or she might respond completely inappropriately to being called one.

Nonverbal communication

Nonverbal messages are transmitted by behaviors other than speech. They include gestures, facial expressions, posture, body movements, tone of voice and intonation, and quite frequently dress. They can occur in conjunction with verbal communication or independent of it and are very often used to reinforce some verbal communication (consider a greeting such as a handshake, for example; even the strength of the handshake can be significant). But nonverbal messages can be and often are independent of verbal communication (consider the person who looks at a watch every 5 minutes during a conversation). A combination of consistent verbal and nonverbal messages produces the clearest communication.

Generally, nonverbal messages are easily interpreted and have meanings that are often determined by social context. Gestures that occur most often along with speech include head and hand movements. They are often used for emphasis; examples include pointing and tracing an object with the hands. Many facial expressions are used to express emotions such as happiness, anger, surprise, fear, sadness, or frustration. Head and hand movements are probably the most frequently used methods of nonverbal communication and are often used by people who have difficulty expressing their ideas or feelings verbally. Gestures expressing anger, such as frowning, are easily interpreted. The angry motorist shaking a fist is another example.

Body posture and movement can also reflect feelings; it can indicate interest and enthusiasm or boredom. Posture can indicate anxiety (consider the person poised on the edge of a chair) or depression. It can indicate joy as well.

Nonverbal communication is important largely because both the sender and the receiver are greatly influenced by what they see. They interpret the meaning of nonverbal messages personally, just as they do verbal messages. The sender's nonverbal cues advise the receiver how one should respond to the message, and the sender uses the receiver's nonverbal clues to gauge the reception of the message. A nod of the head and interested facial expression may communicate to a speaker that a member of audience is interested in talking.

Many people send nonverbal messages that they are not aware of. These messages may not be consistent with the person's verbal behavior. For instance, Diana, an attractive woman, complained tearfully because men were always making passes at her. She felt that they were thinking that she was "available." Diana had grown up in a strict home in which any form of seductiveness was severely admonished. Thus she had repressed her curiosity about this behavior. But even though it had always been forbidden, she had feelings that led her to dress and move in ways that men found attractive. She unconsciously communicated nonverbal seductive behavior. The fact that men responded made her feel guilty, although she was not aware that she was behaving seductively. But the therapist could see the inconsistency in Diana's verbal messages and her nonverbal signal.

There are times that tone of voice, intonation, and speed of speech are also nonverbal communication. They are especially meaningful when they are inconsistent with the meaning of the verbal message. When this occurs, their nonverbal meaning is generally a more accurate reflection of true feelings. This is discussed again in Chapter 4.

SUMMARY

Communication is a process of social interaction in which people attempt to influence each other for the purpose of achieving some more or less specific goal.

Although communication occurs on all levels, true communication can only take place when there is understanding and agreement between the persons involved. Human communication is based on the transmission and reception of stimuli consisting of verbal and nonverbal symbols having predetermined meanings. Its success is determined by the accuracy of the receiver's interpretation of the intended meaning of the sender's message. Messages are encoded and decoded according to life experiences, including culture, education, and socioeconomic status, and according to each individual's psychic system. Clear communication occurs when a stimulus is encoded and transmitted freely and clearly and decoded in such a way that the receiver accurately interprets the meaning. Although it may be easier to communicate with those who share similar experiences, almost any two people have some areas of common understanding that can serve as a primary focus in all communication.

The importance of understanding the communication process, especially its cumulative interactive nature, the meaning and evocative capacities of words and language, and the importance of nonverbal communication, cannot be overemphasized. In crisis communication the clients' messages, feelings, and ideas may be confusing even to themselves, and they may not be aware of what they want to communicate. The ability of the therapist to hear and interpret a client's messages and provide feedback is a most important tool. The therapist must keep in mind the client's crisis state and interpret and respond according to knowledge of human behavior. A person in crisis is experiencing a variety of painful and confusing feelings. The therapist must be able to sort out these feelings and communicate them back to the client in such a way that the client can understand what is going on within himself or herself. The client then receives, digests, translates, and interprets the meaning of the therapist's messages and again responds. Thus the interaction perpetuates itself. If the client feels understood, accepted, and respected regardless of the crisis condition or behavior, a good relationship will result. For both the client and therapist, the willingness to continue to communicate depends on the hope that positive benefits will result to each person involved. When this is no longer believed to be possible, efforts to communicate stop.

Chapter 4 is devoted to the application of this basic model of communication to the process and techniques of therapeutic intervention, especially the initial interview.

REFERENCES

Applebaum, R. L., *et al. Fundamental concepts in human communication.* San Francisco: Canfield Press, 1973.
Davitz, J. R. *The communication of emotional meaning.* New York: McGraw-Hill, 1964.
Trojanowicz, R. C., & Dixon, S. L. *Criminal justice and the community.* Englewood Cliffs, N.J.: Prentice-Hall, 1974.

SUGGESTED READINGS

Cherry, C. *On human communication.* New York: John Wiley & Sons, 1978.
Kadushin, A. *The social work interview.* New York: Columbia University Press, 1972.

CHAPTER 4

Process and techniques of therapeutic interviewing

As we saw in Chapter 3, communication is crucial to the therapeutic relationship and as such is the foundation for interviewing. Within this frame of reference, this chapter discusses a most important skill: therapeutic interviewing. Special attention is given to the first interview, since it is without doubt the most crucial factor in determining whether a therapist will be able to help a client resolve a crisis. Errors or mistakes in subsequent sessions generally do not affect the outcome as much as those in the first session.

It should be borne in mind that although crisis therapy may take place anywhere (on a street, on a bridge, on the telephone, in an emergency room of a hospital, in a home, or in an office), the process of interviewing and treatment are basically the same, given circumstantial variations. The interventive process and techniques in this chapter are not limited to crisis therapy. However, in working with people in crisis they are used much more actively and rapidly. Consequently their use in crisis therapy requires considerable understanding and skill.

PURPOSE OF THE THERAPEUTIC INTERVIEW

The initial therapeutic interview has two purposes: to begin to develop a shared feeling of understanding and to assess the client's condition and social functioning so that the therapist can intervene to help resolve the crisis. Sharing means that the client will learn about his or her own condition through the interaction. The crisis therapist must quickly ascertain information that leads to an understanding and an assessment of the client's problems, condition, and level of social functioning. The process of interviewing is the major medium by which these goals are achieved.

PROCESS OF INTERVIEWING

It should be clear by now that the interaction between therapist and client is the process through which the client benefits and constructive changes occur. The communication process is the heart of the therapeutic intervention, and it depends on the relationship between therapist and client. Thus the first task in therapeutic interviewing is to establish a constructive relationship. Let us look at how this can be achieved.

Therapeutic relationship

Because the therapeutic relationship is so important to therapeutic outcome, the crisis therapist must know as much as possible about it. It differs from a social relationship. The goals of social relationships are fun, mutual stimulation, and satisfaction. The purpose of the therapeutic relationship is to alleviate the client's problems and improve social functioning. It is a relationship that promotes emotional growth and learning. The client is not expected to gratify the therapist's social and psychological needs. Therefore the many amenities of social relationships are omitted from the therapeutic relationship, and the resolution of the client's problem is always in the therapist's mind. Sometimes sugar-coated, light social behavior is believed to be the basis of a good relationship. But a client in crisis is unhappy; he or she is suffering emotionally. Light social behavior may make the client feel that his or her problems are not taken very seriously or that he or she is not important. This does not mean that there is no place for humor, but the therapist must resist the temptation to avoid the client's distress by making light and nonserious conversation. Regardless of the possible humor, this is not the time to say, "It is better laughed about" or "At least you can still laugh about it."

Preinterview factors

Even before the first interview begins, the relationship is affected by several factors having to do with both the client and the therapist. The first is the fact that the client is asking the therapist for help. Even though the client in crisis is more helpless and more amenable to being helped than at any other time in life, his or her feelings and attitudes about asking for emotional help should be considered. Even though society's attitude toward asking for help has greatly improved, many people still feel "funny" about it. Many clients put off seeking help for some time, not only because they are trying to solve their problems themselves but also because of their reluctance to ask for help. This is exemplified by Deborah, who came for help after ineffectively struggling for several weeks with her grief over the sudden and unexpected death of Bob, her husband. She had talked for about an hour and had begun to feel better when she suddenly said, "I'm sorry I had to come; Bob would not have wanted me to be here. He would have considered it a sign of weakness, and he always wanted me to be strong." A client's negative feelings about seeking help should be dealt with, since they generally reflect the client's pride and perhaps self-concept. Therefore they may be obstacles to therapeutic goals.

A second preinterview factor is the therapist's confidence: his or her assurance that he or she will be able to help; his or her wondering whether "nervousness" will be detected. This is of particular concern to new therapists. Self-awareness and a dialogue with oneself regarding the meaning of these feelings will go a long way toward reducing their effect. However, experience is the best long-term cure.

A third preinterview condition worthy of note is initial perception, the impressions gained from first sight to the beginning of the official interview. For better or for worse, people form impressions from the ways other people look, act, and talk before they get to know them. We let new stimuli reactivate previous images, impressions, and experiences to give us some control over new and unfamiliar situations. It is not unusual for a client to look at the therapist and match his or her appearance or physical characteristics with those of someone in the client's past. Or the client may initially feel that a therapist is warm or cold on the basis of some personal characteristics. Such initial impressions are an inevitable part of being human, of the effort to make the unfamiliar familiar. Therapists should strive to be genuine and be themselves in their choice of dress and behavior. But dress should not be so different from the professional norm that it becomes an obstacle. Nor should initial behavior be out of line with the norm. Preinterview conditions can either facilitate the communication process and the establishment of a therapeutic relationship or retard them. The therapist's first task is to be aware of them.

Establishing a therapeutic relationship

As the therapist starts the official first interview, he or she should be aware of the preinterview conditions as a part of the observation procedure. However, these are preliminary; most often the beginning of the real relationship starts with the first official contact with the client in the office or other therapeutic setting. In cases where first contact between client and therapist is by telephone, the communication and relationship start then. Telephone communication tends to increase the importance of the preinterview conditions. In such cases characteristics of a therapeutic relationship are just as operable as in face-to-face situations.

The success or failure of the entire therapeutic process can depend on the opening of the first interview. The therapist should behave seriously, being neither unduly light nor overly friendly. Greetings should be in keeping with personality, but genuinely warm and cordial, in a natural and quiet tone. Overly friendly, loud welcomings should be avoided. Sullivan (1954) states that although he does not overwelcome clients, he does try to convey that they were expected and that he wished to see them. The client should be greeted by title and last name. In the opening phase of the interview, first names should be avoided. If the therapist prefers first names, their use should be delayed until the client and therapist know and feel comfortable with each other. Using first-name greetings before a good relationship has been established can cause a problem for some clients. Consequently the use of first names should never be taken for granted. For some clients the use of first names early in the relationship is felt to be derogatory. The therapist should know the meaning that first names have for clients before they are used routinely.

The personalities of both therapist and client contribute to the outcome of the process. To understand clients and help them, the therapist needs certain qualities (Carkhuff and Berenson, 1977; Rogers, 1957; Truax and Carkhuff, 1967). The kind of person the therapist is, regardless of theoretical orientation or technique, is the key to effective intervention. The therapist's humaneness, values, feelings, attitudes, and behavior all contribute greatly to the therapeutic relationship. Because communication involves mutual interaction, the client is in a position to perceive many of the therapist's true feelings. As Ellis (1955) states:

The personality of the therapist is a most important factor in psychotherapy. . . . The therapist's deepest inner self, as well as his more external characteristics and manner, are, whether or not he is conscious of the fact, inevitably used in his therapeutic relationship; and it is by the use of himself as an instrument that he usually . . . helps effect significant changes in the self of the client.

Perhaps the next question is: How is the therapeutic relationship established? How is it brought about? In addition to being an able communicator, the therapist needs certain facilitative capacities: acceptance, respect, genuineness, nonjudgmental attitude, empathic understanding, and the capacity to tolerate and to elicit painful emotional feelings.

Acceptance. The basis of all therapeutic relationships is the acceptance of the client as a worthy and valuable person. Everyone needs to feel accepted throughout life. Acceptance means to the individual that he or she has worth and value; that he or she deserves the therapist's time and efforts to help. Many persons do not seek help because they are afraid that they will not be considered important. Others approach the setting anticipating being rejected and feeling unacceptable. Consequently the therapist must communicate a feeling of acceptance to the client, not verbally but affectively and behaviorally. The therapist does not have to take any specific action. He or she will communicate feelings verbally and nonverbally when they are there.

The concept of acceptance should not be confused with the blanket approval of all human behavior, especially dastardly acts such as rape, child abuse, assult, or homicide. But although the therapist dislikes those acts, he or she can still accept the individual as worthy of the effort to help. Generally the therapist should be able to accept anyone for two reasons: (1) because the therapist has a need to help others, and (2) because the therapist understands human motivation and wants to understand the client. The therapist knows that all human behavior is motivated, is purposeful, and is an individual effort to meet needs. What the client with the worst behavior needs from a therapist is not condemnation but an effort to understand him or her in such a way that he or she can be helped to meet needs in more constructive ways.

The client, no matter what he or she does, must feel accepted in order to feel worthy and to develop confidence in the therapist. The client must willingly express feelings and must be able to deal with problems and self safely, honestly, and effectively. As Biestek (1957) states: "The purpose of acceptance is therapeutic; to aid . . . in understanding the client as he really is."

It should be clear that acceptance cannot take place unless the therapist is genuine and has respect for the dignity of all human beings. These feelings are basically a product of socialization and life experiences that accumulate before a person becomes a therapist. Training, knowledge, and education only intensify them. If these feelings are not already there in the individual, all the knowledge, training, and education in the world will not make that individual an effective therapist. If, on the other hand, these feelings are there, education and experiences will activate them.

Empathic understanding. Another capacity instrumental to establishing a therapeutic relationship is empathic understanding, which is an extension of the process of empathy. Empathy occurs through identification; the therapist shares the feelings of the client by projecting himself or herself into the client's situation. Although this enables the therapist to feel what the client feels, the therapist still must maintain objectivity and control emotional involvement. It is a form of saying, "I know how you feel."

Empathy is often confused with sympathy. Feeling sympathy connotes feeling sorry for a person, not only for suffering but also because of the hopelessness and inevitability of the condition or situation. Feeling sympathy does not mean sharing feelings. In empathy there are shared feelings, but there is also confidence or hope that something can be done to improve the situation. The therapist who has sympathy rather than empathy communicates a feeling of hopelessness to the client.

The crisis therapist must take empathy one step farther to empathic understanding. Empathic understanding means that the therapist not only has empathy but has the capacity to communicate it to the client. Again, the therapist does not have to demonstrate empathic understanding directly or dramatically. This second human feeling will be communicated if it is there. The client will know when he or she is understood and feelings are shared. Again, the therapist's genuineness and respect for the client play a very important part. Empathic understanding cannot be artificial. If the therapist needs to say, "I understand," it must be at a time when he or she actually feels that way and also feels that the client needs to be reassured. It should never be said simply because it is "good technique."

Sometimes a client will ask the therapist "Do you understand me?" This is important because of its possible meanings. It could mean that the client feels that the therapist is not communicating understanding effectively. Or if the client is accustomed to being misunderstood, he or she may just assume that the therapist does not understand. If so, if the therapist truly does understand, the client's questions should be briefly explored. For example, it might be beneficial for the therapist to say, "I think I understand you quite well. Is there something about me that makes you think that I don't understand you?" These responses give the therapist information about the client's perceptions and whether something he or she is not aware of is being communicated. In addition they help the client become aware of the interaction in the relationship and of interpersonal differences in perception.

Acceptance of painful feelings. A third important therapist characteristic is the ability to elicit and tolerate painful feelings, regardless of content. A crisis, by definition, is an extremely painful emotional state, one that people try desperately to avoid. But for the person in crisis, avoiding the painful feelings is harmful. Consequently the therapist must be able to help the client face these feelings by responses that encourage their maximum expression, regardless of what they are or how painful. The therapist too, must be able to tolerate such painful affect. Helping the client face painful emotional feelings not only facilitates the therapist's understanding of the client's condition, but it is ego strengthening because the client has the support of the therapist to face feelings that had to be faced alone before. If the therapist has difficulty tolerating painful affect, he or she might try to make the client feel better too soon, before the client had sufficiently expressed his or her emotional feelings.

The process of establishing a therapeutic relationship has been discussed. In effect, the capacity of a therapist to do this depends on the kind of person the therapist is. It depends on the capacity to accept people as they are, to be honest and genuine. It depends on the capacity to communicate empathic understanding and on the ability to elicit and tolerate the client's painful emotions.

Quite frequently warmth is associated with a therapeutic relationship. But again, the therapist should not act artificially warm. An expression of warmth should really be the intrinsic feelings of the therapist brought out by the client's need for help. In this regard the therapist should not strive to be warm but simply to be himself or herself and not to be oversolicitous. In the final analysis, perhaps the client wants above all to be accepted and understood. This should be the consequence of a natural human relationship, nothing artificial or contrived.

The techniques of interviewing that facilitate the therapeutic relationship can now be discussed.

TECHNIQUES OF INTERVIEWING

Although the word "technique" has a connotation of mechanical or manipulative approach, it is a precise explanation of what the therapist does. For the purpose of this book the word *technique* is used to identify the skill portion of the therapeutic process, the manner of performance. Techniques are what the therapist does to make things happen and to achieve the therapeutic goal. The four major techniques of therapeutic interviewing are observing, listening, and questioning and exploring.

Observing

It may seem strange to consider observation a technique of interviewing. Nevertheless it is, and it requires a great deal of skill. Observation is a technique used from the beginning of the therapeutic process until the process is terminated. The therapist uses knowledge of human behavior and consciously observes the client to collect information. The first use of the technique of observation is observing the nonverbal signals sent by the client in the preinterview stage. These are the therapist's first clues to understanding the client. What is it about the client that the therapist observes? First, the therapist observes the client's dress and physical and personal appearance. Although there is a great deal of freedom today in choice of dress and personal appearance, they still can be significant. Dress and personal appearance are forms of self-expression. They can reflect an individual's state of mind, body image, self-concept, or membership in a certain cultural subgroup. However, the significance of dress and personal appearance for the crisis therapist is how they reflect the client's condition. Dress is generally consistent with position in life— with age, sex, occupation, culture and socioeconomic status. If dress and personal appearance of the person in crisis vary significantly from the expected patterns, they most often reflect the crisis condition. They may indicate lowered self-esteem, a decreased interest in self and personal relationships. On the other hand, the person in crisis who continues to maintain his or her customary dress and personal appearance may show a higher level of ego functioning, of hope and motivation for help. Concern with maintaining customary patterns of dress and personal appearance indicates the individual's desire to maintain human contact and personal relationships, which are vital needs for the person in crisis. In any event, dress and personal appearance can represent concern for self, interest in others, or the debilitating effect of the crisis.

The importance of the observation of physical appearance is twofold: it can indicate (1) how an individual takes care of himself or herself or (2) whether there is bodily abuse through drugs, alcohol, or inadequate diet.

Second, the therapist observes the client's gait, posture, gestures, nonverbal facial expressions, and affect. These will also be observed during the interview, but the therapist should be sensitive to them from the first time the client is seen. Gait and posture are fairly easy to interpret. For example, a slow methodical gait can show depression, fatigue, discouragement, lack of interest. On the other hand, a rapid gait could represent anxiety, fear, or agitation. Posture, like gait, very often expresses a specific mood or affect, from the person who slumps in a chair to one who perches on the edge of the seat. Also, posture may reflect changes in affect during the course of the interview. An example is the client who rocks continuously in the chair until the therapist says something that is significant, and then stops. Posture can also indicate boredom and disinterest.

Most gestures are hand movements. They can show anger or emphasis (e.g., clenching a fist, pointing a finger, or pounding on the table). They can represent anxiety and depression (e.g., nailbiting, wringing the hands, chain-smoking). The hands can express feelings of confusion, discouragement, or just plain hopelessness. Perhaps the most accurate nonverbal expressions of true feelings are facial expressions, including the eyes. Facial expressions reflect certain feelings; they mirror joy, sadness, pain, unhappiness, approval, disapproval, interest or disinterest, enthusiasm, boredom, anxiety, depression. The eyes also can reflect hope or sadness. They can reflect shyness or low self-esteem. And they reflect feelings about others as well as self. The way that one person looks at another can express love, hate, or curiosity. The individual who is not able to look at another may be indicating shyness or dishonesty. At other times the eyes may reflect mistrust or a desire for privacy. Wearing sunglasses during the interview can mean that the client is trying to hide distress or does not want anyone to know where he or she is looking. Or it could mean only that the person is shy. But the wearing of sunglasses is almost always significant. For certain, it prevents eye contact.

In the interview situation, facial expressions and affect occur simultaneously with verbal expressions. Generally they are used to support, emphasize, or reinforce verbal messages. However, many times there is a discrepancy between verbal communication and facial expressions and affect. Most often when there is a difference between nonverbal and verbal expressions, the former are a more accurate reflection of true feelings than the latter. This is because most nonverbal messages are not consciously sent, and the individual is not really aware of their meaning. The most accurate communication of true feelings occurs when verbal communication and nonverbal communication reflect the same basic meaning. If a person says he or she is angry, nonverbal communication should reflect this anger. If a person says he or she is angry but smiles or does not look or act angry, that person is either not angry or is greatly supressing angry feelings. The appropriate expression of feelings, both verbally and nonverbally, is especially important for the person in crisis. Consequently, not only should there be careful observation of inconsistent verbal and nonverbal messages but also of inappropriate communication. That is, the therapist should observe whether the client is expressing appropriate feelings that are consistent with the precipitating event. If not, the real feelings may be going on internally. When this occurs the therapist should usually bring it to the client's attention. For example, the therapist might say, "You seem to be talking about something that is very distressing to you, but you don't look as if it bothers you as much as I would expect."

Observation is a very important technique, involving constant attention to all of the client's behavior, interpreting its meaning, and using it to help the client. This will become clearer when all of the techniques of interviewing are discussed, since the process is a unified whole.

Listening

A second important technique of interviewing is listening. Listening well is more complicated and requires more than you might think. It requires the therapist's full attention to be alert, observant, and sensitive to the meaning of words and language. Therapeutic listening requires the therapist to put aside personal thoughts to keep the mind from wandering. It requires a genuine and intense interest in the client.

For the therapist, perhaps one of the most important parts of good listening is not taking the client's communication for granted, not assuming that he or she knows what the client means. The therapist cannot assume what the client means simply because a common word is used; that assumption can lead to misunderstanding. Recall that many factors affect the communication process, including a lifetime of experiences. Self-concept, preservation of self-image, educational level, image of the therapist, status relationship, and expectation also influence the way a person communicates. Since each word has a unique meaning associated with the individual's personal experiences, the assumption that they have the same meaning for the client and the therapist is subject to error. Thus the therapist should never take understanding of what the client is saying for granted. The therapist should try to understand what the client is saying from the client's frame of reference, from the client's psychic reality. The therapist must feel free to ask the client what is meant or let the client know he or she does not understand. If a client is using an ambiguous word, the therapist should readily ask what the client means. Even when the therapist is reasonably sure what the client means, he or she should question it if the client seems unsure or vague about what he or she is saying. Such questioning helps the client to focus, to identify problems and put them in clearer perspective. The basis of questioning is listening.

Like observation, listening is a technique for gathering data about the client. It involves hearing what the client is saying literally and understanding what is meant. To understand completely, the therapist must be attentive and concentrate on what the client is saying. The therapist must understand the meaning of words, language, affect, and nonverbal communication. In this regard he or she must be sensitive to emotionally laden words. The therapist should have a clear picture of the client's problems and conflicts and the reasons they exist.

Listening begins with the client's opening statement, and the therapist should pay special attention to it. Some clients start discussing problems right away; others fill the first minutes of the interview with social amenities. Still others start with an expression of doubt or hopelessness: "I don't know whether you can help me, but. . ." or "I don't think anything can be done, but. . ." Sometimes these statements are requests for encouragement or for brief reassurance that the therapist can help or is willing to try. At other times the client expresses concerns forthrightly and requires no response from the therapist.

Regardless of what the client's opening statement is, special consideration should be given to what is being communicated, how, and why. The opening statement sometimes (but not always) establishes what is most important to the client. This initial interaction between client and therapist can determine the success or failure of the interview. Sullivan (1954) calls this the *formal inception* stage.

Once the interview is past the opening phase, the therapist's goal is to understand the client as thoroughly as possible. The therapist first listens to the meaning of each sentence, being careful to hear all emotionally laden words that reflect either the client's feelings about what he or she is saying or a concern that is not being communicated directly. To further understand what the client is saying, the therapist must consider the sum of all sentences over a period of time. The meaning of each sentence is determined by the ones that preceded it.

The therapist should be able to determine the client's basic concern, which may not always be what is verbalized. For example, Larry was overly distressed on hearing the news of the illness of his best friend's father. But his distress was not so much out of concern for the sick person but out of worry for himself. He tends to overidentify with illness and accidents because of his preoccupation with himself. His worry about his friend's father seemed very altruistic but actually had other significance.

The therapist must listen not only to what the client talks about but also to what the client avoids talking about. For instance, the married client who does not eventually discuss the marital relationship is probably not facing something of significance.

In addition the therapist should pay strict attention to the client's nonverbal messages. He or she should listen to changes in tone of voice or in rate of speech. He or she should note the topics covered and the circumstances of each change. Such changes can indicate a change in feelings or a desire to avoid the pain associated with some topic. It is also significant when the client mentions a subject more than once or repeatedly returns to the same subject. This could mean that the topic is so important to the client that he or she is preoccupied with it and cannot move on. The client may be trying to resolve a painful subject by facing it repeatedly, much like the soldier returns to fight a lost battle. Another possible meaning is that the pain associated with the subject matter is so great that the client needs to repeat it because he or she is hurt and disappointed. This is really a form of disbelief or denial. A client may repeat a topic because he or she feels that the therapist is not hearing the message; the client may repeat it until the therapist hears and responds appropriately.

It is very important for the therapist to understand the sequence of the client's messages. If the client is coherent, the facts should be reasonably interrelated. However, this is not always the case with people in crisis, especially when they are emotionally upset. When this occurs the therapist must notice when the client's communication is not clear or is inconsistent or does not make sense. At this time questions designed to help the therapist understand will also help the client to think more logically and to gain a better perspective on his or her condition. By the completion of the first interview, there should be very few, if any, questions about the client that the therapist cannot answer.

Questioning and exploring

Questioning and exploring are techniques used to elicit responses, to help clients talk freely and constructively. They are often used together. In fact, questions are used in exploring.

Questioning has several purposes in therapeutic work: (1) to gather data; (2) to understand the client's condition; (3) to motivate the client to pursue a specific topic or subject matter; and (4) to help the client clarify thoughts. Questioning helps clarify the client's confusion and reestablish logic.

Exploring means delving into a topic in depth. It lets the therapist and client share the client's experiences for as long as the client is willing. It can be used to help the client express powerful feelings that are essential to resolve the crisis.

Exploration requires that the therapist be able to tolerate painful emotions. It means getting the client to share feelings, regardless of how painful. It may even mean getting the client to face his or her own death or the death of a loved one. As Brill (1978) says in the preface to her book:

Soon after the first edition of this book was published, a woman came to see me and asked if I would help her to live till she died and to die with dignity. She had just learned that she had advanced cancer of the pancreas and her time was short. We met once or twice a month, had lunch together, talked, shared readings, ideas, and feelings. She worked as long as she was able, participated in seminars on dying and death, shared her life with her family and friends, died as she had wished.

Success in exploration requires the utmost skill. It should not be confused with probing, a questioning technique without the affective component used to gain information. The purpose of exploration is to encourage the sharing and expression of feelings as well as to gain information.

Two different skills are involved in questioning and exploring: timing and formulating. Timing is the ability to know when to ask a question without interfering with the flow of the client's conversation. A question appropriately timed is not an interruption or obstacle to the client's communication but encourages the client to elaborate on what he or she is saying, to discuss additional feelings and ideas, to continue talking. The therapist should always "stay where the client is." In other words, the therapist should ask questions only at the time that the topic is either on the client's mind or in the conversation. Questioning should not be used to change the subject unless the client has completely exhausted the subject matter. And even though the therapist may need specific information to assess the client, the client always provides clues for a smooth transition from subject to subject. The therapist should skillfully guide the client when necessary by logically sequencing questions based on what the client is saying. Appropriately timed questions give the client the impression that many subjects have been covered but that there has been one continuous interview. If the therapist follows the principle of staying where the client is and always having a purpose for questions, they will almost always be appropriate and relevant.

The second skill in questioning and exploring is formulating, or phrasing. Because the therapist is most interested in the client's expression of feelings and ideas, most questions should be designed to encourage the client to express feelings openly and freely. Thus the crisis therapist's questions should be open ended. That is, they should require explanations and discussion rather than yes or no answers. The therapist's questions should start with what, how, when, or where, not with why. Questions beginning with why require a cognitive answer; they may make the client feel defensive and as if he or she is being examined. Furthermore, it is easy to answer, "I don't know" to a why question. Why questions remind people of childhood, of parents and teachers. They carry blame and accusation. Questions such as, "What brought that about?" "How did that happen?" "What do you think are some possible reasons for your reactions?" "What does that mean to you?" "What happened to make you want to leave?" are more likely to provoke honest, undefensive reactions. They lead people to explore their feelings, to be introspective. For example, if the therapist asks a client, "How are things going?" the client will generally respond with whatever is important to him or her. If the therapist asks a closed question, the client will give a specific answer that may not be very important at the time. Furthermore, the therapist's questions should not be "loaded": they should not require the client to admit to something negative. The therapist should not use leading questions either. He or she should never suggest a "right" answer.

Another part of successful questioning is the nonverbal component. Tone of voice is extremely important in determining how a question is received. A good open-ended question designed to elicit discussion and the expression of feelings may be ruined if tone of voice and other nonverbal signals imply that there is a right answer or that certain answers might be condemned. Just as we discussed, if the therapist's face, tone of voice, or other nonverbal messages are not consistent with verbal expression, the client will usually respond to the nonverbal message. In addition the language and vocabulary used should fit the client's educational level and frame of reference.

Thus far the discussion has focused on direct methods of questioning. There are also other indirect methods such as reflection or restatement. To reflect or restate, the therapist repeats an emotional word or sentence in a questioning tone. Reflection and restatement are used when the therapist wants the client to hear what he himself is saying. They can be used to encourage the client to go into more detail on a subject.

Another indirect method is to form a question as a statement such as, "That sounds really painful" or "That must have been really hard on you." This kind of questioning is used to get the client to share more feelings. It is used when a client may be a little reserved or reluctant to express painful feelings.

A third indirect method is the use of comparative questions. For example, to the wife who says her husband does not love her, the therapist could say, "By 'love' do you mean affection or concern for your welfare?" The question stimulates the client to think about what love is and about whether there are some positive things in the relationship. The direct question, "What do you mean by 'love'?" could make the client defensive and reactivate basic feelings of being unloved.

There are times that the therapist has to ask direct questions, most often to get factual information and demographic data. But even then, each question should be based on the previous discussion. The advice of Bernstein and Bernstein (1974) on formulating direct questions is useful. They state that: (1) the sequence of questions should progress from the general to the specific, (2) the questions should progress from the less personal to the more personal, (3) the questions should be worded to elicit answers of a sentence or more and to avoid yes and no responses, (4) the questions should be worded to avoid bias.

TECHNIQUES OF INTERVENTION

Intervention techniques are the methods used purposefully by a therapist to change or influence an individual's emotional or mental state or behavior. The distinction between interviewing and intervening is rather artificial; in practice they overlap and are parts of the same process. But we will distinguish between them on the basis of purpose. Interviewing facilitates the client's expression of feelings and awareness of experiences. It is done to let the therapist get to know the client as an individual and gather information.

Intervention can have one of four basic purposes: (1) to restore the client's social functioning to a previous level, (2) to sustain a certain level of social functioning, (3) to improve the client's social functioning, or (4) to change various aspects of personality. Sometimes more than one of these goals is appropriate for the same client. However, the basic goal of *crisis intervention* is to restore the client's social functioning at least to the level prior to the onset of the crisis.

We can divide the techniques of intervention into three categories: (1) psychological support, those techniques designed to sustain and support positive aspects of social functioning; (2) cognitive restoration, those designed to alter, change, or modify social functioning; and (3) environmental modification, those that change the relationship between the client and his or her environment. The crisis therapist may use all of these techniques with the same client.

Psychological support

Every therapist uses support in some fashion. In fact, the therapeutic relationship is by nature a framework of support. It helps the client face problems that previously were faced alone. The overwhelming feelings produced by a crisis weaken the client's ability to function; he or she needs ego strength to master the crisis.

When the client needs support above and beyond what is given simply by virtue of the therapeutic relationship, it must be purposefully and skillfully given. The effective use of psychological support requires an understanding of the individual's personality. Giving support does not mean simply giving praise or saying common words of encouragement such as "You did a good job" or "You're a good person." Supportive words should go beyond maintaining the client's self-esteem; they should reinforce, sustain, or encourage positive or constructive feelings and behaviors. Supportive techniques are used to maintain the client's level of ego functioning or to motivate the client to try harder. They provide hope and develop confidence.

The basic skill involved in the use of support is again timing. To know the most effective time to use support, the therapist must understand the individual's personality and decide when the client needs support and will effectively receive it. Not everyone wants to be praised or encouraged, not even all those in crisis. If the client feels guilty or inferior, if self-esteem is low, supportive techniques might be ineffective. Even though the client may like to hear words of encouragement, he or she may not be ready to truly believe them. This is especially true for the depressed client. Remember that people who are depressed tend to turn inward or withdraw. During this time an internal battle is going on, and the client is suffering. For example, a grieving woman who is feeling guilty about her anger toward her dead mother may not want to hear that "everyone feels that he should have treated a lost loved one better." In a situation like this the therapist should listen until the client is ready for active intervention. Often hearing positive support before the client is ready may increase guilt feelings. Other examples of people who cannot accept positive support include the strikingly beautiful woman or handsome man who feels unattractive. They do not feel beautiful on the inside or for the feelings they have. They may feel that they cannot live up to the expectation of the people around them. Another similar example is the very talented individual who feels stupid despite achievements and accomplishments. All of these examples illustrate that the way people feel about themselves is more important in their thinking and social functioning than how others see or feel about them. And this self-image does not yield easily to popularity or premature compliments.

Of course, sometimes a depressed client will actively seek praise and reassurance at the same time that the internal battle of self-blame and guilt is going on. He or she may want to counteract the internal struggles with external praise. But while praise makes the client feel good for a short time, the good feelings generally do not last. Sometimes a client needs to experience painful emotions for a while before he or she can truly receive active psychological support. This does not mean that the client is not being supported at all, but that he or she is not being *falsely* supported. The therapist can refrain from actively praising and supporting the client until psychological needs are understood.

The premature use of support presents other potential problems. It can make the client feel that the therapist does not consider the condition serious or that it is taken too lightly. The client may feel that the therapist underestimates the difficulty of the problem. Premature support may create additional pressure for the client to please the therapist or to be successful too soon.

Clients feeling anxious may be ready for more active support earlier than those experiencing depression. The person who is experiencing anxiety is outwardly directed and actively seeks help from others. He or she is more receptive to direct action of the therapist than is the depressed client. In both cases, however, the use of active support should be purposeful and based on an understanding of the basic personality and needs of the client.

The most effective support comes from the therapeutic relationship and from within the client. Support is always more effective when the client shows readiness to receive the therapist's active support. The client will usually show some signs of being ready. He or she may communicate it nonverbally, with eyes or facial expressions. It is often a good idea to check out the client's feelings about the need for support. Rather than reassure a client that he or she can do something, the therapist can first ascertain the clients feelings about whether he or she can do it. Instead of initially saying, "I think you can manage now," it may be more effective to say, "I wonder whether you can manage now." The client's response can be followed with a test of conviction, such as "What makes you feel that you *can* manage now?" This interaction communicates a shared responsibility for the client's social functioning. At the same time the therapist has other evidence to evaluate the client's condition. Even in situations where the client's behavior is obviously constructive, his or her feelings about the behavior should be ascertained first. The active use of support should be based on three conditions. First, the therapist knows what he or she is supporting and supports only constructive or positive feelings and behavior of the client. (Feelings and behavior that should not be supported can still be accepted. Support means the therapist wants the behavior to continue; acceptance means that the therapist is able to value and respect the dignity of the individual regardless of the behavior.) Second, the client communicates the need to be actively supported and that he or she will be receptive to it. Third, the therapist has already activated any self-support in the client.

Listening. Although listening is a technique of interviewing, it also can be used as a supportive technique. When used as a form of support, the therapist deliberately suspends response to the client and listens attentively to what the client has to say. Often if the client talks freely to an interested therapist, he or she can arrive at an understanding of the condition and very often his or her own solution. When the therapist purposefully refrains from saying anything, the client can benefit and gain strength from talking. The client is forced to rely on what he or she says and hears. Even if the client asks the therapist for a response, the therapist can say something like, "To really get the feel of what you're saying, I'd like you to talk a little longer before I answer your question." Often the client lets the therapist know when simple listening is needed. Nonverbal signals will say, "I want you to just listen." Research shows that the more the client talks and the less the therapist talks, the greater the chance of therapeutic success (Carnes and Robinson, 1948). The therapist's success is not determined by *how much* is said but by *what* is said.

Ventilation. One of the most useful techniques for the crisis therapist is ventilation, which involves eliciting powerful emotions in order that the client can experience and face those feelings and eventually master them. Ventilation involves exploration. For example, a therapist could say, "I can see that your relationship with your husband was truly important to you. I wonder if you can describe to me exactly how you feel now that he is gone." This type of explorative question not only draws out potent feelings but also helps the client face the reality of the situation by not pretending that her husband may come back. The use of ventilation as a technique must be done with empathy and, again, must be properly timed. It must not be done simply for the sake of technique.

Reassurance. Reassurance is a method by which the therapist conveys to the client that he or she can be helped, that the condition is not hopeless, that the perceived danger can be managed and resolved successfully, that the client has more ability or greater strength than he or she may realize. Like all supportive techniques, reassurance should be used only when justified by the therapist's confidence in the truth of his or her statements. The therapist has to anticipate the future, based on both the client's past and the evidence presented at the time. If there is no basis for the therapist's reassurance, it is false and misleading. Like the other techniques, reassurance should be used only after the client's need for it has been determined. The client's lack of confidence or his or her fears should be directly expressed before the therapist gives reassurance. The client should respond to questions such as, "What makes you feel so pessimistic?" or "What makes you feel that you can't do it?" before the therapist gives reassurance. The client may be seeking encouragement before he or she acts by asking, "Do you think I can find a new job?" If the therapist knows that the client thinks that he or she has the ability but just wants to be reassured, the therapist can say something like. "I think that you can find a job, and your past record suggests that you can." If, on the other hand, the client basically feels pessimistic and hopeless, the therapist should not give reassurance but should express acceptance. He might say, "If you truly feel that you cannot find a job and are afraid to try, we'll have to wait until you're ready." The therapist has to determine whether the client is ready for the reassurance.

Reassurance can be used to help the client become aware of his or her potential, of abilities of which he or she is not aware. It can also be used to help the client develop more trust and confidence in the therapist. For example, once the therapist has determined that the client needs reassurance and can be helped, he can say, "By working together I think we can be successful in resolving this problem." This kind of reassurance is often required in crisis therapy. Again, it cannot be falsely used. If a man is in crisis because his wife has unilaterally decided to get a divorce, reassurance that things can be worked out is not justified. Reassurance should never be used in a situation that is uncertain or hopeless. It should also never be used to allow the client to avoid taking the responsibility for behavior or for facing the reality of the situation. Reassurance should be used to motivate the client and to help him or her continue to improve.

Clarification. Clarification is used as a technique of support as well as of interviewing. It is used in interviewing to help the therapist understand the client and the situation. When it is used as a supportive technique, it is designed to get the client to focus on a problem or to recognize that there is something inconsistent or missing in what he or she is saying. It may also indicate that what the client is saying is so important that the therapist wants him or her to explore it further. Clarification helps the client expand perceptions. Often it helps a client face a problem or a feeling that he or she may want to avoid. Clarification should not be confused with interpretation. The former is concerned with the meaning of manifest feelings and behavior, whereas the latter is concerned with unconscious or latent feelings.

Clarification is also used when the therapist asks the client to clarify the meaning of what he or she is saying. For example, the therapist might say, "Would you explain the difference between your feelings at the time of your husband's death and your father's?" Of course, the question should be asked in context and relate to something the client had been talking about. It can be used to reinforce a significant thought or feeling. For example, a therapist could say, "If I understand you correctly, you never had headaches before your mother-in-law came to live with you." There may not really have been anything unclear about the client's statement, but for clarity and reinforcement the therapist repeats the cause-and-effect relationship.

In addition to clarifying the client's statement, clarification can be used to bring forth new material. For example, a therapist might say, "The relationship between your headaches and your mother-in-law is not clear to me." The client's response may lead to a discussion of his relationship with his wife. Perhaps he would say, "When my mother-in-law is in our home, my wife acts differently toward me." This response then opens other areas of concern.

Universalization. Universalization involves telling the client that the experience is a common human one and that his or her reaction is not unusual. It must be used with a clear understanding of its purpose and the client's receptivity to it. While there is strength in commonness, most people also need to be considered unique and different. However, when it is indicated, universalization can be quite effective. It can be reassuring to hear the therapist say, "It's natural for you to feel the way you do," or "If you didn't get angry at that, I'd be worried." Universalization is used *only* when the client is in a common situation and the reaction is typical. It is used only when the client needs reassurance that his or her feelings or behavior are common to all people.

Confrontation. Confrontation is used when the client resists facing the reality of the condition, feelings, or behavior. The client then has to be confronted with his or her resistance and reluctance to face a feeling, behavior, or problem when failure to do so is counterproductive.

Confrontation directly moves the client toward facing something that he or she would rather not face. Thus it must be done supportively, without attacking. The therapist should move slowly at first. If the client responds to mild use of confrontation, more direct confronting may not be necessary. For example, the therapist may say, "For some reason you seem not to act on your dislike for your mother-in-law." In this case the therapist is confronting the client with the fact that, although he dislikes his mother-in-law, he is not doing anything about the situation except complaining. If this nonthreatening exchange stimulates the client to take action, no further confrontation is necessary. But if after a reasonable period of time no change occurs, a more direct confrontation may be indicated. For example, the therapist might say, "Knowing your feelings about your mother-in-law and the effect she has on you, perhaps it's time that we look at what keeps you from doing something about it." If such a direct confrontation is not effective, then the therapist must look for other obstacles that are preventing the client from resolving the situation. In the above case, for example, perhaps the husband cannot do anything about the situation because he actually wants his mother-in-law's love and approval but she will not respond to him the way he wants her to. Perhaps if he becomes aware of his real desires, confrontation will not be needed. An ineffective confrontation may mean that the therapist has to set limits or take some direct action. For example, the therapist may say, "It looks like you can't come to grips with your feelings about your child. On this basis we must take active steps to help you and the child."

Persuasion. Persuasion is another method used to help the client overcome resistance. It is based on (1) the authority of the therapist and the client's trust and (2) the therapist's belief that the client will be successful by carrying out the therapist's wishes. Persuasion is used with people in crisis who are so debilitated by their situation that they need a direct approach. Examples include persuading a teen-aged client to return home or a person with chest pains to go to the hospital. Even in such cases persuasion should be used only after the client's own resources have been judged to be ineffective. For example, the therapist and the client should thoroughly discuss what the client thinks he ought to do about returning home before the therapist tries to persuade him that going home is in his best interest. People who come to their own successful conclusions and make constructive decisions about their own lives are generally happier and stronger for it.

Suggestion. In effect, suggestion is a mild form of persuasion where the therapist is less insistent that the client does what he or she says. With persuasion, the therapist is insistent and persistent. The use of both suggestion and persuasion should be based on the client's personality. Again, clients have greater self-respect when they arrive at their own solutions to problems; guiding a client to make the best use of his or her own resources is always the most effective intervention. Like persuasion, suggestion should be used only after other techniques have proved to be ineffective, even though the person in crisis seems so helpless that it is tempting to tell him or her what to do.

Advice. Advice involves the therapist telling someone—sometimes the client and sometimes a third party—what to do. In this context advice is used to mean more than directive suggestion and persuasion. Its use should not be confused with recommending a course of action for a person in crisis. If a client has refused to respond to suggestion and persuasion and is endangering personal safety or that of others, the therapist may use advice. For example, the therapist might say, "It appears that we can't work things out together. I advise you to immediately seek hospitalization." Or if a client refuses to go to the hospital, the therapist may advise the family to have him or her admitted. Even then, all other alternatives should be exhausted before the therapist resorts to advice. Thus it should be used as a last resort.

Cognitive restoration

The most salient characteristics of a person in crisis are overwhelming emotionality, confusion, and mental debilitation. An emotional crisis results in varying degrees of cognitive dysfunctioning. Therefore one of the major goals of crisis intervention is the restoration of cognitive functioning. Before this can be done there must be some reduction in emotionality. The supportive techniques are designed to help reduce the client's emotionality. Then and only then will the client be receptive to the techniques of cognitive restoration.

A considerable amount of client self-understanding results from interaction with the therapist and the process of interviewing. However, cognitive restoration is achieved by two therapeutic techniques: causal connecting statements and interpretation.

Causal connecting statement. A causal connecting statement is the process by which the therapist connects (or helps the client connect) the cause and effect of two events, conditions, or situations resulting in the client's specific feeling, behavior, or responses. It differs from interpretation in that explanations are based on the client's overt communication and expressions rather than on unconscious inferences. The effect, a causal connecting statement, seeks to establish for the client a causal relationship between a series of events. Consider the following example:

Therapist: Hi! My name is Jack Stein. Can you tell me what brings you here?

Client: The nurse brought me here. I can't do my job. I feel like I'm falling apart.

Therapist: What do you mean by falling apart?

Client: This happened about a year ago. My girlfriend and I were having problems. I took my ring back because she did not do what I wanted her to, and then I tried to kill myself by cutting my wrist.

Therapist: *(casual connecting statement)* It sounds like when you feel like you are "falling apart" it means that you are in such great desperation and feel so hopeless that you think of suicide and attempt to take your own life.

It can be seen that a causal connecting statement ties together for the client the cause and effect of certain events and responses. Consider another example:

Client: I know it's not being a good mother to spank Chris every time that he cusses at me. If I ignored it, he would soon stop. But I can't help myself.

Therapist: *(causal connecting statement)* In effect you are saying that Chris' cussing at you makes you feel you are a bad mother. Could it be possible that you are punishing Chris more for his making you feel like a bad mother than for his cussing?

It should be noted that causal connecting statements as well as interpretations are given with qualifications and tentativeness. This gives the client a chance to participate, to think over, to accept and integrate or to reject. If the client accepts and integrates, it becomes part of his or her cognitive functioning.

Interpretation. Interpretation is the second basic technique of cognitive restoration. Other experiential or affective learning takes place within the structure of the therapeutic relationship. However, interpretation is conscious and purposeful learning. In effect, everyone uses interpretation when offering an explanatory inference of the cause and meaning of some human behavior. When asking and answering why, an explanation is derived from certain data or evidence. This is interpretation. For the person in crisis, identifying what is happening emotionally and situationally is very important in resolving the problem. Interpretation helps the client think and perceive feelings and behavior from a different and more logical perspective. It restores order and structure to the individual's emotional life, which has been out of control. When the therapist identifies what is occurring within the client, some of which is unconscious, and why, the client can understand the situation, which helps reduce the debilitating affect.

Interpretation is the crisis therapist's explanation of the cause and meaning of the client's feelings and behavior for purpose of the client's self-understanding and reestablishment of cognitive control. It gives the client an explanation of his or her behavior in the same way a physician gives a patient the meaning of physical symptoms. Interpretation involves making the client conscious of feelings and behavior of which he or she is not aware; it offers reasons and causes rather than describing what is already known. Interpretation involves relaying information to the client in tentative terms or raising "think" questions regarding the cause, meaning, and purpose of behavior or feelings that the client is not conscious of.

Hammer (1968) says that "other than the relationship-theory aspects (the patient feeling a sense of support, a relationship with someone who cares, a sense of trust) one of the first gains the patient generally struggles to acquire is being able to identify what is going on affectively and rationally." Fenichel (1945) states, "The verbalization of unclear worries alone brings relief because an ego can face verbalized ideas better than unclear emotional sensations." In crisis therapy deep unconscious interpretation is not necessary. What is necessary for cognitive restoration is the explanation of what is going on within the client, which enables him or her to gain cognitive mastery over confusing and overwhelming affect. In this case interpretation can take two forms: (1) informing the client of behavior that he or she is not aware of involving current life situations (e.g., interpersonal relationships involving parents, spouse, and significant others) or conflicts in goals (e.g., self-defeating behavior), and (2) behavior that is a reflection of historical development and experiences involving specific patterns of psychic functioning. This is simply a matter of relating the past to the present. The basis of interpretation is knowledge and understanding of human behavior and a specific interest in helping the client understand his or her behavior.

Consider Scott, a social agency worker supporting a family, who wants to give up his job to enter private practice at considerable personal and financial risk. The therapist might say, "I wonder if your anger about not being able to enter private practice immediately is a result of your competition with me." This response might help Scott look at the meaning of his behavior in a new way. The following dialogue between Martha, a client who developed anxiety while in church, and her therapist is another example of interpretation:

> **Martha:** While sitting in church, all of a sudden I felt faint and I experienced heavy feelings in my chest, began perspiring, and I had to leave the services. I felt better when I got outside.
>
> **Therapist:** How do you explain this sudden attack of anxiety?
>
> **Martha:** Well, I've been on a diet; and yesterday I ate a small piece of pie. It probably upset my sugar balance.

After exploring further, the therapist asked Martha what was going on at the time of her distress. She responded that the choir was singing about Christ's death and resurrection. Based on understanding of Martha, the therapist responded:

> **Therapist:** Could it be that the words of the song stirred up some feelings of your own death, feelings that are frightening to you?
>
> **Martha:** Well, this is Easter, and you know my father died of a heart attack last year at this time. I've always had a weak heart.

This particular interpretive question by the therapist gave Martha the clue to her own anxiety.

Another example of interpretation is, "Could it be that you ran away to test your parent's love for you and to express your anger at them by making them worry about you. Could that be possible?" The therapist's synthesis of the client's bewildering array of feelings helps the client organize thoughts. It facilitates the client's mastery of the condition and situation.

Interpretation should not be used until a good therapist-client relationship has been established. Even then it should be done in a support-ive, nonthreatening manner. How to use interpretation is discussed further in Chapter 5.

Environmental modification

The third technique of intervention is *environmental modification*. It means recommending either that the client be removed from a harmful environment or that the nature of the environment be changed. Exam-ples of removing a client from a harmful environment include the rec-ommendation that a client be hospitalized or placed in a foster home. Changing the environment involves other people in the client's life. The therapist may need to work with a client's parents, spouse, or employer, with a financial agency, or with other social agencies. Environmental modification can be called for by three different conditions: (1) the client is not capable of improving as long as he or she remains in the current specific environment, (2) the client is not able to change the environment constructively, (3) environmental modification is needed as an adjunct to supportive intervention.

To use environmental modification the therapist must be familiar with community resources. Every crisis therapist should maintain an up-to-date file on all community resources, social agencies, and businesses and organizations that serve people.

A cognitive understanding and skill in the use of techniques of inter-viewing and intervention facilitate helping people in crisis. In Chapter 5 we will discuss the process of working with people in crisis.

REFERENCES

Appelbaum, R. L., et al. *Fundamental concepts in human communication.* San Francisco: Canfield Press, 1973.

Bernstein, L., & Bernstein, R. *Interviewing: a guide for health professionals.* New York: Appleton-Century-Crofts, 1974.

Biestek, F. B. *The casework relationship.* Chicago: Loyola University Press, 1957.

Brill, N. I. *Working with people: the helping process.* Philadelphia: J. B. Lippin-cott, 1978.

Carkhuff, R. R., & Berenson, B. G. *Beyond counseling and therapy* (2nd ed.). New York: Holt, Rinehart and Winston, 1977.

Carnes, E. F., & Robinson, F. P. The role of client talk in the counseling inter-view, *Educational and Psychological Measurement,* 1948, *8,* 635-644.

Davitz, J. R. *The communication of emotional meaning*. New York: McGraw-Hill, 1964.

Ellis, A. New approaches to psychotherapy techniques. *Journal of Clinical Psychology,* 1955, *11,* 208-260.

Fenichel, O. *The psychoanalytic theory of neurosis*. New York: W. W. Norton, 1945.

Hammer, E. F. *Use of interpretation in treatment: technique and art*. New York: Grune & Stratton, 1968.

Kalis, B. L., Harris, M. R., Prestwood, A. R., and Freeman, E. H. Precipitating stress as a focus in psychotherapy. *Archives of General Psychiatry,* September 1961, 5(3), 27-34.

Lewis, A. J. Brief psychotherapy in the hospital setting: techniques and goals. *Psychiatric Quarterly,* 1973, 47(3), 341-352.

McGruire, M. T. The process of short-term insight psychotherapy. II. Content, expectation and structure. *Journal of Nervous and Mental Disorders,* 1965, *141,* 219-230.

Menninger, K., with Mayman, M., & Pryser, P. *The vital balance: the life process in mental health and illness*. New York: Viking Press, 1963.

Rogers, C. R. Necessary and sufficient conditions of therapeutic personality change. *Journal of Consulting Psychology,* 1957, *21,* 95-103.

Sullivan, H. S. *The psychiatric interview*. New York: W. W. Norton, 1954.

Trojanowicz, R. C., & Dixon, S. L. *Criminal justice and the community*. Englewood Cliffs, N.J.: Prentice-Hall, 1974.

Truax, C. B., & Carkhuff, R. R. *Toward effective counseling and psychotherapy*. Chicago: Aldine, 1967.

Walker, W. J. Neurocirculatory asthenia. In F. C. Massey (Ed.), *Clinical cardiology,* Baltimore: Williams & Wilkins, 1953.

SUGGESTED READINGS

Hammer, E. F. (Ed.), *Use of interpretation in treatment: technique and art*. New York: Grune & Stratton, 1968.

Kahn, R. L., & Cannell, C. F. *The dynamics of interviewing*. New York: John Wiley & Sons, 1957.

Part II

APPLICATION OF INTERVENTION
TECHNIQUES AND SKILLS

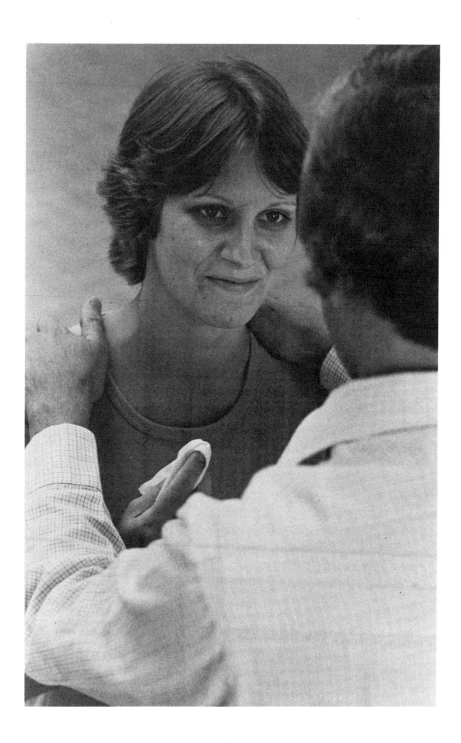

CHAPTER 5

Procedures for working with people in crisis

■ Mabel, age 41, was brought to the emergency service of the mental health clinic by her brother. He reported that Mabel had taken a large dose of a major tranquilizer (Thorazine) 2 hours before. The doctor who was consulted recommended that she be kept in a protected environment for at least 4 more hours. He wanted to prevent Mabel from accidentally hurting herself. Mabel was obviously drug intoxicated. She was quite resistant to his recommendation because she had made plans to spend the evening with friends. Fortunately a therapist was able to get her to stay. Once she had decided to stay, Mabel fell asleep. On awaking several hours later, she decided that she had not had any intent to commit suicide, showed considerable improvement, and was eager to get home.

■ Forty-three-year-old Jane appeared at the crisis center depressed and seeking help. Some 9 months before she had taken a job in a company that she described as closed, negative, and debilitating. She had tried to change the system but to no avail. She felt that to leave the situation would be like running away, and she had never run away from a battle in her life. She had lost weight and hates herself for not being able to do more to change the company.

■ Karen, 45 years old, reported to the crisis center complaining of difficulty eating and sleeping and with poor feelings about herself. She sleeps only 1 hour at night and 1 hour during the day. She can recognize her own considerable anger directed at herself. Her conflict with family members is the source of her anger. Although she currently is living with her sister, she wants out; she feels a need to be more independent. She also feels that her sister had changed since their uncle died and left the sister some money.

■ George, age 31, walked into the emergency service unit of the mental health clinic asking for help for depression and problems with his girlfriend. He felt so depressed that he was afraid that he might do something "silly."

■ The former lover of 24-year-old Phyllis called the Crisis Center to refer her because he was worried about her. He had recently broken off their extramarital affair. She was now so depressed that he feared she might take her own life. The therapist spoke with Phyllis, who at the time was crying but said that she did not know why she was upset. She was given an immediate appointment.

These are samples of calls to emergency services and crisis units. You can easily see that when a person is in crisis, there is considerable confusion. The problems and causes are vague and often ill-defined. You can also see the wide variety of problems that can lead to a crisis, and the human reactions to those problems are innumerable. Contrary to widely held belief, the crisis therapist needs far-reaching knowledge to be able to work most effectively with people in crisis. In the first four chapters of this book the discussion focused on the theory of crisis, human behavior, communication, and the techniques used to improve, sustain, and alter social functioning. In the rest of the book we will focus on using this knowledge in practice as we set forth procedural steps for effective intervention.

BASIC ATTITUDE AND APPROACH

Working with people in crisis requires a different attitude and approach than does traditional therapy. The crisis therapist must be willing and able to see the person in crisis as soon as possible. This is crucial; the client in crisis is most amenable to help at the time of the request for help and at the peak of the crisis. At this time the events precipitating the crisis are most accessible. The individual is less defensive and generally more introspective. In addition, seeing the person in crisis immediately reduces the chance that maladaptive efforts to resolve the crisis will become crystalized and acquire compromise benefits of secondary gains (Kalis et al., 1961).

In addition consider Ben (see Chapter 2), whose crisis was precipitated by his wife leaving him after he had beaten her. At the peak of his crisis he called a local agency, which offered him an appointment 3 days later. In the meantime he attempted suicide and was hospitalized. Since the crisis was not resolved but the threat of suicide was abated, the psychiatrist at the hospital referred Ben back to the same agency. This case shows the importance of knowing when a person is in crisis. It is my premise that a crisis is subjectively defined by the individual. That is, initially a person is in crisis when he believes that he is in crisis, feels that he is unable to function, and turns to someone else for help. At this point some assessment and evaluation are needed, even if over the telephone. If an appointment can not be given immediately, the client should be referred to someone who can see him or her. In Ben's case the therapist who spoke with him should have made some effort to evaluate him rather than routinely giving him the next available appointment. If the therapist could not see Ben, referral to another agency with some assurance that he got there was in order. What if Ben's interim suicide attempt had been successful? Most important, the case of Ben illustrates the need for staff and agencies to have a structure that allows people in crisis to be seen immediately. In fact, this should be a part of every helping agency, because people in crisis may not always call a crisis center. They often call agencies whose names and services are familiar to them.

Of course the question can also be raised of those people who believe everything is a crisis and want to be seen every time they are upset. Most often these people are overly dependent on the agency and have not learned from previous crisis experiences. Assessment and evaluation and knowledge of these clients, too, are needed for appropriate responses. It seems important to evaluate why they are not becoming more independent and functioning better. The therapist needs to determine what the behavior of the client means. What prevents the client from making progress? People who are always in a crisis state are possible candidates for long-term psychotherapy. When not possible, the crisis model will probably have to suffice. But this may be a smaller price to pay than total breakdown or hospitalization.

Another necessary approach is early assessment and evaluation of whether the individual needs hospitalization or whether he or she can be helped on an outpatient basis. This is a question that concerns many crisis therapists, especially novices. From the first contact with the client through termination, the crisis therapist needs to keep this question in mind.

The crisis therapist *must* be self-confident. The multitude of problems presented by people in crisis can be very frightening as well as taxing. We have already seen the significance of confidence to client improvement. Anxiety and lack of confidence tend to be contagious, and the opposite is also true. A calm, confident therapist who is hopeful is very reassuring to the person in crisis.

STEPS FOR WORKING WITH PERSONS IN CRISIS

We now have a frame of reference for our discussion of how to help people resolve a crisis and become functional again. We will divide this process into steps to make it easier to remember. To become a competent crisis therapist, you need to be able to gauge the completeness of your intervention. Knowing the steps of process helps you make that judgment. Furthermore, working with people in crisis has two parts: an intellectual process and an empathic process. The empathic process is generally the easiest; it is furthered by the client's vulnerability and need for help. The intellectual process is more difficult because it occurs at the same time as the empathic process. This means that the therapist must think at the same time that he or she is feeling and reacting emotionally. Learning by procedural steps helps to develop the intellectual process; the steps provide a cognitive road map for intervention. Later in the chapter we will see the works of some beginning therapists who did not know what to do after the opening greeting because they were not familiar with the steps of intervention. This does not mean that helping people emotionally is not a unified process; the intervention techniques represent a continuum of interaction in which a therapist uses self, knowledge, and skills to help an individual resolve a crisis and improve social functioning. Bear in mind also that these orderly procedures are not rigidly fixed; at times they overlap. The nine procedural steps for helping people in crisis are:

Step 1: Rapidly establish a constructive relationship
Step 2: Elicit and encourage expression of painful feelings and emotions
Step 3: Discuss the precipitating event
Step 4: Assess and evaluate
Step 5: Formulate a dynamic explanation
Step 6: Cognitive restoration
Step 7: Plan and implement treatment
Step 8: Terminate
Step 9: Follow up

Step 1: Rapidly establish a constructive relationship

The process of establishing a relationship is discussed at great length in Chapter 4. To review, the therapist should keep in mind the preinterview conditions. The person in crisis is not only suffering and struggling with his or her own problems but may also have feelings about having to turn to a stranger for help. The time between the onset of the crisis and the request for help varies greatly. During this time the individual in crisis is struggling to resolve the crisis without help. Finally having to call someone for help means that the individual cannot resolve the problem alone. He or she goes through a process of "giving up" in anticipation of help. Between the request for help and the first appointment, the client will again have to manage in whatever way he or she can, even though the request for help can be a source of strength. However, the greater the time between the request for help and the first appointment, the greater the opportunity for distortion and confusion regarding the precipitating event (Kalis et al., 1961). This point was illustrated in the case of Joanne (see Chapter 1), who felt that her deceased husband would consider her weak if he knew that she was seeking outside help.

The major task of the therapist at this point is to present himself or herself to the client as a helpful person. This means that the therapist must feel genuine respect for the client as a human being. The client should be greeted with respect, acceptance, and eagerness. Last names with appropriate prefixes should be used, unless the client gives only his or her first name.

It should be remembered that the person in crisis generally feels frightened and often hopeless. He or she has lost the sense of mastery over self and the condition. Self-esteem is generally low. The client may or may not be trying to compensate or save face. The therapist must be sensitive to his or her own initial effect, which may reflect the client's low self-esteem (e.g., using first names before the client is ready). If there is a long walk between the waiting room and the therapist's office, the therapist must be wary of small talk. This is a serious situation, and silence between the waiting room and the therapist's office is more effective than trying to fill the time with artificial small talk. Perhaps the most important aspect of the therapist's task at this point is sensitizing himself or herself to the client's feelings about seeking help, about the helplessness of the client's condition and the degree of debilitation. The therapist should be responsive to the client's dependency needs, since they are generally heightened by needing to turn to another for help. Sometimes also, people in crisis may seek help but feel very pessimistic about the results. Initially they may need reassurance that they can be helped or that they are in the right place. They might say, "I don't know if you can help me," or "I don't know if I'm in the right place or not." In such cases the therapist can respond by saying, "Let's discuss your situation first and then decide what we can do." Still other people in crisis may present the message, "Here I am, take care of me." In such cases the therapist must communicate to the client the feeling that the situation is not hopeless and that by working together something can be done about it. These situations require the therapist to motivate the client. The therapist must use whatever capacities the client has available at the time. To do this the therapist uses those capabilities of the client that are not affected or are the least affected by the crisis. For instance, sometimes anger can be used as a motivating force. Consider the case of Doug (see Chapter 2), who flunked his doctoral comprehensive examinations. His anger could be used as a motivating force by the therapist saying something like, "It seems to me that your committee was setting you up to see how motivated you really are. The way you are handling this situation, it will appear to them that you tend to give up very easily. Is this what you want them to conclude?" Such a statement would, of course, be based on a careful assessment and evaluation, with some notion that what is said will be effective. On the other hand, this might not be a very good motivating statement for the severely depressed, the self-defeating, or the masochistic. The very masochistic person would probably say, "See, you think I'm no good too." Whatever the therapist says should be purposeful and predicated on knowledge and needs of the client. Still other individuals approach therapy with ambivalent feelings about the helping process for various reasons. One, they may feel hopeless. Some people feel that, since they cannot help themselves, no one else can either. There is also at times a competitive striving in which a client dares someone to help. The client may be ambivalent about the whole process because of rumors or heresay (i.e., what friends, TV, or the press says about therapy). In addition the client may be worried about what will happen to him at the crisis center or what he will find out about himself. The latter is less of a problem in crisis therapy than in traditional therapy, but nevertheless it occurs, as we saw in the case of Joanne (see Chapter 1). To rapidly establish a relationship, the therapist must be sensitive to these possibilities. In traditional therapy the therapist does not have to aniticipate as much, since there is time to wait and see what manifests itself. The time required to establish a constructive relationship can be decreased by the therapist's anticipation coupled with the helplessness and need of the client as manifested and revealed in the communication process.

Another factor important in rapidly establishing a constructive relationship is the client's expectations of the helping person. The client no doubt comes to the interview with a preconceived idea or image of the therapist. It may be based on the client's own notions and feelings about helping professionals, on TV images, or on just plain self-esteem. A client may expect to see a younger person, an older person, a shorter person, a taller person, a man or a woman, a psychiatrist, a psychologist, or a medical doctor. The point is that the therapist must be sensitive and perceptive to the client's fears, misgivings, misunderstanding, and lack of knowledge. These can block a constructive relationship and must be dealt with before the client and therapist establish the kind of relationship that is conducive to the goals of crisis treatment. You might not think that a person in crisis would be concerned about some of these factors. But people can be proud to their last breath, even when it is an obstacle to being helped. Consequently such obstacles must be worked through very quickly. This requires a therapist who is not easily threatened or intimidated, one who has confidence in his or her ability and who can accurately interpret human communications. Understanding is the key to accepting the client as he or she is and not needing to react with judgmental attitudes and behaviors. Consider the following illustration:

Therapist: Hello, I am Mr. Phillips.

Client: Hello, I am Connie Fleming.

Therapist: Will you tell me how you see your problems?

Client: You look pretty young to be a psychiatrist.

Therapist: I'm not a psychiatrist. Were you expecting to see a psychiatrist?

Client: Yes. They told me at the emergency room that psychiatrists were on duty here.

Therapist: I am a psychiatric social worker, and if you're willing to discuss your concerns with me, we can determine whether you need a psychiatrist or whether you and I can work things out.

In this case the therapist is not offended or defensive but is confident in his ability and communicates this confidence to the client. Some clients, regardless of condition, feel that they must have the "best," the highest status professional. Nonmedical therapists must deal with this attitude and very often explore the feelings that lead clients to want a highest status professional. Sometimes these feelings are based on self-esteem, other times on their feelings about how bad off they are. Still other times it is lack of knowledge about the helping professions. Remember that a long explanation of the differences between various helping professions serves very little if any purpose; the client will not generally remember it anyway. What is necessary in such a situation is a simple statement of the professional identity of the therapist, an exploration of the basis of the client's feelings and feelings about working with the therapist present. All of this done in a confident and accepting manner helps establish the constructive relationship quickly. The therapist's goal of seeking to understand the client regardless of behavior helps to minimize behavior of the client that could be considered to be a personal attack on the therapist.

Rapidly establishing a constructive relationship is achieved by the therapist's accepting the client as he or she is, communicating this acceptance through affective and other nonverbal behavior, projecting a genuine interest and natural eagerness to help the client, and feeling confident in ability to understand and to help the client. But how do you know when a constructive relationship has been established? First, the client feels comfortable with the therapist and speaks relatively freely, consistent with what is expected in the crisis condition. For example, a depressed client may not speak freely completely but within the limits of the condition will respond to a genuine interest and concern. Other signs of a constructive relationship are mutually positive feelings and the client's beginning identification with the therapist, especially therapeutic goals. In effect a good relationship is established with the person in crisis when he or she is willing to accept the therapist as an alter ego or self. When signs of a constructive relationship are not apparent, the therapist should find out why.

Step 2: Elicit and encourage expression of painful feelings and emotions

Although this step is closely associated with discussing the precipitating event, it is discussed separately here because many beginning therapists miss it in the effort to quickly get to the "facts," the precipitating event. This is a particular problem of the beginning therapist. The precipitating event and significant aspects of the client's life should not be explored until painful feelings and emotions are thoroughly ventilated and are actively flowing. Almost all people in crisis come to the first session manifesting some painful or distressful affect. (If they do not, they are either not in crisis, suppressing appropriate crisis affect, or it is a sign of a different problem). The client should be encouraged to express these feelings before moving to the precipitating event. Consider this example:

Therapist: Hello, I'm Ms. Fox.
Client: Hello, I'm Pat Knight.
Therapist: Please tell me what bothers you, Ms. Knight.
Client: *(depressed and crying)* My best friend told me I should come here.
Therapist: I can see that you are very upset. Can you tell me what you are feeling right now?
Client: I'm feeling sad, lonely, and empty—like nobody cares about me. (NOTE: An expression of feeling "empty" generally means a feeling of being unloved.)

Here the therapist encouraged expression of the painful feelings. After sufficiently expressing the painful feelings, the client can be easily guided to their cause. Following the sequence above:

Therapist: Now tell me, what is causing you to feel the way you do?

Eliciting and encouraging painful feelings lets the individual in crisis gain mastery over feelings that have been overwhelming. The client now faces them with the support of the therapist. A thorough expression of emotions not only facilitates mastery over affect but is also a source of ego restrengthening and the beginning of cognitive restoration. This is achieved through the therapist's skillfully encouraging and guiding of the individual toward ventilating feelings on the one hand and toward thinking in order to respond to the therapist's supportive questions. To encourage a client to express painful feelings the therapist must use questions that elicit feelings. For example, for the client who feels he or she is falling apart, the therapist needs to know what this feels like. Such statements are based on feelings that need to be explored. Consider the following statement by Menninger (1963):

The man who feels himself "falling apart" or "going to pieces" has some vague sense of the unity and integrity of his personality. He feels rather than knows this to be a normal or ideal characteristic of life. By "being upset" or unbalanced or "going to pieces," he describes by implication an awareness of an equilibrium which we may well call "the vital balance."

Hence a response would be, "Can you tell me what this feels like?" or "Can you describe for me what this feels like?" This kind of exploration helps the client talk about what it feels like to fall apart, and it can be associated with something more concrete or relatable. It also helps the therapist understand what the client means and whether it is real or a figure of speech. Most important, it facilitates empathy, providing the therapist with something to relate to and identify with. Consider this case excerpt:

Therapist: Hi! My name is Jack Stein. Can you tell me what brings you here?
Client: The nurse brought me here. I can't do my job. I feel like I'm falling apart.
Therapist: What do you mean by falling apart?
Client: This happened about a year ago. My girlfriend and I were having problems. I took my ring back because she did not do what I wanted her to, and then I tried to kill myself by cutting my wrist.
Therapist: Is that similar to what's going on now?

In this case the therapist did not explore what falling apart really feels like for this individual, and the client associated it with a previous experience. Even if the therapist did not explore with the individual what it feels like to be falling apart, we can get some idea by following the client's associations. To this client "falling apart" means attempting suicide. At this point we cannot be sure that this is what he meant to say, but that is how he responded to the question "What do you mean by falling apart?" This would be a good opportunity to use the technique of clarification, for example, "Are you saying that when you have this feeling like you are falling apart, that is when you attempt to take your own life?" This is also the beginning of some cognitive restoration, because the therapist has asked a causal connecting question. It is also information for assessment and evaluation. Exploring feelings also enables the therapist to better understand what the client is feeling; he or she can empathize with the client's description. The techniques used during this step include ventilation, encouragement, clarification, questioning, exploring, and listening.

There are times that people in crisis may not want to face painful feelings. They may want to handle them by denial or suppression. In such cases the use of suggestion, reassurance, and universalization may be helpful. For example, a therapist might find it helpful to say, "I know you have said that you want to forget about what has happened to you because it makes you feel worse; but if you can face your feelings about it with me now, it will be better for you in the long run." Or, "Bringing your feelings out in the open is always better than keeping them inside, all alone." Universalization is used much less often than other techniques to initiate and maintain a person's expression of feelings. But sometimes it is useful to let a client know that the expression of the kind of feelings he or she is experiencing is not only necessary but common to all people going through what he or she is going through (or has gone through).

The need to encourage a person in crisis to express painful feelings and emotions before moving on to other steps cannot be overemphasized. It requires patience and the capacity to tolerate painful feelings. This is another problem of the beginning therapist. It is very easy for such a therapist to avoid or shorten this step in eagerness to relieve the client of suffering or to move from painful feelings to facts. But the therapist must actually participate in the expression of these feelings through encouraging, eliciting, questioning, exploring, and clarifying such feelings and emotions.

Step 3: Discuss the precipitating event

Following a thorough discussion of painful feelings and emotions, the therapist moves to the causes of these feelings, the precipitating event. Recall that crisis theory assumes that social functioning is a continuous activity of maintaining and reestablishing equilibrium in the face of daily upsetting internal and external events. This homeostatic process is achieved through the functioning of the individual's psychic system, through specific coping mechanisms and habitual patterns of adaptation. Only when some event is perceived to be so dangerous or threatening to the individual that he or she cannot cope as effectively as before the event does a crisis develop. It follows therefore that the therapist should find out what this event is, when it occurred, how it occurred, the circumstances surrounding it, and as much information leading up to the event as needed to understand the individual in crisis. For example, it would be very enlightening to know in a bereavement crisis the nature of the relationship between the client and the deceased, certainly immediately before the death and also historically. In other situations it is important to know how the client contributed to the occurrence of the precipitating event and what it means. If we recall the case of Ben (see Chapter 2) we can see why this is so significant. In Ben's case the precipitating event was his wife leaving him after his beating her.

It is also very important for the therapist to ascertain how the client has tried to resolve the crisis and how he or she has been trying to cope since its occurrence. Most important, the therapist should determine what made the client seek help at the time that he or she did. The therapeutic benefit of discussing the precipitating event, its meaning and circumstances surrounding it, is unestimable. It not only provides for emotional release, but it facilitates cognitive restoration and is the basis for assessment and evaluation, as we shall see later. However, ascertaining the precipitating event is not always easy. Sometimes it requires considerable search on the part of the therapist and the client. This is most true when the individual is very upset or when a series of significant events occur at the same time or in succession. This helps to evaluate the level and adequacy of psychic functioning. It identifies those functions of the psychic system that are impaired and those that are functioning and to what degree. This is illustrated later in the case of Alice, who had a series of traumas in a short period of time. She was unmarried and pregnant and had been rejected by her boyfriend. Her mother hated the boyfriend and had secured a lawyer to force him to pay medical expenses. Further compounding her problem, her mother died unexpectedly.

In cases of multiple problems, the therapist must search for the one event that is the primary cause of the crisis. In Alice's case the therapist did not explore her feelings sufficiently to provide a clue. However, if the sequence of association is followed, it would appear that the boyfriend's rejection and being uncertain about keeping her baby appear to be the actual precipitating events. Alice did not mention her mother's death until near the end of the interview. However, given a series of successive events, without adequate exploration and clarification of feelings, we are still not certain which is the precipitating event ("the straw that broke the camel's back"). The most important event to the client in cases of successive events is generally reflected by present affect and feelings. This is why a thorough exploration of feelings and causes should be completed before the therapist moves to the facts of precipitating events. Regardless of how difficult it is to discover, it is a premise of crisis therapy that a precipitating event invariably exists. It is not unusual for the client to be unable to sort out the precipitating event in this chainlike process. Furthermore, people in crisis generally do not seek help immediately after the precipitating event. Consequently it is not unusual for the individual in crisis to not be readily able to identify the precipitating event. The therapist may need to discuss events and circumstances that took place several weeks before the onset of the crisis.

Discussion of the precipitating event properly starts after painful feelings and emotions have been ventilated and are an integral part of the therapeutic session. Specific attention should be given to the manner in which the individual in crisis explains and accounts for difficulties. Herein lies the client's reason for being upset. The key is to stay with the client in his or her emotional state and inquire about the precipitating event simply as a part of it. If the client is inconsistent and illogical, interviewing techniques should be used to help him or her clarify feelings, perceptions, and thinking. As Menninger (1963) states:

No one can know all of the reasons for his behavior, and yet almost anyone can give many reasons for specific acts. Over and beyond the reasons he gives, there are many reasons which he doesn't give. There are reasonable but unmentioned reasons, and there are unmentioned and unreasonable reasons, reasons depending upon emotions or biological processes of which the individual has no full knowledge.

At this time also, recurring patterns, what is expressed and what is unexpressed, should be observed. Self-defeating or self-punishing behavior characteristics should also be observed. In discussing the precipitating event, the client is revealing his or her psychic functioning.

Although this may seem simple, it can be difficult in practice to maintain the emotional flow as the client is moved to discuss the precipitating event. Consider the following interview with Alice:

> **Therapist:** What is your name?
> **Client:** Alice.
> **Therapist:** Hi, Alice, what brings you in today?
> **Client:** *(tearfully)* My lawyer made the appointment. He thought I should come and talk with someone.
> **Therapist:** Your lawyer?
> **Client:** Yes. He made the appointment; he told me to come here.
> **Therapist:** He feels you need to talk to somebody. How do you feel about that?
> **Client:** I guess so *(sigh)*.
> **Therapist:** What is it that you feel that you need to talk about?
> **Client:** *(tearfully, long silence)* I don't know.
> **Therapist :** Confused about what you feel?
> **Client:** *(sobbing)* Yes.

It can be seen that this therapist did not encourage Alice to express painful feelings in spite of the fact that she was obviously upset and in distress. Neither did the therapist search for the precipitating event. The question about the lawyer making the appointment may have been appropriate for a captive client such as a juvenile delinquent sentenced to see a therapist or a school administrator who has told parents that their child cannot come back to school until he or she has gone to the child guidance clinic. In this case, however, we are interested in what the lawyer observed about the client to recommend that she come to the crisis center, since she was not aware of the need herself. The next question should have been, "What do you think are your lawyer's reasons for sending you here?" A more effective approach, however, would have been for the therapist to first recognize the client's upset and encourage her to express these painful feelings, followed by exploring the causes of these feelings. Consider another example that has been discussed before in which a therapist did not explore feelings:

> **Therapist:** Hi! My name is Jack Stein. Can you tell me what brings you here?
> **Client:** The nurse brought me here. I can't do my job. I feel like I'm falling apart.
> **Therapist:** What do you mean by falling apart?

The therapist should have said, "Tell me what that feels like?" He or she should have followed that with ascertaining what was causing the client to feel like he was falling apart and if he had ever fallen apart before and under what circumstances.

By examining these two interviews, you can see that eliciting and encouraging the expression of painful feelings and determining the precipitating event are not simple tasks.

There are three possible reasons why a therapist has difficulty with these steps: (1) to avoid the painful feelings in the client, (2) to get facts too quickly, or (3) the therapist needs more practice functioning intellectually and empathically at the same time. Furthermore, these two examples illustrate how the therapist's opening comments set the stage for what follows. Since crisis is an affective state, opening comments should be formulated to bring out feelings and emotions first, followed by events and information.

Historical information. Gathering feelings, experiences, and facts about the client's past life is very therapeutic even for the person in crisis. Lewis (1973) most adequately expresses this author's position on the value of historical information even though he is discussing brief psychotherapy. He states:

A skillfully taken history can have the effect of holding a mirror up to the patient, thereby helping him to develop a much clearer picture of himself as an historical being than he had before. He may be compelled to look at certain recurrent problems in his life which he has not been able to look at before by reason of denial or cognitive disorganization. A careful history, with persistent questioning as to the patient's feelings about life events, and motivation for life decisions, may lay bare a pattern that he cannot avoid facing for the first time in his life. He may become aware, for example, of patterns of recurrent failure or self-destructiveness, a tendency to regard himself as a passive victim of circumstances, a tendency to create problems for himself, or a tendency to blame others for his inadequacies.

It should be clear that historical information is obtained in the context of the crisis and not as a separate entity. As the individual mentions past events, parents, and so forth, historical information is gathered. This information helps in understanding the basic personality of the individual, the relationship between the past and present, and the assessment and evaluation. The therapist should also observe the attitude associated with the information. Although historical information may appear to be objective, it is always loaded with feelings that are more therapeutic when offerred in the context of the crisis. If it is not at least somewhat emotional, the therapist should regard this as significant. For instance, in the case of Alice the death of her mother was not revealed until some 45 minutes into the session. Until that time she appeared to be distressed only about not knowing what to do about her boyfriend's rejection of her pregnancy. The therapist did not direct her into the causes of her distress. As we move into the assessment and evaluation phase, remember that the therapist must have enough information about the nature of the crisis, the precipitating event, and the life of the client that all significant questions about the client can be answered. This is necessary for assessment and evaluation, especially for identifying the nuclear problem.

Thus while discussing the precipitating event and searching for the nuclear problem, historical information that lets the therapist understand the individual's usual coping mechanisms and patterns of adaptation can also be ascertained. The following outlines some of the information needed to understand, assess, and evaluate a person in crisis.

Current life situation
A. Interpersonal relationships
    1. Marriage or other long-term heterosexual relationship
        a. How did they meet? What was the attraction?
        b. How long did they know each other before marriage? What was their relationship while dating?
        c. Try to learn some feelings about spouse.
        d. Ascertain any changes in marriage or personality of respective spouse.
        e. Attempt to ascertain feelings about significant others (e.g., friends).
    2. Family, children
B. Employment
    1. What, where, how long, degree of functioning, satisfaction.
    2. Relationship with co-workers, supervisor.
C. Background information
    1. Number of siblings and line of birth. Place of birth. Childhood experiences. Developmental facts if unusual, accidents, significant events, separations. Unusual childhood illnesses or the typical ones if there was some adverse effect.
D. Parents (discuss mother and father separately)
    1. Relationship and feelings about parents; childhood memories of them. Take particular notice of how the client describes each of his or her parent's personality and how the client feels he or she was treated by each parent.
    2. Nature of parent's relationship. How parents got along with each other. Were they happy? If not, why not? How did the client feel about parents' feelings about their marriage?
    3. Education: how much, how functioned, undue difficulty with any teacher. Activities in school, dating (ascertain parents' feelings about dating). Activities at college.

All of this information may not always be necessary for working with people in crisis. But often much of it is necessary for a complete understanding of the individual and the nuclear problem and to ascertain the client's usual level of social functioning. It is presented here as a guide to some areas that might be explored for better understanding of the individual in crisis. There are, of course, times when the therapist does not have time to gather all of this information, especially in the first interview. However, the more that is known about the client, the better the therapist is able to help. For example, if a person was abandoned or threatened with abandonment in childhood, a current situation may reactivate those old fears. When this happens, the perception and reactions to the previous experiences replace current reality, which generally compounds the problem. It is generally not possible to solve current problems with past unresolved methods and coping mechanisms. Again, historical information is only necessary in relationship to the crisis and as needed to understand the individual's psychosocial functioning. When it is needed, much of this information can be obtained very quickly and therapeutically when the therapist stays affectively where the client is. A discussion of history is most therapeutic when the client is helped to relate the present to the past when it is appropriate.

Step 4: Assess and evaluate

Assessment and evaluation really begins with the first contact with the client. However, by the time the therapist "officially" reaches this step, he or she has observed the client, listened attentively, elicited and encouraged the expression of painful feelings and emotions, identified and explored the cause and meaning of the precipitating event, and obtained sufficient information about the client, his interpersonal relationships, and other significant aspects of his life. At this point the therapist must systematically use this information to assess and evaluate the client's current level of functioning and capacity for future functioning and determine some understanding of the client's usual habitual level of functioning. This information becomes the basis for treatment planning and implementation. In sum, during assessment and evaluation the therapist draws conclusions regarding the cause of the individual's crisis, the degree of debilitation, and the potential for recovery.

Determining the cause of the crisis condition. Recall that the cause of the crisis is not specifically the precipitating event but the reaction to the event. Hence the first step in determining the cause of the crisis is for the therapist to identify the nuclear problem. The nuclear problem differs from the precipitating event or present problem. Although treated with acceptance, understanding, respect, and empathy, the precipitating event is the way the client perceives and reacts to the current situation. It is of necessity a subjective view of distress and is contaminated by cognitive debilitation, distorted perception, and emotional confusion as a consequence of trying to resolve the crisis alone. It can be compared with trying to repair a television set with hundreds of tubes without knowing how. Although you try to remove all of the tubes at the same time in an orderly fashion, putting them back in the right place is complex. Once you get one out of place, they all become confused and your problems are compounded. Finally the television set blows up, and a professional television repairman has to be consulted.

The nuclear problem, on the other hand, is the underlying reason that causes the individual's reaction to the precipitating event. It is really the client's unknown personal meaning given to the precipitating event. In effect, our understanding of anxiety and depression and their derivatives gives us a foundation for understanding the nuclear problem. As we said in Chapter 2, almost all reactions to crises are manifested by anxiety, depression, or their derivatives. So the behavioral and affective manifestations of the person in crisis locate the area of the nuclear problem. For example, we know that depression results from (1) loss or threatened loss of a loved object or other ego value; (2) loss or threatened loss of self-concept or self-esteem; (3) the failure to live up to internalized expectations, standards, values, or goals; or (4) the violation or wish to violate some significant moral code (i.e., to engage in or the desire to engage in something personally unacceptable). Although this understanding locates the area, the specific problem is the meaning to the client of the behavioral or affective manifestations. Consider the case of Ben (see Chapter 2), who became depressed and suicidal after his wife left him because he beat her. What is the specific meaning of his depression to him? Is it the loss of a loved object that threatens him? Or the loss of self-esteem? Since Ben contributed greatly to the precipitating event, it is logical to conclude that he had some wish for his wife to leave. If so, why did he get depressed and react as if he were hurt by the loss of his wife? A possible answer is that he felt considerable conflict over loving his wife versus loving his mother. The conflict could be resolved by his wife leaving him. On the other hand, going to live with his mother was consciously unacceptable, and he really could not accept this feeling. Because he attempted suicide, it is logical to conclude either that this conflict made him feel contemptuous of himself or that the suicidal gesture was symbolically directed at another person, probably his mother or his wife. (As Freud stated, every suicide is a homicide.) Consider the case of Kay, a 35-year-old attractive woman, who developed a crisis because her husband's employer arranged a working retreat at a famous resort for only the executives of the company. Kay felt strongly that the wives should go also. The precipitating event occurred while she was vociferously expressing her feelings to her husband, who in effect communicated to her both affectively and behaviorally that he did not want her to go. He was in support of his boss; he wanted to go with "the boys." Although Kay complained of the "fear" of being left alone (Kay was not left alone, since she had a 14-year-old son at home), the nuclear problem was a deep feeling of rejection and loss of self-esteem, on the one hand, because her husband did not want her to go, and on the other hand, she was concerned about whether her husband would be involved with other women. This was supported by Kay's talk about having an affair herself, which was a retaliatory defense against the loss of self-esteem she associated with the possibility of her husband's having an affair, and a fear of herself because the possibility of it happening to her was a threat.

A reliable way to find the nuclear problem is to determine the underlying meaning to the reaction to the precipitating event. Anxiety and depression provide the beginning. The therapist should be careful to look for the sometimes multiple meanings and purposes the nuclear problems serve. As we saw in the case of Ben and Kay, many unacceptable desirable feelings previously handled by keeping them out of conscious awareness can be reactivated by certain external events. When this happens, unacceptable desirable feelings must be defended against or controlled. In Ben's case he wanted to live with his mother but needed his wife to defend against this desire. There are times that the nuclear problem may be tied to the nature of the individual personality and developmental history. In such situations the precipitating event reactivates a previous forgotten conflict. When this happens the individual reacts to the current crisis in the same way he or she reacted to the old conflict.

These situations respond very well to cognitive restoration. Although we are providing areas that can be explored, which helps to understand the individual, the therapist should be interested in gathering meaningful and significant information that is germane to understanding the individual and his or her problems. But we should also keep in mind that discussion of significant historical information, especially that of interpersonal relationships, is very therapeutic.

Assessing degree of functional debilitation. An assessment and evaluation of the seriousness of the individual's crisis condition and capacity for social functioning can be made as soon as the precipitating event and the nuclear problem are understood.

Before the crisis the individual was able to use the function and capacities of the psychic system: intelligence, perception, judgment, and so forth. He or she related and adapted to the social environment. The crisis interrupted these processes. We are interested at this point in which of the functions have been interrupted and to what degree. We are interested also in those functions that are not impaired or that are the most functional.

The first step in assessing the seriousness of the individual's crisis state is to observe and estimate the degree of debilitating affect or emotions: depression, anxiety, and their derivatives. The therapist should get answers to such questions as: How depressed does the individual seem? How anxious? How angry? Is he or she homicidal or suicidal? Remember that the greater the depression, the greater the internalized anger. As a general rule the deeper the depression, the less likelihood of suicide. The depression immobilizes the individual because of the anger that is turned inward. Consequently the danger of suicide for the depressed is not during the depth of the depression but while going into and coming out of the depression, when the individual has more energy. More will be said about suicide later in this chapter and in Chapter 6.

The overwhelming effect of emotions on the functions of the psychic system determines the degree of functional dibilitation. Hence to find the client's capacity for social functioning resulting from overwhelming emotionality, the degree of debilitation of the various functions of the psychic system must be assessed and evaluated.

The functions of the psychic system that make possible unique and idiosyncratic social functioning and adaptation are cognitive functioning, perception, memory, reality testing, judgment, thought processes, impulse control, adaptive efforts, and coping mechanisms. By assessing and evaluating these various functions and capacities of the psychic system, the therapist not only identifies the impaired functions, but they become a focus of treatment, reinforcement, and restrengthening. Again, the functions of the psychic system are an integrated whole and overlap. They are separated here for the sake of study and learning.

COGNITIVE FUNCTIONING. By cognitive functioning we do not mean IQ. We mean the use of information processing, thinking ability, perception, memory, planning, and problem-solving methods. An estimate of cognitive functioning can be determined through several clues: (1) the methods the individual uses to try to resolve the crisis; (2) the adequacy and consistency in discussing events preceding the onset of the crisis; (3) the logic and consistency with which facts and reasons are discussed; and (4) the capacity to comprehend, understand, and make logical responses to the therapist's questions and explanations. We know from the nature of a crisis that these cognitive functions will be impaired to varying degrees. Hence we are interested in evaluating the degree. We are also interested in assessing and evaluating the individual's capability to receive, digest, and interpret new information. This provides some estimate of how much cognitive capacity has been restored.

REALITY TESTING. Reality testing is important to adequate social functioning because it requires reconciling the internal world with the events and conditions of the real world. When reality testing is impaired there is confusion, and in extreme cases, psychosis. Reality testing is the individual's ability to distinguish between what is in his or her mind and what is in the objective world. In effect, two realities exist in every human being: psychic or subjective reality, that which is in our minds, and objective reality, that which is in the real world. Theoretically these two realities should be the same. But this is not always possible. Each person's view of reality is influenced by inner processes, thoughts, imagination, wishes, beliefs, fears, hopes, memories, desires, and experiences. Consequently it is not easy to consistently see reality as it really is. However, adequate social functioning requires a certain degree of success in reality testing. The individual's inner processes must be relatively consistent with objective reality, and he or she must be able to reasonably accurately appraise objective reality as the basis for behavior and adaptation. When people are able to successfully test reality, their social functioning is generally good. On the other hand, when reality testing is impaired, what is in the individual's mind is projected onto external reality. Reacting accordingly, that becomes the person's total reality. An example is the individual who develops hallucinations or delusions. He or she reacts as if they are reality. Since they actually contradict reality, the individual develops great problems in social functioning. Psychosis is the extreme form of impaired reality testing. In more common situations, you can probably recall a time where your imagination, projected onto reality, created a seeming nightmare for you. Even more common are the use of magic and superstition as reality even when objective reality contradicts them.

For the crisis therapist the concept of reality testing is not only important for assessing and evaluating the individual but also for understanding him or her. Consider the example of an individual who says (and does not mean it as a figure of speech), "I'm scared to death of taking beginning tennis lessons." This person has also made the same statement about flying and sickness. Is that person's reality testing impaired? To a certain extent it is, since the same danger is associated with beginning tennis lessons as with flying and sickness. In other words, the individual projects inner fears onto tennis, which become reality as far as tennis is concerned. Often the person in crisis does the very same thing. Impaired reality testing can be estimated by the degree of inaccuracy or misinterpretation of objective reality.

Whatever is in the person's mind is his or her reality. Although we may want to change it, we first should accept it and feel empathic. Pain and suffering in the mind hurt just as much as they do when they have an objective cause. The husband who feels that his wife does not love him despite objective evidence to the contrary feels just as unloved as if it were true. The physician who is depressed because he feels that he did not do all that he could to save his patient in the face of evidence to the contrary feels just as bad as if he had failed. Very often making the individual in crisis aware that he or she is reacting to the events of the real world based on psychic reality can be quite effective, *if* the pain has been accepted and empathized with first. Thus reality testing is used not only as a means to assess and evaluate capacity for social functioning and understanding the individual in crisis, but also for treatment in specifically cognitive restoration.

The extreme form of impaired reality testing is loss of a sense of reality. This is reflected in psychosis, depersonalization, and the heavy use of drugs.

PERCEPTION. Perception is the basis of reality testing and a part of the cognitive process. In simple terms it is the way an inidvidual sees reality. Of interest, it is based on experience and memory and greatly influenced by specific intrapsychic functioning, need, and motivation. It follows therefore that perception affects reality testing and judgment.

IMPULSE CONTROL. Impulse control refers to the ability to control intense emotions and urges (e.g., sexual and aggressive drives). Assessment and evaluation are especially important to the individual who is very angry or aggressive, as in homicide, assaultive behavior, or physical abuse. An example is the individual who is angry at a spouse or child. Perhaps the first factor in assessing and evaluating an individual whose impulses have been precipitated by a specific event is to estimate the strength of the impulse in relationship to strength of the ego and other countercontrol mechanisms. For example, a person with a relatively strong conscience, though very angry, may be less likely to lose control than a person with a weaker conscience.

A second factor in assessing and evaluating impulse control is history. People who have a history of poor impulse control are more likely to lose control than people with a history of good control. The exception is the overly controlled or rigid individual. The individual who has a history of rarely getting angry or not showing normal emotions should be evaluated thoroughly, and caution should be taken.

Another factor to be considered in assessing and evaluating impulse control is the meaning to the individual of the event precipitating the threat of loss of impulse control. Is it loss of self-esteem? Is it personal hurt? Is it perceived as exploitation or being taken advantage of? Or is it taking away something that is an important ego value, for which the individual must take revenge? In those situations, unless the individual has effective counterforces against the impulse, loss of control or retaliation should be a serious consideration.

Another factor is to try to ascertain whether the precipitating event really activated feelings that were meant for another source. For example, a parent battering a child could be having feelings about a sibling or some relationship with his or her own parents.

Not all problems of impulse control involve rage, aggression, or hostility. Sometimes they involve sexual impulses and the threat of unacceptable sexual indulgence or acting out, heterosexually or homosexually. In such situations the therapist must be careful to hear what the client is saying. In those situations, if an individual comes for help, it is almost always because there is conflict over the impulse, that is, the desire to indulge versus the feeling that it is wrong. Regardless of how liberal or traditional the therapist is, he or she should not impose personal feelings or views on the client but identify the conflict, hear what the client is asking for, and help the client resolve the conflict. The potentiality and consequence of losing control of impulses other than aggressive ones should be thoroughly evaluated also. Specifically, focus should be given to what is provoking the threat of loss of impulse control in all cases.

THOUGHT PROCESSES. Thought processes are important in the evaluation when they reveal an incipient psychosis or impending break with reality. In such cases the individual's thought processes may appear to be reasonable but on close scrutiny are either illogical or inappropriate. There may be disproportionate emphasis on something insignificant. Thoughts may be preoccupied with small physical complaints. Often a client may give specific and exacting details of normally embarrassing subjects such as sex practices before he or she really knows the therapist. New words may be used. The client may be distractable and have a poor attention span. Perseveration may be present; that is, the client may persistently repeat an idea or thought. The client may give trivia or irrelevant details about other subjects along with the main point or idea. As thought processes progressively deteriorate, they become incoherent and disorganized. The final stage of deterioration is psychosis manifested by delusions, hallucinations, or both, the recognition of which is easy. But recognizing the early stages of psychosis requires a constant sensitivity to the communication process. The therapist must be sure of what the client is saying, and if questions to clarify it do not succeed, serious disturbance in thought processes should be suspected and serious deterioration should be ruled out. Disturbances in thought processes are probably the best indicators of incipient psychosis. As long as an individual's thought processes are understandable or can be made understandable by logical responses to questions, the ego or self-system is reasonably intact.

EFFORT AT ADAPTATION AND COPING MECHANISMS. We have seen that through the socialization process people develop habitual patterns of adaptation and coping mechanisms. Under normal conditions these enabled them to function and to restore equilibrium when it is upset. In the development of a crisis, both of these break down, forcing the desperate individual to resort to less effective adaptive efforts and coping mechanisms. They are less effective because usual cognitive functions are impaired by overwhelming affect and because the most successful adaptive efforts, the ones habitually used, have become ineffective. It is like a solid foundation moved from under a person, leaving him or her suspended by uncertainty. Given the degree of cognitive impairment, an important index of the degree of debilitation is how the individual is attempting to deal with the crisis. This is a question the therapist must be able to answer. The therapist must also answer the question of what defense or coping mechanisms the client is using. Is the client using the defense mechanisms of projection, denial, reaction formation, or rationalization more than is beneficial? These are mechanisms that keep people from assuming responsibility for their behavior and from facing the reality of the situation. How are they functionally being used? What purpose do they serve? What are the consequences of the client's efforts to deal with the crisis? When greatly regressed, a person relies on primitive behavior patterns. If the therapist can identify the characteristics of these behavior patterns, he or she can identify the level of psychic functioning. For example, the person who resorts to excessive dependency needs or submissiveness is functioning characteristic of an early phase of life. The impulsive acting-out client is another who is functioning at a level characteristic of early life. It simply means that the ego has become ineffective and that the individual is dominated by emotions. When this occurs it is generally an indication that the therapist must attempt to restore self-control or take active steps to ensure self-control.

In some cases an individual will attempt to deal with the crisis by being overcontrolled. The use of the mechanisms of intellectualization and isolation are examples. Being overcontrolled, in the long run, can often be just as ineffective in consequence to the client as losing control. Consequently, being overcontrolled should not be viewed as a source of strength, and efforts should be made to help the person deal with the crisis in a therapeutic way, that is, to face it and to express the painful emotions.

The final area to be assessed is the individual's residual capacity to function and to adapt. This evaluation comes at the end of the session with the therapist. By now a great deal of treatment has gone on since the beginning of the session. The client should be different at the end of the session than at the beginning. So the question now is: How integrated is the client? What is his or her capacity to tolerate the effect of the crisis now? How much has ego or cognitive functioning improved? Which of these and other ego functions are operable now? Which are still impaired? To what extent has the client been able to integrate the content of the session? Is the client able to be sent back to his or her environment until the next appointment?

These questions cannot be answered until the client's external resources have been assessed and evaluated. These include relatives, significant others, friends, and other helping professionals. Relatives or significant others and external sources of support should be assessed and evaluated carefully, including the client's feelings about and relationships with them. Some of this may have taken place while gathering historical information during the affectual release early in the session. Many people are in crisis because of conflict, disappointment, or rejection by significant people in their lives. If the evidence suggests the involvement of others, it should be discussed thoroughly with the client. If the therapist indicates that relatives should be involved and the client is opposed to this suggestion, it should be treated as a form of resistence and worked through if possible. Whether the therapist acts against the client's will depends on the degree of need for involvement of others in the client's crisis and the consequence if they are not involved. Another factor to consider is the client's right of self-determination, within his or her capacity for reality testing.

The result of the assessment and evaluation process should enable the therapist to recommend the kind of treatment that will further alleviate the crisis and restore the client's social functioning to at least the precrisis level. In order to do this the therapist must be able to synthesize a wealth of information into some understandable causal explanation. He or she must then communicate it back to the client in such a way that the client receives, understands, digests, and integrates it.

Step 5: Formulate a dynamic explanation

We have conceptualized social functioning as being determined by the psychic system, the array of functions and forces that receives its stimulus for action from both internal and external sources. The word "dynamic" is used to mean the interplay of the functions and forces of the psychic system and the social environment that unite to cause specific ways of social functioning and patterns of adaptation. Hence the therapist must understand and explain the significant forces that are causing the person's crisis condition. The therapist must understand both internal forces and environmental factors that are important to precipitating the crisis as well as those sustaining it and preventing the client from resolving it alone. The dynamic formulation explains certain affective states and identifies specific defense or coping mechanisms, how they are being used, and for what purpose. Through the dynamic formulation the therapist comes to understand the relationship between the precipitating event and the psychic forces it mobilizes.

The dynamic formulation is the basis of cognitive restoration and treatment planning. It is the basis of client insight and understanding of the crisis condition and reaction. It is also the basis for the type of treatment needed (e.g., crisis psychotherapy or environmental manipulation). In sum, the dynamic formulation is the therapist's understanding of the cause of an individual's reaction to an event precipitating a crisis condition. It is not *what* (e.g., the loss of a loved one) but *why* the client reacts the way he or she does. It establishes the therapist's rationale for how the crisis can be resolved and the client restored to at least a precrisis level of social functioning. It seeks to answer the following questions: What is the core or nuclear problem (i.e., the condition that causes the reaction to the precipitating event)? What is its basic meaning to the client? Why does the client perceive the precipitating event as he or she does? What are the implications to the client's basic personality structure of the meaning of the event and the way he or she tried to resolve the crisis?

Sometimes the dynamic formulation can be made with a minimum of facts and information about the client. At other times it requires a great deal of historical information. Whatever it requires, the therapist must arrive at as accurate a dynamic formulation as possible as the basis of treatment planning and implementation.

Step 6: Cognitive restoration

A great deal of therapeutic work has gone on before the process of cognitive restoration begins. Generally by this time a person in crisis has gained some relief from painful emotions and tension by expressing them to an interested and concerned person. He or she has begun to use some cognitive facilities again by talking about traumatic experiences and painful feelings. Cognitive facilities have been forced into further use by responses to the therapist's "think" questions. The therapist's effort to thoroughly understand the individual, the nature of the crisis, the nuclear problem, and the significance of the precipitating event have all served this end. Now the client is ready to know what is wrong, why, and what can be done about it. Hence cognitive restoration is the process in which the therapist conveys to the person in crisis an explanation of the causes of the crisis, of the meaning of the nuclear problem, and why the way the individual attempted to handle the crisis was ineffective. In effect, cognitive restoration is an empathic intellectual process somewhat like a physician's explaining to a patient what is physically wrong. Consider the following example from Walker (1953):

If on completion of the history and physical examination, the patient is believed to be suffering primarily from an anxiety reaction or psychogenic cardiovascular reaction, he is informed somewhat as follows: "Mr. Jones, after a thorough examination I do not believe you have any serious heart disease, although you have suffered from distressing chest pain and are naturally concerned about it.

The pounding and skipping of your heart, I believe, result from a nervous reaction rather than from disease in your heart. For instance, if you walked down a dark alley at night and a masked bandit suddenly stuck a gun in your ribs, I am sure your heart would beat very fast and hard—not because it was bad, but in response to the nerve impulse that went out because of the fear you were experiencing. Your breath would also come short and fast and your hands would be wet and shaking as they were when you came into the office. Prolonged worry, tension, anger or anxiety can produce the same nervous impulse as intense fear. That this is probably a factor in your case is suggested by the appearance of your symptoms shortly after the arrival of the new foreman with whom you are having trouble. . . . You are afraid that your heart is bad, and as a double check I suggest we get an electrocardiogram, chest x-ray, blood test and urinalysis as a part of a complete medical evaluation. I expect they will be normal and even if they aren't, I am sure most of your symptoms result from nervous causes since no form of heart trouble can completely explain your symptoms while a tension state readily can."

As McGuire (1965) states:

Of those patients who eventually gain insight, nearly all begin their own mental ordering and analyses of conflicts in the period between the evaluation and the start of therapy.

Cognitive restoration is needed because the emotional state resulting from the precipitating event is so painful that the client's goal is to avoid or defend against the painful affect, not resolve the crisis. The premise of cognitive restoration is the belief that knowledge and understanding, after a thorough ventilation of feelings, reduce emotional overloading, restore cognitive functioning, and facilitate regaining cognitive control. In other words, by providing an explanation to the client of the reason for the crisis state and the meaning of his or her behavior, the therapist helps the client to regain mastery of his or her life.

When the therapist has sufficiently completed the first five steps, cognitive restoration is indicated. It generally occurs near the end of the first session, after the therapist has a thorough understanding of the client and the condition and has formulated in his or her own mind what is causing the client's problems and why. Cognitive restoration involves the techniques of interpretation and causal connecting explanations. For example, an explanation of the cause of the pessimism is presented to the client in simple, clear, and concise statements using words that the client can understand rather than professional jargon. The explanation can be either short or long, depending on the complexity of the client's crisis condition and personality structure. Consider the following cognitive restoration statement:

■ Fred, a 55-year-old man who 3 years ago had a laryngectomy, came to the center in a crisis precipitated by his wife's final threat to leave him. For the past 4 months Fred had felt uncontrollably forced to spend the last three nights of each week "with the boys," nightclubbing, drinking, and having a good time. The other four nights he worked two jobs, rarely coming home before 11 PM. During the session Fred insisted that he loved his wife and did not want to lose her, as evidenced by his seeking immediate help. When the therapist reached the cognitive restoration phase, he tersely said, "The cause of your condition is that you seem to be living your life as if it is coming to an end soon." Fred eagerly returned for his next session, feeling very pleased with himself. He had returned home to his wife, did not go out with his friends for the weekend, and quit one of his two jobs. Although he returned for two more sessions, he made such a quick recovery that the therapist asked permission to see his wife, who confirmed his change. She was pleased and thought the therapist was a "miracle worker." In follow-up contact with Fred, he was asked what he thought the therapist did that helped him most. He said it was explaining to him that he was living like his life was coming to an end.

It is very difficult to explain all of the variables that made the cognitive restoration phase so significant for Fred. It could have been that perhaps he had some latent feelings of impending death, as he had had cancer. But at the same time his doctor felt that Fred was in good health. The important point is that the therapist's cognitive restoration statement enabled Fred to regain control over his emotions and behavior.

In sum, cognitive restoration helps the client regain control over cognitive facilities and social functioning by providing an explanation of the causes of the crisis condition and an understanding of how he or she reacted and why.

Step 7: Plan and implement treatment

Many crises situations can be resolved in one session. In these cases no further treatment is necessary and the therapist can move on to termination and follow-up in the first session. In most cases, however, further treatment planning and implementation are necessary.

After the therapist has provided the client with some understanding of the causes and reasons for the crisis condition through cognitive restoration, treatment planning can be recommended. Based on the assessment and evaluation of the client's condition, specific psychic system, and capacity for social functioning, treatment planning is the therapist's professional judgment of what is needed to help the client resolve the crisis and improve social functioning. Specific treatment plans that use the client's motivation, strengths, and capacity should be shared and discussed. The therapist has three basic choices of treatment plans: additional crisis therapy, environmental modification, and referral.

Additional crisis therapy. Additional crisis therapy is indicated when the assessment and evaluation reveal that the individual can safely be treated outside of a hospital and needs additional sessions to further resolve the crisis and restore social functioning.

If additional sessions are indicated, they should be recommended in ways that the client can understand and accept. Using the word "psychotherapy" or other professional jargon should be avoided. Also, a definite appointment should be given at the conclusion of the first session. In other words, the client should not be asked when he or she would like to come back or can come back. It should be stated as, "I would like to see you again tomorrow at 10:00 AM." A recommendation of crisis therapy could be handled like this: "I believe that you and I, through discussions like we had today, can work things out for you. What do you think about that?" Or the therapist might say, "You seem to be feeling better and looking at things differently now, and I would like to have a few more sessions with you like we had today. I would like to see you tomorrow (or next week) at 10:00 AM. Is that all right?" Or "I think if we can meet a few more times and pursue further some of the things we talked about today, maybe we can make things like they used to be. I can see you on Wednesday at 9:00 AM. Is that a good time for you?"

If involving significant others is indicated, that recommendation should be stated with confidence along with an explanation and due consideration to the individual's feelings about it. This can be sensitive, since many crises are precipitated by conflict and problems with significant others. Assessment and evaluation of the nature of the client's relationship with relatives and other significant others and consequences of involving them should be done before the recommendation or permission is sought from the client.

Thus far we have been discussing those things that happen or could happen in the first session. Now more definitive action on the part of both the therapist and the client are set forth in goals established from the assessment and evaluation process. Keeping within the framework of crisis theory, the individual's crisis should be resolved within the next five sessions or 5 weeks. The causes of the crisis state have been identified and thoroughly discussed, and the goals have been laid out and explained to the client in the first session. The therapist can move toward definite action designed to further resolve the crisis, based on an idea of what is causing the crisis. In other words, the cause of the crisis and capacity for social functioning suggest the solution. This dictates that both the therapist and the client become active in the further resolution of the crisis, doing whatever is necessary to improve psychic functioning. The therapist should try to increase the client's self-esteem. This can be done through supporting the client's ego when it is appropriate and indicated and by empathically communicating a feeling that the client has worth and value. This means that the therapist continues to be sensitive to the client's needs, desires, fears, and conflicts as he or she communicates them overtly and covertly. The therapist motivates and encourages, keeping in mind the dictates of psychological support and cognitive restoration. He or she reinforces and bolsters strengths and weakness where needed and provides the insight that helps the client regain cognitive control. The therapist does not wait for the client to develop insight as in traditional psychotherapy; he or she imparts it personally. Insight occurs through the cognitive restoration process, specifically, the use of causal connecting statements and interpretation. The success of interpretation is based on three factors: timing, clarity of expression, and the receptiveness of the client. Timing refers to making the interpretation at the most effective point, that is, when it is current in the client's mind and can be connected to current feeling or behavior. It is ineffective to tell that client that he is expecting his wife to treat him the same way as his mother if he is not emotionally feeling it at the time of the interpretation. There must be evidence that he is doing it. In other words, there must be some evidence, behaviorally or affectively, to support the basis for the interpretation. The therapist should also elicit the client's interpretation of the meaning of his or her feelings and behavior, most often before the therapist gives his own.

Clarity of expression refers to the therapist making the interpretation in the most concise and succinct manner possible. It should be recalled that the shorter and simpler the therapist's statements, the greater their impact. Sometimes the use of parables or analogues is quite effective.

Receptiveness refers to the client being ready to accept the interpretation. Usually this is less of a problem with people in crisis than for those in traditional therapy. People in crisis are generally less defensive. Even so, the therapist should try to anticipate and gauge the effect of his or her interpretation. The therapist should try to make sure that the interpretation does not unduly decrease self-esteem. Nor should it be too anxiety provoking, keeping in mind that an optimal amount of anxiety can be a positive motivating force.

Environmental modification. Environmental modification involves recommending that the client in crisis be removed from his or her environment because it is holding back improvement or because the client cannot function in it safely. As we saw in Chapter 4, there are three basic reasons for recommending environmental modification: (1) the client is not capable of improving as long as he or she remains in the current environment, (2) the client is not able to change the environment constructively, and (3) environmental modification is needed as an adjunct to supportive intervention. Involving significant others is a form of environmental modification.

If hospitalization is indicated, rarely if ever should the client be trusted to report to the hospital alone. Another person should accompany the client to the hospital. Recommending the removal of a child from his or her home or from a foster home is another delicate and sensitive proposition that should be done only after thorough assessment and evaluation of the situation. This process requires a great deal of knowledge and skill because of the extreme defensiveness of those causing the situation, coupled with society's implication of blame and anger. It is imperative that the therapist in such situations remain as nonjudgmental as possible and recognize even before contact with the client that he or she will be perceived as a representative of society who is angry, condemning, and punitive ("Just wanting to take my child away"). In such situations the therapist must work through the client's feelings of anticipated blame, defensiveness, resistance, and other negative experiences before real therapeutic work can begin. Regardless of the nature of the crisis, the therapist's purpose is to present himself or herself as a helpful person.

Step 8: Terminate

After the crisis has been resolved and the individual has returned to the precrisis level of functioning, termination is indicated. Although crisis therapy is over, the client should have learned from the experience. He or she should have learned through the process of self-understanding how to better cope and how to go about solving the next upsetting event, preventing a crisis condition. The client should have learned that he or she has ability and capacity, can do something about his or her life, and can live a good life within personal limitations and those of the environment. The client should have learned that he or she must take responsibility for what is wanted, for wanting that which is achievable, and for engaging in behavior that will achieve those ends.

Termination should be concluded with the client feeling that the therapist will be there if needed again, such as the case of Joanne (see Chapter 1). Knowing that the therapist is available if needed is often a source of support. However, in most bona fide crises it is rarely needed.

Step 9: Follow-up

At the end of the last session the client should be informed that the therapist will be interested in how he or she is getting along and will contact him or her at some time in the future. Generally clients feel good about such interest and welcome the information. Some crisis therapists, however, believe that such a follow-up prolongs dependency feelings. However, this has not been proved, and the advantages the client gains from this interest usually outweigh questionable negative consequences. Furthermore, such follow-up lends itself to evaluation of results, which becomes the basis of new knowledge for working with people in crisis.

In Chapters 6 and 7 we will look at ways of working with specific crisis situations.

REFERENCES

Bernstein, L., and Bernstein, R. Interviewing: a guide for health professionals. New York: Appleton-Century-Crofts, 1974.

Biestek, F. B. The casework relationship. Chicago: Loyola University Press, 1957.

Brill N. I. Working with people: the helping process. Philadelphia: J. B. Lippincott, 1978.

Carkhuff, R. R., & Berenson, B. G. Beyond counseling and therapy. New York: Holt, Rinehart and Winston, 1977.

Ellis, A. New approaches to psychotherapy techniques. *Journal of Clinical Psychology*, 1955, *11*, 208-260.

Fenichel, O. The psychoanalytic theory of neurosis. New York: W. W. Norton, 1945.

Hammer, E. F. (Ed). Use of interpretation in treatment: *techniques and art*. New York: Grune & Stratton, 1968.

Kalis, B. L., Harris, R. M., Prestwood, R., & Freeman, E. H. Precipitating stress as a focus in psychotherapy. *Archives of General Psychiatry*, 1961, 5(3), 27-34.

Lewis, A. B., Jr. Brief psychotherapy in the hospital setting: techniques and goals. *Psychiatric Quarterly*, 1973, *47*(3), 341-352.

McGuire, M. T., The Process of short-term insight psychotherapy. II. Content, expectation and structure. *Journal of Nervous and Mental Disorders*, 1965, *141, 219-230.*

Menninger, K., with Mayman, M., & Pryser, P. *The vital balance: the life process in mental health and illness.* New York: Viking Press, 1963.

Paul, L. Treatment techniques in a walk-in-clinic. *Hospital and Community Psychiatry*, 1966, *17*(2), 49-51.

Rogers, C. R. Necessary and sufficient condition of therapeutic personality change. *Journal of Consulting Psychology*, 1957, *21*, 95-103.

Sullivan, H. S. The Psychiatric interview. New York: W. W. Norton, 1954.

Truax, C. B. The effective ingredients in psychotherapy: an approach to unraveling the patient-therapist interaction. *Journal of* Counseling Psychology, 1963, *10*, 256-263.

Truax, C. B., and Carkhuff, R. R. Toward effective counseling and psychotherapy. Chicago: Aldine, 1967.

Walker, W. J. Neurocirculatory asthenia. In F. C. Massey (Ed.), *Clinical cardiology*. Baltimore: Williams & Wilkins, 1953.

SUGGESTED READINGS

Kalis, B. L., Harris R. M., Prestwood, A. R., & Freeman, E. H. Precipitating stress as a focus in psychotherapy. *Archives of General Psychiatry*, 1961, *5*(3), 27-34.

Paul, L. Treatment techniques in a walk-in clinic. *Hospital and Community Psychiatry*, 1966, *17* (2), 49-51.

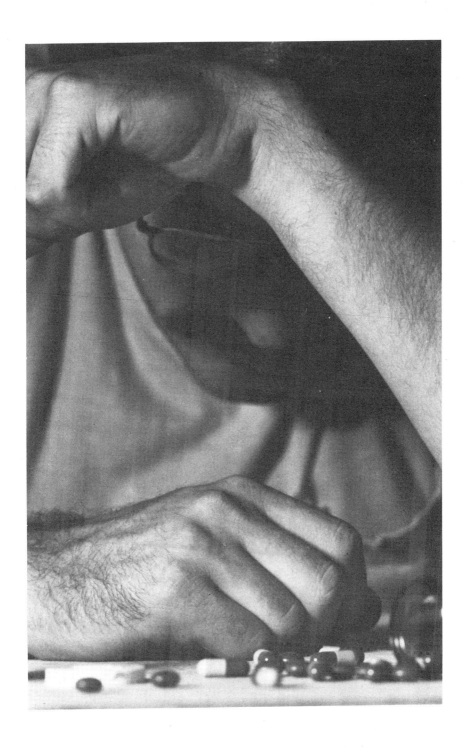

CHAPTER 6

Common crisis reactions

This chapter is designed to expand our knowledge and understanding of common crisis reactions and to make some suggestions for treatment. We have seen that it is the reaction to an event that causes a crisis and not the event itself. Consequently, effective crisis treatment requires treatment of the *reaction,* because the reaction is really the cause of the debilitation. Remember that once a person is unable to resolve a problem by usual methods and coping mechanisms, he or she feels overwhelming emotional pain. As far as the person is concerned, his or her goal now is to alleviate this pain, and solving the problem situation is abandoned. For example, if a husband's crisis is precipitated by his wife leaving him, he is usually not interested at first in why he is reacting in that way or what it means to him to be dependent on his wife. He is interested only in what to do to get his wife back so that his pain will be relieved and he can return to his precrisis status. Of course his wife is a critical part of that. It follows therefore that the goal of the therapist is to alleviate the client's pain by doing whatever is necessary. The therapist may need to help get the wife back or may need to help the client see the difference between objective reality and his inner feelings that are making him feel that he cannot live without her. The point is that the painful emotion is the cause of the debilitation. Thus it must be treated first. The first of the common emotional reactions that we will discuss is anxiety.

ANXIETY

Anxiety is basically a spontaneous response that acts as an alarm system, preparing an individual to defend against a potential danger. As we know it, anxiety develops whenever a person feels a threat to existence as a human being or to the values perceived to be necessary for existence. It follows therefore that anxiety will develop whenever someone feels that life or life-sustaining values or personality integration are threatened.

Anxiety, regardless of how irrational it is, can be the most painful of all

129

human experiences. Its pain is intensified because its source is generally unknown. Furthermore, the human body cannot tolerate anxiety indefinitely. Prolonged anxiety must be alleviated by some psychological mechanism or it turns into a psychosomatic ailment. Laughlin (1967) reports the following case of death from panic anxiety:

A 54-year-old man was admitted to the hospital because of marked anxiety accompanied by depression. He did not respond to treatment, and the anxiety increased. Rapidly he became severely anxious and agitated. Sedatives seemed powerless. He was apprehensive of death and he presented a clinical picture of the most acute anxiety. This unfortunate state continued unabated for well in excess of 48 hours, when he suddenly collapsed and died. The immediate cause of death was on postmortem examination reported to be "coronary insufficiency," accompanied by massive pulmonary edema. Pathologically, however, his coronary arteries were otherwise excellent. It was also difficult to explain the massive edema from any strictly pragmatic viewpoint. Seemingly, this patient had tolerated all of the acute anxiety of which he was physically, physiologically, and psychologically capable, and then death had supervened.

This case illustrates the importance of anxiety to psychic functioning. However, it is not the mere existence of anxiety that is a problem (as we saw in Chapter 2), since a certain level of anxiety can be constructive and motivating. It is only excessive anxiety that is debilitating, and that is what we are concerned with here. When a crisis is manifested by overwhelming or excessive anxiety, the meaning is always the same: the individual feels relatively helpless to cope with a perceived danger to survival. He or she is simply speaking, "scared to death." Remember that in using the word *anxiety* we imply that the cause of the reaction is subjective and that there is no objective threat to survival. If there is an objective threat that is real in fact, we call the reaction *fear*. Thus cognitive restoration takes the form of reconciling the person's internal reality with objective reality.

There are three basic situations when a crisis is manifested by anxiety, that is, when the individual subjectively (if it is objective it is *fear*) feels that (1) life is threatened, (2) control of a sexual or aggressive impulse is about to be lost, or (3) body integrity is perceived to be threatened.

Anxiety may arise when a person feels that life is threatened. This includes also the loss or threatened loss of a loved one who is perceived to be needed for survival (e.g., children who need parents for survival). It may also include the need for love.

We can make functional differentiation between reacting to loss of a love object with anxiety and with depression. If one reacts with anxiety, the meaning of the loss has to do with survival needs; if one reacts with depression, the meaning of the loss has to do with the need for love and self-esteem.

Anxiety may arise when an individual feels that he or she is about to lose control of a sexual or aggressive impulse. In such situations the usual methods of impulse control are progressively more ineffective, and anxiety develops to warn the person to do something quickly. Again, the threat of loss of impulse control is most often an unconscious cause of the anxiety, although some people can verbalize it. Verbalization is a good sign because conscious steps to avoid the loss of control can be taken. Two common examples of a fear of loss of impulse control are parents who develop anxiety over hurting their child and people in a homosexual panic. Consider the following case:

■ Mrs. Applebaum called the crisis center asking that her 3-year-old son be placed in a foster home. Mrs. Applebaum was obviously upset and crying profusely. After considerable difficulty she said that the reason that she wants to put her son in a foster home is because he has been crying all day and she is afraid that she may harm him. Discussion of the precipitating event revealed that the night before she had gone out with friends and her ex-husband took care of their son. After she returned, he made a disrespectful comment regarding her "running around." She became so angry that she broke a window. She was unable to sleep all night, and her son's crying all day was too much for her to handle.

Mrs. Applebaum had enough cognitive functioning to take preventive steps. Although she could verbalize that she was afraid that she would harm her son, she did not.

A fear of losing control of impulses that the person finds unacceptable or repugnant can sometimes result in depression rather than anxiety. At these times the conscience is operable in psychic functioning, in effect punishing the person for desiring the unacceptable. The notion of lust is an example.

Anxiety can reach crisis proportions when body integrity is perceived to be threatened. Recall that a negative reaction to forthcoming surgery is fear and not anxiety, because there is probably some danger inherent in all surgery requiring anesthesia.

The following two cases illustrate crises manifested by anxiety.

■ John, a 55-year-old accountant, requested an emergency appointment because his "nervousness" was affecting his performance on the job. When he was seen a few hours later, he appeared tense and restless; he was trembling. He said that he did not know what was wrong with him. He had vague feelings of uncertainty and said there were times that his legs felt so "rubbery" that he thought he was going to fall to the ground. He was having difficulty sleeping and had begun to lose weight because of loss of appetite. When asked to describe how he felt, he related feelings of uneasiness, tenseness, anxiousness, and nervousness. John related his condition (precipitating event) to the sudden and unexpected notice that he was going to be transferred to his company's office in Arizona. He had been with the company in the same city for 24 years and had achieved the successful position of chief accountant. In the new position he would be the only accountant, performing the same duties as a beginner. In addition a younger man was going to take John's position. All of this made John feel that he was being pushed out. This sudden and unexpected loss of position after 24 years, coupled with his considerable ego investment in the job and company, caused John considerable insecurity and tension. He did not know what to do. It all came so fast, so unexpectedly.

■ Brooke, a 29-year-old man, called the emergency services expressing a desperate need to talk to someone. He appeared anxious, red faced, and drained. The precipitating event causing his condition had occurred two nights before when his wife had told him that their marriage was over, that it was a mistake, and that she was bad for him. She then took off her wedding rings. Although they had only been married for a year, they had had a series of serious problems: his wife's hysterectomy, a step-daughter's operation for curvature of the spine, and the loss of his job, although he has one currently. The wife's leaving was "the straw that broke the camel's back." Brooke expressed feelings of shakiness and an inability to sleep caused by his desperate need to be with his wife. He believed that if he could talk to her they could correct the situation, but she refused to talk with him. Brooke was sent home from work because his supervisor noticed his trembling and poor concentration. He believed that Brooke was too upset to work around machinery. It was at this time that Brooke called the emergency services.

Both John and Brooke reacted to their precipitating events with anxiety. John, for example, described feelings of nervousness, tenseness, restlessness, tremors, uncertainty, weakness in the lower extremities, loss of appetite, and sleeping difficulties, all characteristic of anxiety. Reacting this way meant that John basically perceived the event as a threat to his survival. It is understandable why John would react with anxiety. For one reason, he could feel that his transfer was the first step toward being fired and that after 24 years with one company he might not be able to get another job. Just as we can wonder why John reacted with anxiety, he probably also searched his mind for possible meanings of the precipitating event. This search can become the heart of the problem for the person in crisis. As the person searches his or her mind, imagination may take over. The person projects fears onto reality and reacts to them accordingly, often increasing the degree of anxiety and debilitation.

We treat the individual who reacts to a precipitating event with anxiety with the same nine steps discussed in Chapter 5. The therapist can safely be and should be more psychologically supportive in treating anxiety than depression. In anxiety the person feels helpless, weak, and not confident. He or she feels scared and does not know what to do. The person cannot remember usual strengths and capacities. The therapist in such cases can actively encourage the client and reassure him or her of strengths. He can help provide the client with hope and self-confidence again.

While the therapist is eliciting and encouraging the expression of painful feelings and emotions, he or she should focus on the physical symptoms, including a description of the physical sensation. If the client has chest pains or stomach pains, the therapist should ask the client to describe the feelings. (We are assuming that there are no organic causes for the client's physical symptoms. In such cases the therapist may want to inquire about the client's state of health or the last time he or she has seen a doctor.) If the individual simply says, "I feel anxious" or "I feel tense" or "I feel uneasy," the therapist should try to localize the feeling by asking, "Where do you feel tense?" or "Where do you feel uneasy?" This focus is therapeutic; it makes the client feel better because the therapist shows an interest in what the client is most concerned about now: the physical symptoms. It also satisfies the client's dependency needs and gives reassurance that he or she can be helped.

Having the client describe and discuss physical sensations can often be important in assessment and evaluation also. The physiological symptoms may at times be significant. For example, stomach pains can represent a perceived danger to dependency feelings; heart palpitations can represent guilt and anticipation of punishment (e.g., heart attack, death). Headaches can represent unexpressed anger and tension. Back pains and weakness in the legs can represent a desire to be dependent and to be completely helpless, confined to home or even to bed. The therapist should determine whether the anxiety symptoms are habitually expressed through the same physical system. If so, they are move likely to have idiosyncratic psychic meaning and value. Anxiety that is diffuse and manifested in several systems is less likely to have idiosyncratic meaning.

Another therapeutic value of focusing on the sensations of anxiety is the cognitive benefit. It forces the client to identify the pain, which helps to reduce the effects of feeling that the source of pain is unknown. At the same time it tends to make the client aware that what is being experienced is anxiety. As the individual's anxiety decreases, the therapist moves to discussing the precipitating event and gathering information for the other therapeutic tasks (i. e., assessment and evaluation, identifying the nuclear problem, cognitive restoration, treatment planning, and implementation).

During cognitive restoration it is effective to explain the meaning of anxiety in words that the client can understand (see Step 6 in Chapter 5). The client should understand that when he or she gets these feelings called "nerves," he or she is experiencing anxiety. The client should immediately recall what anxiety means and search internally and externally for the cause. He or she should compare what is in his or her mind with what is in the outside reality. In cognitive restoration, the relationship of the precipitating event to the crisis response should be clearly made.

Individuals vary in their ability to tolerate anxiety. However, those whose anxiety is overwhelming generally respond to steps we have discussed, especially to the therapist's encouragement to ventilate. Consider for example, the case of Vernon, who experienced homosexual panic:

■ Vernon, a 35-year-old professional man, called the crisis therapist requesting an immediate appointment. He started the session by saying that he was worried about his masuclinity. He had recently developed thoughts that other men were thinking that he was "queer." As a consequence, he had to be careful that his behavior was not open to suspicion, that he could not notice another man scratch himself or pull up his trousers as they slipped down, for fear that they would wonder about him. He said that he was not worried about being a homosexual but was a little concerned about becoming one.

The therapist encouraged Vernon to express his feelings and concerns. After exploring the client's feelings, the therapist asked about the circumstances in which Vernon's panicky feelings were heightened. As expected, it happcnod when he was with a group of men, as his job required. He was still able to function, however, but had become incrcas ingly worried that one of the men would notice and would see that Vernon was worried about his masculinity. The therapist used cognitive restoration to help Vernon recognize that he was attributing to others what was in his mind and not real in fact, that he was reacting as if what was in his mind were real. Vernon's insecurity regarding his masculinity had started several weeks before when his wife left him. As the precipitating event, this was related to his condition, which was further reinforced by the nature of his job. The therapist suggested that his wife's leaving undermined his confidence and his masculine self-concept. Since he said that he had never had any homosexual experiences, the problem was one of impulse control. This was stated to him in terms that he could understand. The therapist offered to refer him to a physician who could prescribe medication that could help him with his control problem. Vernon said that the session was very helpful and that he felt he was in control again. Another session was scheduled for the next day, one 3 days later, and one each for the next 3 successive weeks. Persons in homosexual panic should be seen frequently until the panic subsides, and they generally respond to a crisis model. However, two conditions should be considered in treating such individuals: (1) they are capable of being reactivated, and (2) in some, homosexual panic is the beginning of a schizophrenic process.

If anxiety is so overwhelming that all the therapeutic procedures, including ventilation, do not reduce its debilitating effects, referral to a physician for an antianxiety drug may be necessary. Other times environmental modification may be necessary. One example is to place the client in a controlled environment that may reestablish feelings of safety and security. Final treatment planning should be based on the client's response to the therapeutic intervention, including the treatment planning and restoration. If there is sufficient reduction in anxiety and cognitive functioning is restored, the client can continue to be treated in crisis therapy.

DEPRESSION

As discussed in Chapter 2, people whose crisis is manifested by depression suffer from an overwhelming mood disturbance. Feelings such as dejection, sadness, despair, and self-depreciation are debilitating. Events that can precipitate a depression of crisis proportions are innumerable. However, there are four basic causes of debilitating depression: (1) loss or threatened loss of a love object; (2) loss or threatened loss of self-esteem, self-concept, or other ego values needed for psychic equilibrium; (3) failure to live up to internalized standards, expectations, values, or goals; and (4) violation or wish to violate some significant moral code or dictate. At the same time that the depressed person withdraws from people, he or she wishes for contact and gratification, often making repetitive complaints that help keep contact with others. The capacity to evoke in others a desire to help is both a danger and an aid. It is a danger in that gratification and attention from others are pitted against the internal feelings of unworthiness and guilt. In other words, the depressed person attempts to alleviate the pains of negative internal feelings of unworthiness and so forth by soliciting or demanding support and praise from others. The stronger the negative internal feelings, the greater the demands for attention from others. At the same time the depressed person's need for others renders him or her very amenable to help. This dynamic understanding of the depressed should be the basis of treatment.

Treatment. In treatment of a depressed individual, the therapist should initially proceed with caution, at least until a firm and constructive relationship has been established. Once a therapist, in effort to support a depressed client, said, "Well, at least you're trying to do something about your situation by coming here." The client responded, "Even a dog will obey most of the time." The therapist should try to gauge the effects of intervention, particularly with severely depressed individuals. In such cases dramatic improvement without corresponding time and effort could be a warning sign of suicide. It usually does not take very long to establish a constructive relationship with a client who is not severely depressed. The individual will throw out feelers very early on the qualities in the therapist that he or she wants to relate to. For example, about 5 minutes into the session another depressed client said, "I went to the emergency room of Morton Hospital, and the guy they assigned to me was a trip; if I wasn't crazy when I went to him, I would have been when he finished with me." Although the therapist did not discuss this comment with the client, it raised questions as to the type of person the client wanted to relate to. To know what the client wants, the therapist simply needs to listen and truly hear what is being communicated. Until the therapist understands the depressed client, including what the client expects to get from the therapist, and how the client uses interpersonal relationships, and his or her need for punishment and degree of masochism, the therapist should not actively give psychological support. The natural response to seeing depression is to use psychological supportive techniques such as reassurance or praise to negate the client's feelings of hopelessness, self-depreciation, guilt, or inferiority. But initially a constructive relationship is inherently supportive enough. The therapist's genuine interest, respect, empathy, and desire to help the client will come across to the client. More active psychological support should be used sparingly and only when the client needs it and is willing to accept it as a source of hope and motivation.

A therapist at this point should be concerned with eliciting and exploring feelings, especially physical complaints. The therapist should inquire into the daily activities of the client. A very beneficial process with the depressed is to explore history material. To ascertain experiences and feelings of past interpersonal relationships, moving from husband or wife or loved ones to parents, siblings, and friends. This process helps the establishment of a constructive relationship, since it gratifies the client's dependency needs. Further, it facilitates the therapist's development of empathy and empathic understanding. This process is more than beneficial for the client; it helps the therapist to understand his or her psychic makeup and functioning. Furthermore, this focus interrupts the client's feelings of hopelessness and despair. Often the client will smile as he or she talks of past happy experiences or relationships. The therapist should not be overly concerned about the depressed client's dependency needs, since this is a positive way to rapidly establish a constructive relationship. More important, it makes the client feel that relating to the therapist is going to be beneficial and worthwhile. Such a relationship not only gives the cognitive restoration process more impact, but it serves the function of reducing dependency after needs have appropriately been gratified.

Some depressed people will not be aware that they are depressed. They may feel "sad," "blue," or "down." In such cases it is therapeutic to suggest to the client that he or she is depressed. For example, the individual who talks about constant fatigue, loss of interest in activities, and depletion of energy can gently be told that it sounds as though he or she is depressed. A frequent response is, "I've never thought of it that way." Sometimes a depressed client will feel that the therapist does not understand the seriousness of the condition. Sometimes this comment is designed to solicit sympathy or to make the therapist worry or feel guilty. The therapist who truly understands need not be manipulated by such an effort. Rather, he or she can reassure the client of understanding and can express the hope of helping the client overcome depression.

Another factor in treating the depressed is that they are generally not aware of intense anger. Of course the fact that they have turned their anger inward is the cause of the depression. This is not to suggest that clients be encouraged to express anger simply as a technique. Anger should unfold naturally in the treatment process. The depressed individual tends to attribute to others what he or she feels about self. For example, one wife constantly talked about how dissatisfied her husband was with her. She spoke of how critical he was of her and how she was unable to please him. When pressed for specific examples of how he was dissatisfied with her, she said that he did not notice when she had cleaned out his closet. When she demanded that he recognize her effort, he said, "Having a clean closet is not that important to me." This comment, she said, proved that he was unsatisfied with her. Appropriate cognitive restoration can be used to help the client become aware of how he or she attributes feelings about self to others. A therapist should be wary of trying to talk a depressed person out of guilt feelings by logic. This whole process serves as self-punishment. After the client has indulged in self-punishment, the therapist can relate the need for self-punishment and self-depreciation to the anger turned into the self. Also the therapist can discuss the individual's feelings about anger, helping him or her to recognize why he or she cannot express anger outwardly. The therapist can then point out that the client will continue to feel depressed until the anger is expressed outwardly and about its real source.

The therapist should observe carefully the individual's reaction to what is said and let that guide what he or she pursues. In treating depression, the therapist must use any hope and positive feelings that the client shows. The therapist must be careful that, if he or she uses positive past behavior or performance of the client, the client is ready to receive it. It is generally best if hope is oriented toward the future. For example, Vivian, a 32-year-old doctoral student, had written all but the last chapter of her dissertation but felt unable to complete the last chapter. She appeared hopeless and incompetent. Rather than refer to the fact that she had completed all but one chapter, the therapist could support her hope and future accomplishments. For example, the therapist at one point said, "When you receive your Ph.D. you may be able to get the job with the new presidential administration." It should be pointed out that getting a job with the Department of Health, Education and Welfare was her career goal and the basis for aspiration for a doctorate.

Some suggestions have been offered here for treating the depressed. Closely related to treating the depressed is the subject of suicide, which we will look at next as we turn to the subject of violence.

CRISIS REACTIONS WITH POTENTIAL FOR VIOLENCE

Regardless of the setting or training, anyone working as a crisis therapist is likely to have as a client someone who is threatening or has the potential to commit violence (suicide or homicide) or who is a victim of rape.

Suicidal behavior

For simplicity we will use the phrase *suicidal behavior* to mean suicidal ideation, potential, and attempt. Every crisis therapist will encounter a person who is considering suicide as a solution to a crisis. At the same time, every person who considers suicide, in whatever form, is at some point ambivalent or does not want to take his or her own life. In fact, the individual whose motivation for suicidal behavioral is failure at love relationships or interpersonal domination and control most assuredly does not. However, because everything that the individual has done to resolve the crisis has failed, and he or she has reached a point of desperation and cannot think of any other solution, the individual feels hurt, angry, and hopeless.

The majority of people with suicidal behavior seen by the crisis therapist are depressed. That is, they are disappointed in love relationships or by other interpersonal relationships. Virtually all such persons have an interpersonal problem, even those who contemplate suicide because of a feeling of personal failure. In such cases the dynamics are the same as in an overt interpersonal relationship. Specifically, the disappointment in oneself represents a loved one's disappointment. In all suicidal behavior the individual feels a loss of love and affection and a painful sense of rejection. The suicidal individual reacts with anger and a wish for retaliation. The attempt at suicide is basically designed to achieve interpersonal domination and control: to make the loved one feel guilty, or to force her to love him, or for revenge, and so forth. The dynamics of the act remain the same. That is, the intense anger at the loved one is turned against the self. The specific reasons for this course of action can be found in the person, and the search is a very beneficial therapeutic process.

Clearly, suicide is the reverse of homicide. Rather than violence against another, it is violence against self and symbolically against the loved one. As we saw in depression, suicidal thoughts and attempts result from the tremendous need of people for other people. Again, a psychosocial need achieves a life-or-death value.

For some reason suicidal behavior is increasing. Successful suicide has increased among the young, especially those between 15 and 20 years of age. Even some 22 years ago, in his forward to *Clues to Suicide*

(Shneidman and Farberow, 1957), Menninger stated:

Once every minute or even more often someone in the United States either kills himself or tries to kill himself with conscious intent. Sixty or seventy times each day these attempts succeed. In many instances they could have been prevented.

Menninger is not including unconscious intent or suicides camouflaged as accidents. It is clear that suicide and suicide attempts are very prevalent and serious acts of desperation and distress. Inspite of its seriousness, suicidal attempts can evoke anger and fear in crisis therapists because they feel responsible for their clients and because of the unpredictable behavior of individuals who consider suicide. In addition it is individually caused and self-inflicted. When people who want to live are dying at alarming rates from diseases and poverty, it is often difficult to have empathy for the person who threatens to take his or her own life to solve a problem. To control their own anxiety, sometimes therapists will quickly categorize a suicidal attempt as manipulation or a way of getting attention. However, all suicidal acts or thoughts should be taken seriously. Many people who sought "attention" died before someone got to them. Suicide attempts are serious because they indicate a breakdown in cognitive functioning; the individual feels so helpless and desperate that he or she cannot think of another way to solve a problem. It is on this basis that a suicidal person deserves empathy and understanding from the therapist. The therapist should be especially sensitive and receptive to what the client is communicating. He or she should search for answers to the questions: Why is the client so desperate? What is wrong with his thinking that he cannot think of other ways to resolve problems? Why has he become so hopeless?

Assessing suicidal potential. Perhaps the greatest concern to the crisis therapist is assessing the degree of suicidal risk. The first step is to take all suicidal threats seriously. In a study of people who actually committed suicide, Shneidman and Farberow (1957) found that three fourths had previously threatened or attempted to take their own lives. Some communication of suicidal intent is almost always given. The first task of the crisis therapist is to rapidly establish a constructive relationship. Suicidal behavior is the result of a failure in interpersonal relationships. Consequently a good therapeutic relationship can provide hope for the suicidal individual so he or she can want to go on living.

This leads to the second task: decoding the individual's communication. The client's communication contains a message of why he or she is distressed, the motive for suicidal thought, and what is needed to relieve distress. This point is illustrated by the case of Rosemary (see Chapter 2), who came to the crisis center because she found a note written by her husband implying that he was going to commit suicide. First of all, nobody believed him, and second, what he needed to relieve his distress was a divorce, which Rosemary refused to give him. It is the fact that no one hears the suicidal cry that makes it necessary for the individual to resort to suicide. He or she simply feels that there is no hope left. As Farberow and Shneideman (1961) found, suicidal attempts are a cry for help. The cry, however, has to be decoded and interpreted. Inquiry into its meaning is therapeutic and ego reinforcing. To recognize and evaluate suicidal potential, the therapist must get involved in the client's mind by asking questions. Expressing his or her thoughts and feelings separates in the client's mind the thoughts from the actions. With the support of the therapist, talking about suicidal thoughts can reduce the individual's feelings of helplessness and despair. Perhaps the first questions would involve suicide plans. The therapist could ask, "Do you feel so hopeless that you have thoughts about how you would take your life?" The more specific the plans, the greater the danger. And the greater the lethal method, the greater the danger. Dwelling on thoughts of suicide is more serious than having transitory thoughts. If the individual says something like, "I've thought about suicide, but I'm too scared," it can be a good sign. Another consideration is the client's residual interpersonal relationships, those with significant others. A client who is concerned about the negative effects his or her death would have on relatives is showing some positive signs. If the therapist feels that the client has invested in him or her to the point that the relationship is meaningful, that is a very good sign. These are advantages of rapidly establishing a positive relationship. The client who denies that he or she will commit suicide is usually being truthful and can temporarily be relied on. Physical signs such as insomnia, weight and appetite loss, constipation, and lack of sexual interest are important in the evaluation of suicide danger. The greater the self-depreciation, the greater the danger. Going into and recovering from episodes of depression are also danger points. Other danger signs are a family history of suicide, repeated attempts, financial worries, and a sudden change in a significant relationship, for example, divorce or separation. The risk of successful suicide has been found to be higher among men (Susser, 1968), although women make the most attempts. Homosexuals are prone to be suicidal, especially when depressed. People who live alone are more likely to commit suicide. Regan and Small (1969) summarize clues to suicide as follows:

Classically, the therapist has many descriptive clues which help him to decide how much suicidal protection should be provided. More severe depressions, characterized by self-depreciation, feeling of worthlessness and hopelessness, nihilistic delusions, persistent self-destructive thoughts (especially of an aggressive nature), early morning awakening, anorexia with marked weight loss, amenorrhea, loss of sexual desire, and history of previous suicidal attempts by the patient or his relatives are major indications for instituting precautions to avoid self-harm.

It is incumbent on the crisis therapist to alert relatives and responsible friends of suicidal potential. They should share the responsibility of prevention. Sometimes this concern can reverse the whole process. If suicidal potential is so severe that hospitalization is warranted, the client should be told and the family should be involved. A suicidal client should never be left to go to the hospital alone. The client should be given a feeling of being protected.

Homicidal behavior

We will use the phrase *homicidal behavior* to mean potential for or threat to commit physical harm to another individual.

A client that presents a threat of homicide can be frightening for the therapist. At the same time, a therapeutic response requires a calm, confident therapist who can take charge of the situation. The therapist should keep in mind that a threat of violence is an indication that the individual is struggling against losing control of self and is very frightened. Sometimes this fear may be hidden or covered up by a preoccupation with aggression or with boisterousness. Any person or situation that immediately counteracts this fear of loss of control is reassuring. Our concern here is with the individual who wants help because he or she is afraid of committing a violent act (e.g., "I'm afraid I'm going to kill my child" or "I'm afraid I'm going to hurt someone"). Just as we have seen with anxiety and depression, the potential for homicide is also a consequence of an inability to cope with a crisis.

Again the first task in intervening with a person who is potentially violent is to rapidly establish a constructive relationship. If the individual is obviously upset and angry and the therapist knows how the client feels, he or she can move to the precipitating event or causes of the condition. If the client does not show the obvious emotions normally associated with violence, his or her present feelings should be explored before moving to the causes of the need for violence. If the client's emotions are not consistent with the thought of violence, he or she may be planning future action. Consequently, thoughts and feelings should be examined before moving to precipitating events. Finding causes is extremely important for ego building and cognitive restoration and very important for understanding the client's psychic structure and for determining the nuclear problem. For example, if the precipitating event or cause of the individual's need to resort to violence is infidelity, humiliation, or insult, it is clear that he or she has ego needs involving self-esteem and feelings of worth and value. This means that the client is a very sensitive person who feels unduly inadequate or inferior and must protect himself or herself from the pain of these feelings. When an incident occurs that breaks down defenses against these feelings, the basic reaction to feeling hurt is to hurt back. The therapist must keep this kind of sensitivity in mind while actively getting involved with the client.

In working with the potentially violent, the therapist must act decisively and often directly. The therapist must be in charge. To do so, he or she must gather a great deal of information and evaluate quickly. The therapist cannot hesitate to ask specific questions regarding the client's violent potential and life experiences. It is the information gained from these questions that the therapist uses to assess and evaluate the risk of violence. Furthermore, it opens up cognitive functioning, again suggesting the need to be aware of consequences, a search for alternatives, and the provision of hope.

Certain historical patterns and experiences can act as predictive clues to homicide. Some people who experience severe emotional deprivation and rejection in early childhood will resort to violence in a crisis situation (Menninger and Modin, 1972). This is understandable in light of the emotional satisfaction necessary for satisfactory psychic development and control of impulses. At the same time, not all people who experience severe emotional deprivation have so little impulse control. If emotional deprivation is a factor in homicidal tendencies, it generally will have been reflected in previous homicidal acts. Thus a history of homicidal behavior or past problems of impulse control are reliable predictions of future homicidal behavior. The exception, of course, is the overly controlled, inhibited, shy, and passive person whose excessive control breaks down under the impact of the crisis. If such a person seeks help just before defenses break, he or she should be evaluated as at high risk, and caution should be taken. However, in such cases the reason that the person seeks help for a lifelong problem at this point is important to understanding the individual. Seeking help is generally a positive sign, unless the client is coming to the therapist simply to achieve some other goal such as to get a spouse back. Hellman and Blackman (1966) found that people with a childhood history of enuresis, fire setting, and cruelty to animals are more likely to be homicidal risks.

As when assessing suicidal behavior, the first step in ascertaining potential for violence is to take all threats seriously. Second, a discussion of the client's plans for violence should be thoroughly discussed. The question should be formulated in terms of the future, such as, "Since you have not been able to think of any other way to feel better, have you thought about how you might hurt John?" This question also suggests the reason for the violence. It simply reflects the natural human tendency to want to hurt back when one has been hurt. Careful consideration should be given to the precipitating event or the cause of the violence. MacDonald (1967) found that the more illogical or unjustified the reason for the homicide threat, the greater the risk. Conversely, the more logical and justified the reason for the threat, the less the risk. Also, the more diffuse the direction the homocidal impulse takes, the less the risk. When the threat is directed at a specific person or object, especially if specific plans have been made, the risk is greater. In cases where the homicidal threat is directed toward a specific person, the nature of that relationship should be thoroughly explored. This helps the therapist understand the meaning of that person to the client as well as the client's psychic functioning. When homicidal thoughts are directed toward a loved one, that person should be interviewed when possible. Menninger and Modlin (1972) suggest that often in such situations the loved one unconsciously encourages the client to act violently. Sometimes when problems involve loved ones, they can be worked out or resolved conjointly. When the situation can be improved by involving another person, be it a loved one, minister, or friend, that person should be brought in when it is therapeutic and in the best interest of the client.

Another factor that should be considered as the therapist actively gathers information for the evaluation is the client's capacity for satisfying interpersonal relationships. How does the client relate to people? Does he or she tend to have good feelings about people? Does he or she appear to have a conscience or to feel remorse? Does the client feel bad about what he or she feels like doing? Specifically, how does the client relate to the therapist? Is he or she superficial and mistrustful? Does he or she have a close friend? Or is the client overly self-centered as a defense against feelings of inadequacy or inferiority? What is the client's relationship with members of the opposite sex? If the client is a man, does he unduly need women to sustain his ego and to meet dependency needs on the one hand, while being violently angry at them on the other? (This question applies to women also. However, more men than women become homicidal in reaction to disappointment in love relationships.)

Another consideration in evaluating homicidal potential is the client's culture. The client who is a member of a culture in which violence is considered acceptable is more likely to act out violently. Also, the client who is sociopathic is more likely to be homicidal. Obsessive homicidal thoughts are common in parents who fear that they are going to hurt their children. If these parents deny that they want to do so and appear to have good impulse control through defense mechanisms such as undoing, reaction formation, denial, or rituals or compulsive acts, the risk is less. However, if the immediate problem cannot be alleviated in the usual crisis time limit, referral to traditional therapy should follow.

In sum, a homicidal threat should be taken seriously. All of the clues suggested here should be explored as part of the assessment and evaluation process. Treatment then should be formulated and implemented accordingly.

Treatment. Treatment of the homicidal client follows the same procedures and steps as other crisis treatment. Cognitive restoration allows the client to understand the meaning of the behavior, separating thought from action. The therapist must appeal to and relate to the positive ego functions and strengths. Before seeking help, the client has been simply acting. The cognitive restoration process enables the client to think about his or her actions. Chances are he or she will do that throughout the session, but at this point, with the help of the therapist, the client can cognitively relate behavior and think about reasons and alternatives.

The first act of the treatment process is to decide, based on the assessment and evaluation, whether the client needs protective custody. He or she may need hospitalization or go to a halfway house of a mental health facility.

If the client needs hospitalization for self-protection, he or she should be informed and relatives should be notified and brought into the situation. They should assume responsibility for getting the client to the hospital if they can. Sometimes referral to a physician is necessary. If hospitalization is not necessary but some control is needed, the therapist can assess whether the family can provide the needed protection. Sometimes this can be combined with medication, in which case referral to a psychiatrist should be made. As well as possible, the therapist ensures that the client will go to the psychiatrist.

If at the conclusion of the session the therapist believes that the threat of homicide can be worked out by crisis therapy, he or she proceeds accordingly. However, the therapist should especially be concerned with helping the client ventilate as a means of reducing aggressive impulses. The therapist should help the client recognize the reason for the desperation. He or she should work toward increasing the client's cognitive functioning, especially perception, judgment, and reality testing. When reality testing is poor, people are unable to recognize the consequences of their behavior. Environmental manipulation should be used to make the client's life less stressful. The therapist should consider interviewing the loved ones involved. Most violent acts are against loved ones and friends rather than strangers. Understanding the threat of violence toward loved ones can be very effective in preventing it. If removing the client from the environment is indicated, it should be recommended. For example, the therapist might recommend that a potentially brutal husband move in with friends for a few days while he works on his problem.

Rape

Rape is the third form of violence to be discussed in this chapter. For our purposes, *rape* is defined as an act of sexual intercourse between a stranger and a female, against her will and under the threat of violence or physical harm. It is the fastest rising violent crime in the United States (McCombie et al., 1976; Rada, 1978). Yet the victims of rape are just now beginning to receive the attention from the community that they deserve. This increased attention is due more to the Women's Movement than to the increase in incidence of the crime.

The victim of rape needs the therapeutic help of a comprehensive support system more than the victims of other violent crimes do. Ideally a rape crisis therapist should be a part of or immediately available to every hospital emergency room. One should be assigned to each police unit answering the call of rape. Consider the following case*:

---

*From *Sisters in crime* by F. Adler. Copyright © 1975, McGraw-Hill Book Co. Used with permission of McGraw-Hill Book Co.

If I had to do it again, I would never have gone through with the prosecution. "I wouldn't even have reported it," said one twenty-seven-year-old woman who suffered through months of legal proceedings and publicity only to see her rapist found innocent because she was unable to prove that she did not consent to the act. Despite extensive body bruises and a wound in her forehead that took six stitches to close, the defense attorney argued that "vigorous love play" did not necessarily indicate nonconsent and, in fact, could even indicate enthusiastic approval and passionate involvement in the act.

"From the beginning I had this feeling that I was the one who was on trial rather than the guy they picked up and charged," said the woman, raped by an intruder who entered her apartment through a window, from an adjacent rooftop. She was at the time sleeping in the nude, a fact that is frequently alleged in rape cases to prove "willingness to have intercourse."

Right after it happened . . . I mean, here I was lying on the floor, my face was streaming with blood, I was damned near hysterical when I called the police. They arrived and the very first question this one guy asked me was, "Did you enjoy it?" "Did you really try to resist the guy?"

Then the questions really started. I couldn't believe what they asked me. About five officers were crowded into my bedroom. They said things to me like, "Lay on the bed exactly as you were when the guy came in. Why did you spread your legs if you didn't want to be raped? Did you see his penis? Describe it. Did you touch his penis? Did you put it in your mouth? Did you have an orgasm?"

Then there was the hospital they took me to. There were maybe three dozen people sitting around in this large ward. This one guy in a white coat takes my name and he yells down the ward, at the top of his lungs, "Hey, Pete, I got a rape case here. Check her out, will you?" It was just incredible. The guy checking me out left me sitting on this table for like an hour. One of his questions was, "Did you give the guy a blow job or what?"

Later at the police station. They caught the guy from my description. He was sitting there, and one of the cops went out to get him a cup of coffee and gave him a cigarette. They told me, "Sit over there, lady, we'll get to you in a minute."

Over and over again, the police, the district attorney, the defense attorneys, even my own goddamned private lawyer asked me the same thing: "Are you sure you really resisted? Did you really want to get raped subconsciously?"

In the end the guy who did it got off. They even brought in this one boy—a man now—that I knew in high school. That was ten years ago. He testified he had intercourse with me, after a prom. The defense attorney said, "She was pretty easy, wasn't she?" The guy just grinned and shook his head.

Although there has been an increase in the number of rape crisis centers, all victims do not go to these centers first or even know that they should go there. Access to needed services is determined by the community. There is still a large percentage of rapes that are not reported for various reasons, including feelings of guilt or shame or lack of knowledge. Greater sensitivity to the emotional and psychological effects on the victim needs to be developed by the support network, especially the police and lawyers. Rape is a reprehensible crime that not only violates the victim's human rights but can result in irreparable psychological damage, not to mention physical harm and even death. People in the helping network must be sensitive to this danger to prevent psychological damage and to reduce the victim's fear of reporting this hideous crime.

Some characteristics of the rape victim. Burgess and Holmstrom (1974) found several physical and emotional characteristics generally manifested by the rape victim. Physical symptoms resulting from trauma were soreness and bruises all over the body, especially on the legs, arms, chest, thighs, and neck. Physical symptoms also occurred in the area of the body that was the focus of attack. For example, victims who were forced to have oral sex reported irritation to the mouth and throat. Those forced to have vaginal and anal sex reported experiencing vaginal discharge, itching, burning sensations on urination, generalized pain, and rectal pain and bleeding. Tension headaches, sleep disturbances, stomach pains, appetite loss, and increased motor activity are also common manifestations.

Contrary to expectation, Burgess and Holmstrom (1974) did not find the shame and guilt were the primary reactions. Understandably, it was fear of physical injury, mutilation, and death. The primary feeling of fear was also associated with a variety of other symptoms such as humiliation, shame, guilt, anger, and a desire for revenge.

Treatment. The first step in the treatment of the rape victim is to rapid establish a constructive relationship. This requires considerable sensitivity and empathic understanding. She may have a variety of ambivalent and confusing feelings including guilt, self-blame, shame, fear, anxiety, uncleanliness, and feelings of being damaged. Sensitivity is greatly facilitated by the therapist's perception of rape as an act of violence with the potential of serious damage. It is possible for a male therapist to have the same degree (if it could be measured) of empathy as a female therapist; however, the fact that the client has been victimized by a man can pose some problems. In a broad sense, one problem can be overreaction on the part of each: the male therapist becoming oversolicitous and the victim overly angry at the therapist simply for being a man. It is not always possible, though preferable, for the rape victim to be assigned to a female therapist. When a male therapist is assigned, he should be sensitive and aware of whatever feelings the victim has about seeing a man. He should explore her feelings early to help establish a constructive relationship.

The second step in working with the victim of rape is dealing with the emotional reaction. As in every crisis, there is an initial state of upset. For the rape victim it is initially anxiety, fear, and shock, all contributing to psychic disequilibrium and a threat to personality disintegration. From our understanding of anxiety, we can see that the rape victim is at first overwhelmed with fear for her bodily integrity and survival. During this phase the therapist works toward a complete expression of her painful feelings and emotions. While eliciting maximum ventilation of painful feelings, the therapist begins the third step by having the victim discuss the assault (the precipitating event). During this time the therapist also encourages the victim to discuss what happened, how, and the circumstances surrounding it. The therapist must understand the victim's total perspective of rape. The therapist needs to know what happened to her. If there is any misinformation or erroneous sexual knowledge, it should come out as she talks about what happened. Thoroughly discussing the precipitating event—the rape—is very important regardless of how painful it is. It is a basic premise of crisis theory that to successfully resolve the crisis, the individual must face the precipitating event and thoroughly express her feelings about it, no matter how painful.

Discussing the assault lets the therapist and the client share the client's experiences. It is at this time that the circumstances surrounding the rape are described. Information on the setting and how the act occurred is obtained to help in assessment and evaluation of the problem. The victim should talk about her personal contribution, if any, to the rape in terms of acts omitted and committed. Was the victim unusually careless? Was she in a strange neighborhood at a time when she would be vulnerable? Did she take undue chances? There may be times that a victim will not want to discuss the horrible experience and say that she wants to forget it. Instead, she should be encouraged to discuss and face it, as she can never forget it. As emotions flow, the therapist must be supportive and empathic as he or she tries to help the client sort out the difference between her feelings and reality. Universalization is used to support the victim's feelings and to let her know that she is not alone in her feelings; that it is natural for her to feel what she is feeling after being assaulted.

Step 4, the assessment and evaluation phase, is modified somewhat for the victim of rape. During this phase the therapist is most concerned with identifying the nuclear problem, which is the meaning of the rape to the victim, rather than purely the causes of her reaction. We see that basically the rape has two meanings, as the client moves from manifestations of anxiety to depression. Most rape victims move from initially being overwhelmed with anxiety, that is, concerned with bodily integrity and survival, to depression, where they are concerned with feelings of loss, loss of a loved one, self-esteem, shame, and other interpersonal relationships. The victim often degrades herself, which is characteristic of the depressed. The therapist should allow her to experience the pain of her own recriminations. The therapeutic task here is to share the victim's pain, understanding and accepting how she can feel the way she does. She needs to do this as a part of the restoration process. Part of this need for recrimination is due to the natural feeling that she could have done more to prevent it. Such feelings of self-blame are also characteristics of the depressed. We see such feelings in the bereaved and in people experiencing other kinds of personal losses. The other aspect of the assessment and evaluation phase is to determine whether the victim's responses are average and expectable or whether they indicate incipient psychosis or other clinical syndromes.

Step 5, formulating a dynamic explanation, involves reconciling the meaning of the event to the victim and the circumstances surrounding its occurrence. Here we are concerned with objectively understanding whether the victim contributed to the occurrence of the event by not taking "reasonable" precautions or whether it was impossible for her to prevent it. If the victim was careless and did not take all possible precautions, the therapist is interested in determining what this means to her psychic functioning. This is not because the therapist is any less sensitive or empathic. It is because he or she wants to understand the psychic structure of the individual in crisis and what her behavior means to her overall psychic functioning and to her future social functioning. Such behavior may indicate the need for long-term psychotherapy.

The therapist should assess and evaluate the victim's own supportive resources, especially loved ones, family, and close friends. This means that the therapist may need to help the victim resolve any ambivalence or reluctance to tell loved ones what happened. After discussing with the victim who she will tell, the decision needs to be made as to how this will be accomplished. The victim can decide to tell other people herself, the therapist can do it for her, or they can do it together. The victim's feelings regarding the loved ones' reactions will need to be handled and worked through if necessary. There are times when negative reactions of husbands or relatives will require therapeutic work for the victim's benefit.

It should be emphasized that step 6, cognitive restoration, is implemented only after lengthy and complete ventilation and expression of feelings and emotions. This phase for the rape victim can take two directions. The first is to help the victim understand the meaning of her posttraumatic behavior. This is necessary to help her integrate the experience. The second direction is to help the victim cognitively accept the event. In these situations cognitive restoration involves helping the victim accept the fact that there was nothing that she could have done to prevent the event and to reconcile reality with her emotional feelings, her psychic reality. Inherent in both of these tasks is still the realization that a violent act has been committed and that, regardless of circumstances, any person ought to be able to go anywhere he or she wants at any time and under any condition and not have his or her body violated. But such is not a fact of life. Additional treatment in this session should involve helping the client with practical arrangements.

Practical arrangements. After the crisis has subsided and some cognitive functioning has been restored or improved, the therapist should help the rape victim with some necessary practical tasks that she should attend to. Although the therapist should encourage the victim to do everything that she can for herself, the therapist should be there for support, encouragement, and to do those things that the victim cannot do herself. The first task is medical treatment. If the victim has not received medical treatment, the therapist should arrange for her to have a physical examination including tests for venereal disease. Slaby and associates (1975) recommend several methods to prevent pregnancy. Such medical matters can be discussed with the victim's attending physician. A female physician is recommended when possible.

Another practical task that the therapist should help with is securing an attorney. This should be done whether the victim presses charges or not. In many cases the therapist will have to help the victim through ambivalent feelings about pressing charges. There are numerous reasons for such indecisiveness, including police procedures, which can be very dehumanizing. Fox and Scherl (1972) relate a willingness to report the crime with a degree of self-blame.

Sometimes it is therapeutic for the rape crisis therapist to accompany the victim to the medical facility and the police station. In any event, the victim should not be left to go to those places alone.

Perhaps the final practical arrangement is to help the victim deal with anticipated consequences of the assault. Court trials are notoriously brutalizing, and she will be subjected to a defense attorney who is trying to prove that no rape occurred and who may resort to all the dirty tricks in the book. The victim should be aware of what she will have to go through. Other upsetting consequences include fear of returning to the same location or fear of another assault. Reasonable precautions that would alleviate these fears can be discussed. It is often therapeutic to suggest that the rape victim not stay alone for a few nights if she lives by herself.

Not all rape victims need more than is discussed in the first session. However, the first session can take hours. After the anxiety over bodily integrity and survival have passed, the victim may again become depressed, and additional sessions will be required. Much of the anger at the attacker or at a nonaccepting judgmental husband or relative is turned inward. The victim may still feel guilty, unclean, or damaged. She will need help in working through these feelings. If they are too intense, too tenaciously held, and do not respond to usual therapeutic techniques, she may be showing signs that a clinical syndrome is developing. Further evidence of this would be reflected in her overall social functioning, her interpersonal relationships, functioning on her job, personal habits, and thought processes.

Just as with any other crisis condition, when the rape victim is restored to her preassualt level of social functioning, therapy can be terminated. Sometimes this occurs after the first session; other times it requires several sessions. If the victim does not return to her precrisis level of social functioning, she should be referred for traditional psychotherapy. The exception, of course, is if another precipitating event associated with the original assault occurs. Examples include becoming pregnant or separating from her husband as a consequence of the rape.

BEREAVEMENT AND GRIEF

■ George died at age 55, swiftly and unexpectedly. Joanne, a professional nurse, appeared strong and unshaken as she dramatically carried out the practical arrangements of the funeral and greeting the many sympathizers and mourners. When a friend remarked about how well she had been holding up under the stress and strain, she said, "These tranquilizers are doing a great job. I have to be strong for the children. George would have wanted it that way." Several months after George's death Joanne came to the crisis center, saying that she could no longer go on living.

Joanne did not allow herself to experience the normal grieving process, never getting beyond the shock and denial phase, refusing to emotionally accept her loved one's death.

Bereavement is the loss of a loved one through death, and grief is the emotional and behavioral reaction to the loss. Grief is a universal phenomenon. It is based on the inevitability of human mortality and the innate capacity and need of people to attach themselves first to parents and later to others. Let us look further at why grief is such a painful but necessary process. Through introjection and identification, these attachments become an integral part of the psychic system. They are instrumental in social functioning, specifically in meeting emotional needs and maintaining psychic equilibrium and happiness. Therefore when people lose a loved one, they in effect lose a part of themselves. Although there are normal characteristics of the grieving process (to be discussed later), specific patterns of reactions are influenced by three basic conditions. The first is the nature and meaning of the survivor's relationship to the deceased. This includes the ambivalent feelings inherent in every close or intimate relationship, the love and hate, dependence and independence, repressed anger, and overdependency. The meaning of the relationship refers to the significance of the deceased to the psychic system and functioning. The spouse who is overly dependent on the deceased will have, as a rule, a more difficult grieving process than those who are appropriately dependent.

The second condition is the degree of identification with the deceased. Identification is part of the love process, but in this case identification with the deceased refers to the survivor's projection of self in the place of the deceased. However, problems occur when there is overidentification. In this case the survivor sees self too much in the position of the deceased, preventing the appropriate management of the grief process and participation in the practical arrangements, a very important part of the grieving process. In fact, this is the purpose of funerals; they are for the benefit of the living. Consider the example of Fred, a 44-year-old successful lawyer who could not visit his wife in the hospital while she lay terminally ill, let alone make funeral arrangements for her when she died. While all of this was going on, he disappeared for more than 9 weeks, simply living the life of a recluse. He was drinking himself into oblivion until he was able to face the reality of the situation. Relatives and friends condemned Fred's behavior, since they were not able to understand or accept the way he handled his grief. Fred could not only not face his wife's death, he could not face her, since he overidentified with her. She reminded him of his own mortality.

Underidentification is more difficult to observe because of the social pressure and expectation to grieve. Furthermore, it can have many causes, including relief that the "loved one" has died, or even happiness. In underidentification the survivor is concerned with the benefits gained from the death of the deceased. Perhaps a common example is the terminally ill loved one who is conscious of impending death and lingers on and on, creating hardships for the survivors. Living with this kind of awareness is no doubt very painful for the terminally ill, but it is also painful for people who love him or her. They may become angry and wish the person would die quickly so they can "get back to normal." After the death they may feel guilty about those reactions.

The third condition is the age of the bereaved. The grieving process is generally more difficult for the very young and the elderly. The reason, of course, is that young people and old people often are quite dependent on others. It is more difficult for them to adjust and fill the void. This is especially true of the elderly, who now must deal with less resources than they once had and fewer chances of developing new relationships to replace the old one.

Grief as a normal process. Some characteristics of a normal grieving process can be identified. Lindemann (1944) declares:

The picture shown by persons in acute grief is remarkably uniform. Common to all is the following syndrome: sensations of somatic distress occurring in waves lasting twenty minutes to an hour at a time, a feeling of tightness in the throat, choking with shortness of breath, need for sighing, an empty feeling in the abdomen, lack of muscular power, and an intense subjective distress described as tension or mental pain.

Lindemann also adds as common characteristics a slight sense of reality, a feeling of increased emotional distance from other people (sometimes they appear shadowy or small), and intense preoccupation with the image of the deceased. If we examine these characteristics, it becomes clear that the grieving process involves emotional and behavioral manifestations of anxiety and depression (see Chapter 2). Depression in grief is somewhat different than depression caused by other events. Guilt and anger may be present in grief but less intense. At one level the grieved remains hopeful that the pain will eventually pass. Grief involves rational expression of feelings. A grieving person does not feel inferior or less of a person because of the loved one's death; self-esteem is not greatly altered. Crying spells are related to feelings about the deceased and preoccupation with self (e.g., "I don't know what I'm going to do"). The grieving person evokes sympathy but is often more concerned about the pain of others. It is not unusual for the grieving person to wish he had treated the deceased better or told him that he was loved and so forth.

It is not unusual for normal grief to last from 6 months to 1 year. Lindemann (1944/1965) states that the length of the grieving process depends on how well the individual does his or her grief work, specifically, how well he or she emancipates himself or herself from the bondage to the deceased, readjusts to the environment in which the deceased is missing, and forms new relationships. Normal grieving is successful when there is emotional and psychological acceptance of the loss of the loved one, when there is a return to psychic equilibrium and social functioning is directed once again toward personal goals and the pursuit of happiness, when memories can be recalled without pain but with joy, pride, or pleasure.

Grief as a crisis condition. Grief reaction is a crisis when the deceased is so significant that the loss is overwhelming and causes overall social dysfunctioning and mental debilitation. It may become a crisis when the nature of the relationship between the survivor and the deceased was one of ambivalence and unacceptable hostility on the one hand and guilt on the other. It becomes a crisis when the death of the loved one cannot be emotionally accepted. It becomes a crisis when painful feelings of sorrow, hurt, and loneliness cannot be adequately expressed.

Treatment of grief as a crisis condition. The treatment of grief as a crisis condition follows the basic steps set forth in Chapter 5. Most important are eliciting and encouraging the expression of painful feelings, including crying. Tranquilizers should not be used unless necessary, since they prevent the maximum expression of feelings. No feelings should be discouraged, not even idealized ones or the need to review the past. The bereaved should be helped to remove the obstacles to natural grief work. The client must be helped to do grief work and encouraged to express feelings and emotions. The client should be allowed to talk about the deceased in whatever way he or she wants. Expression of feelings and emotions may take two to three sessions before the dynamic formulation and the cognitive restoration phase. The dynamic formulation involves determining the reason for overreaction. The answer can generally be found in one of the three conditions discussed earlier: (1) nature and meaning of the relationship, (2) degree of identification, and (3) phase of the life cycle. The use of cognitive restoration may have to be delayed until later sessions. It is determined by the bereaved's readiness for emotional lifting. The therapist may encourage and motivate the bereaved to get back into normal social relationships. Some direct advice and prescription of what to do may have to be offered. If the client offers resistance to recovery, it has to be dealt with. The therapist should be alert and sensitive to the expression of any suicidal ideation or bizarre behavior. The distinction between depression proper and grief work should be observed. Family and relatives should be used as resources when indicated. Termination can occur when there is an emotional acceptance of the loss and restoration of psychic equilibrium and adequate social functioning.

In this chapter we have discussed some common reactions primarily involving the individual in crisis. As we move to the next chapter, more than one individual in crisis will be discussed, namely, the family in crisis. We will also discuss three major crisis conditions associated with the task of the life cycle, specifically, adolescence, middle age, and old age.

REFERENCES

Adler, F. Sisters in crime. New York: McGraw-Hill, 1975.

Burgess, A. W., & Holmstrom, L. L. *Rape: victims of crisis*. Bowie, Md.: Robert J. Brady, 1974.

Farberow, N. L., & Shneidman, E. S. *The cry for help*. New York: McGraw-Hill, 1961.

Fox, S. S., & Scherl, D. J. Crisis intervention with victims of rape. *Social Work*, 1972, *17*, 37-42.

Hellman, D. S. & Blackman, N. Enuresis, fire-setting and cruelty to animals: a triad predictive of adult crime. *American Journal of Psychiatry*, 1966, *122*, 1431.

Kubler-Ross, E. *Death: the final stage of growth*. Englewood Cliffs, N. J.: Prentice-Hall, 1975.

Laughlin, P. *The neuroses*. Reading, Mass.: Butterworths, 1967.

Lindemann, E. Symptomatology and management of acute grief. In H. J. Parad (Ed.), *Crisis intervention: selected readings*. New York: Family Service Association of America, 1965, pp. 7-21. (Reprinted from *American Journal of Psychiatry*, 1944, *101*).

MacDonald, J. M. Homicidal threats. *American Journal of Psychiatry*, October 1967, *124*(4), 475-482.

McCombie, S. L., Bassuk, E., Savitz, R., & Pell, S. Development of a medical center rape crisis intervention program. *American Journal of Psychiatry,* April 1976, *133*(4), 418-421.

Menninger, R. W., and Modlin, H. C. Individual violence: prevention in the violence-threatening patient. In J. Fawcett (Ed.), *Dynamics of violence.* Chicago: American Medical Association, 1972.

Rada, R. T. (Ed.). *Clinical aspects of the rapist.* New York: Grune & Stratton, 1978.

Regan, P. F., & Small, S. M. Brief Psychotherapy of depression. In J. H. Masserman (Ed.), *Current psychiatric therapies* (Vol. VI). New York: Grune & Stratton, 1966.

Shneidman, E., & Farberow, N. L. (Eds.), *Clues to suicide.* New York: McGraw-Hill, 1957.

Slaby, A. E., Lieb, J., & Tancredi, L. P. *Handbook of psychiatric emergencies.* Flushing, N.U.: Medical Examination Publishing, 1975.

Susser, M. *Community psychiatry: epidemiologic and social themes.* New York: Random House, 1968.

SUGGESTED READINGS

Bach-y-Rita, G., Lion, J. R., Ailment, C. E., & Ervin, F. R. Episodic dyscontrol: a study of 130 violent patients. *American Journal of Psychiatry,* 1971, *127,* 1473-1478.

Burgess, A. W., & Holmstrom, L. L. *Rape: victims of crisis.* Bowie, Md.: Robert J. Brady, 1974.

Evans, J. *Living with a man who is dying.* New York: Taplinger Publishing, 1971.

Fox, S. S., & Scherl, D. J. Crisis Intervention with victims of rape. *Social Work,* January 1972, *17,* 37-42.

Kubler-Ross, E. *On death and dying.* New York: Macmillan, 1969.

Lindemann, E. Symptomatology and management of acute grief. In H. J. Parad (Ed.), *Crisis intervention: selected readings.* New York: Family Service Association of America, 1965, pp. 7-21. (Reprinted from *American Journal of Psychiatry,* 1944, *101.*)

Prichard, E. R., Collard, J., Orcutt, B. A., Kutscher, A. H., Seeland, I. & Lefkowitz, N. (Eds.), *Social work with the dying patient and the family.* New York: Columbia University Press, 1977.

Shneidman, E., & Farberow N. L. (Eds.). *Clues to suicide.* New York: McGraw-Hill, 1957.

Verwoerdt, A. Death and the family. *Medical Opinion and Review,* September 1966, *1*(12), 38-43.

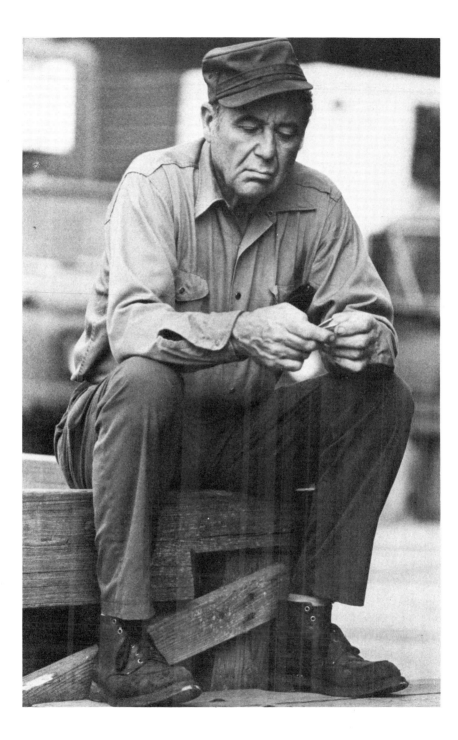

CHAPTER 7

Family and life cycle crises

The discussion thus far has focused on the individual in crisis. This chapter will expand our knowledge and understanding of crisis theory and techniques to include the family and certain life cycle crises, specifically, adolescence, middle age, and old age. These times of the life cycle seem to be common points for the development of crises because of significant psychosocial and biological changes that occur at the same time.

The underlying definition of the family in crisis is the same as for the individual. That is, the family is assumed to be in equilibrium and functioning satisfactorily until a significant event occurs that threatens its stability. The event is perceived to be so dangerous to family stability and functioning that the family's usual coping methods are ineffective, causing a crisis. More will be said about this later.

A life cycle crisis is caused by an individual's inability to successfully adapt to the tasks and changes brought on by maturation (see Erikson [1963] for the adaptive tasks of each phase of the life cycle). Again, crisis in this context means functional debilitation or ineffectiveness resulting from the occurrence of some event, in this case the events and condition of the aging process. It does not mean the characteristic "upset" associated with all significant changes in life, as in the popular use of the phrase "middle-age crisis."

THE FAMILY

A family is an organized system of interacting personalities with characteristic ways of functioning. It has several important functions. The first function of the family is the socialization of its children. Next comes the satisfaction of the emotional and affectional needs of its members. The family provides love and security, which we know are critical to psychic development and social functioning. Third, the family is an economic unit that ensures the physical survival of its members. Finally, the family ensures the continuity of society by incorporating the society's values, traditions, and laws into its system.

The family system is responsible for meeting these four basic purposes. Let us briefly review how a family system develops as a first step in understanding family functioning. A marriage, the prelude to a family, begins when a man and a woman from different families legally agree to live together. They agree to attempt to meet each other's needs. These two people bring to this relationship their own socialization experiences, their own individual psychic systems, and their idiosyncratic needs, expectations, and ways of loving, giving, and receiving. To be successful in marriage they must fuse their individual psychic systems into one, while at the same time each must maintain his and her own identity and individuality. To do this well, both partners need to agree on and adjust to new roles, a somewhat difficult task. Much of the conflict found in marriages and families is caused by people losing their own identities (or being confused about them). We saw an example of this in the case of Anne (see Chapter 2), who felt considerable conflict over being "just" a housewife and mother and wanted to get a job so that she could feel worthwhile and of value.

If marriage requires psychological adjustments and adaptations, the birth of children requires even greater change. For one thing, there are two additional roles to fulfill, those of mother and father. However, the need for personal identity and individuality never changes. How an individual functions as a mother or father is influenced by childhood relationships with parents, by personality development, and by individual needs, feelings, and goals, all subject to change as the individual passes through the life cycle. As a unit each family joins the diverse backgrounds and traits of its members to develop habitual patterns of functioning and coping with life stresses. Each family also develops needs, values, and goals. Like the individual, each family will develop specific behavioral patterns that it uses to achieve its goals, to meet its needs, and to adhere to its values. At the same time the family, just as the individual, must deal with events that threaten its equilibrium (e.g., a child being unjustly picked on at school, an illness of one of its members). As long as the family can satisfactorily function, equilibrium can be maintained. To keep equilibrium, each family develops a homeostatic process. Riskin (1963) supports this view, stating:

The family is viewed as an ongoing system. It tends to maintain itself around some point of equilibrium which has been established as the family evolves. The system is a dynamic, not a static, one. There is a continuous process of input into the system, and thus a tendency for the system to be pushed away from the equilibrium point. . . . Over a period of time, the family develops certain repetitive, enduring techniques, or patterns of interaction for maintaining its equilibrium when confronted by stress. This development tends to hold whether the stress is internal or external, acute or chronic, trivial or gross. Those techniques, which are assumed to be characteristic for a given family, are regarded as homeostatic mechanisms.

Family as a system

A family can be easily understood as a system. Olsen (1968) defines a system very clearly:

A social system is a model of social organization that possesses a distinctive total unit beyond its component parts, that is distinguished from its environment by a clearly defined boundary whose subunits are at least partially interrelated within relatively stable patterns of social order. Put even more simply, a social system is a bounded set of interrelated activities that together constitute a single entity.

The concept of the family as a system implies that a change in one member brings about a corresponding change in the rest of the system, in this case the other members. Each member has a different role and function. The quality of the functioning of any overall system depends on the functioning of the largest subsystem. In the case of the family, this is the marital pair. The marriage is the heart of the family, and all other subsystems revolve around it. It is the basis for understanding the organizational structure of the family as well as the dynamic interaction of its members. The family system also develops rules and procedures to keep it organized and to guide it in fulfilling its purpose and functions. There are dynamic forces, emotional exchanges, that govern the emotional and affectional atmosphere of the family.

To understand a family's structure and functioning, we look at its communication and interaction patterns.

Family in crisis

All families experience upsetting events, and all of them have some degree of strength to cope with the stress. However, some upsetting events produce a crisis in some families and not in others. Goldstein and Giddings (1973) state:

A crisis-proof family must have agreement in its role structure, satisfaction of the physical and emotional needs of its members, and goals toward which the family is moving collectively. Having all of those, the family is adequately organized and has crisis-meeting resources. Lacking them, the family is inadequately organized, and likely to prove vulnerable to crisis-precipitating events. If a family has deficiencies in crisis-meeting resources, they will tend to experience and define hazardous circumstances as crisis.

While Goldstein and Giddings place a great deal of the responsibility for a family developing crisis on its structure, we should realize that the development of any crisis, family or individual, does not depend solely on the strength of the family or individual. It depends on the subjective meaning of the event. This means that any family or person has the potential to develop a crisis if the right event occurs, regardless of strength. As stated in Chapter 1, crisis theory confirms human vulnerability to stress. History is replete with examples of people overcoming the greatest of hardships only to succumb to the most common events.

A family in crisis is defined as a functionally debilitated family system. The crisis is precipitated by its reaction to some event perceived to be so dangerous to its existence or to its equilibrium that it is unable to fulfill its functions or to meet the needs of its members. Consequently the family's reaction to the event leaves the members feeling helpless and unable to function as effectively as they did before the event. Although in a family crisis each member is affected individually and each member's method of coping varies, it is the threat to total family functioning that is the major focus. Family crises develop from two basic sources: external and internal events. External precipitating events are natural catastrophes, death, illness, the birth of a handicapped child, and so forth. External events, as a rule, do not tear the family apart emotionally as do internal events, although they can. In most cases external events cause the family to band closer together. However, the crisis is caused by the family's perception and interpretation of the event as being dangerous to its existence as a unit, and it lacks the capacity and resources to adequately handle the situation. Internal precipitating events are those that are caused by one or more members of the family. They threaten the internal functioning, emotional equilibrium, or values, goals, or existence of the family as an integral unit. Examples of internal precipitating events are the mental illness of a member, changes in role relationships and status, an adolescent running away, a child leaving home, infidelity, the introduction of a new member to the family system, and so forth. The field of family therapy is based on internal precipitating events. Although we have classified precipitating events of family crises, it should be emphasized that any event can precipitate a crisis in the family if it is perceived to be dangerous to its existence or to its internal functioning.

Treatment of family in crisis

Crisis as a family problem. The first step in family crisis treatment is to clearly establish that the problem is a family problem. Regardless of the precipitating event and who appears to be responsible, it has to be clearly understood that the precipitating event affects all of the family members. This means that all family members capable of contributing to family functioning should be included in the session. Sometimes a parent or older child will say, "It's Mike with the problem, so why do I have to come?" The answer, of course, it that it is a family problem, affecting all the members and how they are getting along with each other and carrying out their responsibilities. If very young children are not contributing to or reacting to the crisis, they may be left out of subsequent sessions. Most families in crisis are eager to participate. They may have felt a great deal of self-blame and guilt long before they appear for help. Once the crisis is perceived to be a family problem, the next step for the therapist is to rapidly establish a constructive relationship with the family. This means that the therapist relates positively to each member at the same time that the members may be competing with each other for the therapist's support.

It is important for each family member to feel that the therapist is an ally. Hence the therapist must present himself or herself as a helping person to all. This requires considerable skill, especially in families with a definite political power structure. The therapist has to guard against over-identifying with one member. In some agencies for runaway adolescents, for example, therapists tend to overidentify with the adolescent to the point that the parents are often alienated. In child guidance clinics some parents' self-blame keeps them from perceiving the part their children play in the family problem.

Focus on precipitating event and identify problem for family. While the family is gathering, the therapist watches their seating arrangments, looking for possible significant patterns. Once the family is gathered, the task of the therapist is to elicit and encourage the expression of whatever affect or emotion is present. If none is present at the time, the therapist can begin by discussing the precipitating event. If discussing the precipitating event brings out feelings, each member should be encouraged to ventilate them before pursuing the precipitating event further. The therapist should pay particular attention to who speaks first and how that is determined. He or she should observe the members' different perspectives, especially if there are differences between mother and father or parent and child. In addition the therapist should get everyone's views and reactions.

Generally, the family will respond differently to external precipitating events than to internal ones. As previously stated, they tend to band together and are probably easier to work with as a total unit. In such cases the therapist must understand how the event is perceived by each family member. Consequently he or she should get everyone's view and reaction. Individual family members may react to the reaction of other family members and not specifically to the event itself. This is especially true of children. If the family crisis is precipitated by the loss of a loved one and all family members are not grieving appropriately, the therapist should elicit and encourage those who are not to express painful feelings. It should be remembered that family crises precipitated by external events pose a threat to family existence as a unit as well as the threat to love relationships and affectional tendencies. Consequently, eliciting and encouraging the expression of painful feelings and the meaning of the event to each family member is a major therapeutic task.

Internal precipitating events caused by a family member that threaten family equilibrium and functioning are more complex and require the therapist to intervene in the family's patterns of interaction. Consider the following example:

■ Mr. and Mrs. Sargent brought their 16-year-old son John to the crisis center for help before they put him out of the home. The problem was precipitated by John physically attacking his mother for not letting him have the car. Mr. Sargent stated that John's attacking his mother was a sign that he was dangerous and had a "screw loose." John and his mother have not gotten along for the past 3 years. Since John received his driver's license, the relationship between him and his mother has grown destructively worse. However, this was the first time that he had physically attacked her.

In a case like this, what is the real precipitating event? We know that on the surface it was John not being able to get the car. Did John's mother provoke him beyond his capacity to not react? What was there about this situation that was so threatening to the family system that the parents wanted to handle it by removing John if he could not continue to function as expected in spite of his movement toward independence? As we can see, a family crisis can be precipitated when habitual patterns of functioning are threatened. Although a family is an organized system, within its structure it must have room for change. John's movement toward independence was a threat to the family equilibrium. His parents were not ready for change. A family must be ready for change in the dynamic interrelationships and roles of its members brought on by the life cycle. The precipitating event provides significant clues to the nature of family functioning.

Determine nuclear problem. The next step in working with the family in crisis is to determine the nuclear problem. In the case of the Sargent family we know that something happened that was extremely significant to John, since this was the first time he had ever attacked his mother. A discussion of feelings and events leading up to the precipitating event can help to illuminate the nuclear problem. Was his mother trying to maintain her control over John? Was she angry at her husband? What is the nature of their relationship? Is John being used to hide a poor marital relationship threatened by his impending emancipation? These questions and others are answered as the family members talk and communicate with each other. As the session progresses, the focus of the family moves from the precipitating event to intrafamilial feelings, behavior, and interactions.

It is by looking at the family communication process and interactions that the family is understood and the nuclear problem is manifested. As the therapist observes and listens he or she discovers the nuclear problem, that is, the underlying cause of the family's crisis.

Assess and evaluate family structure and functioning. As with working with the individual in crisis, assessment and evaluation of the family begins with the first contact. By now the therapist has a wealth of information on which to base assessment and evaluation. This phase properly begins with identifying family structure. This is important for evaluating the family's potential for fulfilling its purpose and functions. Generally, family structure consists of a mother, father, and one or more children. A crisis can be precipitated by a threat to family structure such as the introduction of a new member or the loss of a member. The single-parent family is vulnerable to the development of a crisis because of a deficit in structure. It is deprived of a resource that generally gives strength and support to family structure. The strength of family structure is determined by how each member fulfills functions and roles. In this regard the heart of family functioning is the marriage. The therapist assesses the contribution of the marital relationship to the family crisis. What is the relationship between husband and wife? Are they together or disunited and competitive? A divided family cannot be a strong family. Is the marriage an unwillfully dominate and submissive relationship? Revolving around the marital relationship are the functions and roles of the children. What are the children's roles and expectations individually and collectively? Are they perceived as respected individuals, or are they used by one or both parents? If so, how and in what way? For example, is one a scapegoat who is keeping the family from total disintegration? What is the nature of feelings and emotional atmosphere in the family? What is the nature of the communication process? How does each member feel about the others and about the relationship of others in the family? What needs are being met in the family? What needs are not being met, and how are members reacting to unmet needs? In sum, the assessment and evaluation of the family requires the evaluation of the family as a total unit and of each individual's contribution to its total functioning. The therapist needs to answer such questions in order to know the degree of debilitation and what areas of family functioning have been affected. Furthermore, it identifies areas of weakness requiring treatment and sources of strength that can be used to help reestablish equilibrium and strengthen family functioning. Synthesizing this information enables the therapist to formulate a dynamic explanation of the causes of the family crisis.

Provide family with self-understanding. By this time some of the upset should be reduced, and the therapist can move to cognitive restoration. In this phase the crisis therapist will give the family an explanation of the cause and reasons for the family crisis. He or she should identify the positive aspects of the family functioning and the negative ones, as revealed in how they communicate. He also can identify various role assignments, their consequences, and why they are no longer functional, thereby causing family conflict. Hence the therapist helps the family move toward new roles.

Plan and implement treatment. If the precipitating event involves a threat to overall functioning, the family must be helped to work through threats of its disintegration. For example, if the crisis is caused by the loss of a member on whom the family depended for survival, they must be helped to grieve as a group and individually. In all aspects of therapy with a family in crisis, the therapist must assess and use the strengths of the family. The therapist should identify a potential leader as a source of strength for reequalizing or reintegrating the family as a whole system. Every group, to be functional, must have a leader.

In the subsequent treatment sessions, the family as a group must agree to work together to continue to resolve the crisis, that is, to change roles, rules, and so forth, that will facilitate growth and restrengthening. If the precipitating event is a loss of a family member, then the task is to complete the grieving process and directly or indirectly delegate another family member to assume the unfilled roles and responsibilities. If the family crisis is a life cycle problem such as child leaving home or resistance to the emancipation of children, the family must be helped to cope with such a disequalizing event and to reintegrate in another acceptable fashion. By this time each member should be aware of his or her own significance and responsibility to the family. Family members then should be willing to compromise for the sake of the group.

Termination and follow-up. The family is ready for termination of therapy when the crisis is resolved and the family has returned to a precrisis level of functioning. It is to be hoped that they have learned a great deal about themselves as a family and individually and that they have also learned new ways to resolve problems. At the point of termination, the family should be advised that they will be contacted in a specific period of time (1 month, 3 months, 6 months) to learn how they are doing. This not only suggests an interest, but it also suggests that help is available if another crisis occurs. If the crisis is resolved but long-term therapy is indicated, referral should be made. The success of such a suggestion depends on how it is presented. After one to six sessions (or 1 to 6 weeks) with a family, the therapist has a great deal of knowledge about them. The way a referral is recommended should be based on this knowledge of why the referral is necessary and what it hopes to accomplish.

THE LIFE CYCLE

The life cycle is the maturational sequence that each person goes through during the normal passage from birth to death. Each phase in the cycle involves certain psychosocial tasks and adaptations to certain biological conditions. The phases are not discrete; there is some overlapping. The success achieved in each phase is related to the success attained in each previous phase. The common phases of the life cycle are shown in Fig. 2.

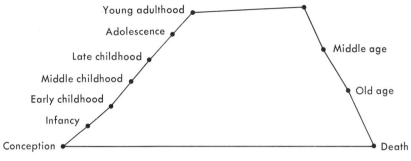

Fig. 2. Life cycle.

Erikson (1959) refers to each phase of the life cycle as a crisis:

Each stage becomes a crisis because incipient growth and awareness in a significant part function goes together with a shift in instinctual energy and yet causes specific vulnerability in that part. One of the most difficult questions to decide, therefore, is whether or not a child at a given stage is weak or strong. Perhaps it would be best to say that he is always vulnerable in some respects and completely oblivious and insensitive in others, but that at the same time he is unbelievably persistent in the same respect in which he is vulnerable.

Erikson is using the term *crisis* as a problem-solving process. However, the term is appropriate because of the vulnerability of people at various phases of the life cycle, particularly those that are turning points. Although a crisis can develop at any point in the life cycle, we will discuss three very vulnerable phases: adolescence, middle age, and old age.

According to the life cycle model, all that is needed to understand human behavior is to compare the behavior of the individual with the expected behavior of the appropriate phase of the person's life cycle according to chronological age. But chronological age is less important in understanding behavior than is the individual's emotional maturity. Chronological age provides only a baseline; it lets you know the adaptive task the person should be working on. In other words, a person's specific behavior and feelings indicate where he or she is *emotionally,* according to the life cycle model. If a middle-aged man feels and acts like an adolescent is expected to feel and act, adolescence is his emotional level. Of course, in mature psychic functioning the individual's feelings and behavior are reasonably consistent with position in the life cycle.

Adolescence

An adolescent in crisis creates a family crisis. At times the adolescent engages in crisis-producing behavior as a means of trying to restore family equilibrium. Consider the following example:

■ Sixteen-year-old Jack called the crisis center, requesting an appointment. When he was seen he said that he was distressed by the way that he was getting along with his mother. The conflict between the two was getting unbearable. She was always criticizing the work he did at home and school. He had no freedom to do the things that the rest of his friends did. For instance, he could not use the family car. She picked at him all of the time, and their relationship had begun to affect her marriage, since his father defended Jack when he was at home. The crisis therapist saw this as a family problem. She and Jack agreed that the whole family should be called in; however, the mother refused. Some 2 weeks later, Jack ran away. He was gone for a little over a month. As he kept on the move, he would call his dad or write a postcard letting him know that he was all right. After weeks of roaming around the nation, he went to his uncle's home in Florida. When his parents picked him up, they agreed to seek family treatment.

We will discuss some of the common problems of adolescence that cause crises for adolescents themselves. But before discussing the adolescent in crisis, let's review some characteristics of adolescent development to help distinguish between average expectable adolescent turbulence and the adolescent in crisis.

What is adolescence? Adolescence is the individual's total psychosocial reaction and adaptation to puberty. Puberty is the biological event of sexual maturation, during which full genital and reproductive maturity are reached. Adolescence generally begins around the age of 13 years and continues until full independence is achieved. Thus the conclusion of adolescence can vary considerably; it is not solely the function of chronological age. For example, the person who goes to work right after high school may be independent and assume adult responsibilities 4 years before someone who goes to college and remains dependent on his or her parents.

In general, the assumption of adult responsibilities marks the conclusion of adolescence as long as sexual maturation is complete. How adolescents develop in Western society is influenced by three factors: (1) biological and physical changes, (2) resultant changes in the psychic system, and (3) the social environment, specifically parents and the culture. We will briefly consider all three.

The onset of adolescence is marked by puberty, which in turn is manifested by the first appearance of secondary sex characteristics and marked physical changes and growth. Puberty in girls (which occurs earlier than in boys) involves the appearance of pubic hair, the enlargement of breasts and nipples, the growth of genitalia, and most significantly menarche (the first menstrual period). Most American girls reach puberty between the ages of 10 and 16 years. Engel (1962) states:

On the average, there is a lapse of two to four years after menarche before ovulation finally takes place and conception becomes possible. Full reproductive capacity in the girl is not achieved for another two to four years after ovulation has been initiated.

Engel's statement refers to a statistical average; girls as young as 11 years have borne children.

The onset of puberty in boys is marked by a rapid growth spurt, muscular development, voice change, genital growth, and appearance of pubic and facial hair. It occurs around the ages of 12 to 14 years, some 2 years later than in girls. However, boys' changes are very rapid, and their physical strength and growth in height generally occur very rapidly.

Throughout adolescence girls move toward emotional adulthood more quickly than boys. They are generally attracted to older boys rather boys of the same age. Each adolescent's pattern of internal growth is inconsistent. This often gives them the feeling of strangeness or awkwardness. As Blos (1962) states:

This lack of uniformity in physical development, called *asymmetrical growth,* often puts extreme demands upon the physical and mental adaptivity of the individual.

This asymmetrical growth not only makes it difficult for many adolescents to control their bodies, but it affects body image as well and influences the degree to which adolescents compete and make comparisons with their peers.

This is only a brief description of the human biological and physical changes that occur at the onset of puberty. These changes greatly affect the adolescent's psychic functioning, often making average expectable behavior turbulent and unstable. However, it is not solely physical changes and sexual maturation that make adolescence so difficult. The difficulty is also caused by changes in the psychic system.

Adolescent psychic system. By the time the child reaches adolescence, most of his or her growth and development have taken place. The child has had a wealth of experiences, all contributing bits and pieces to his or her psychic system. During the relative quiet periods of middle and late childhood, the psychic system has been integrating and solidifying an enormous amount of learning and achievement. The child has had a great many experiences in dealing with the social environment, specifically, in relating to peers, and the school and other institutions, generally with the support of parents. As stated earlier, human development is an evolutionary process in which the success of each phase depends on success in the preceding phases. Consequently the individual's ability to cope with adolescence basically depends on the degree of success during preceding phases of growth and maturation. But regardless of the quality of psychosocial development before adolescence, some conflict and problems are inevitable. The onset of adolescence in many ways dismantles and rearranges some of the parts of a psychic system that has been completed over a number of years. This system served the child well while growing up in a variable social environment. Now it must withstand the onslaught of adolescence, but not without some turbulence for all. However, this final renovation of the psychic system before adulthood offers the individual the opportunity to enter adulthood stronger and more capable. It also provides the opportunity to turn back if the individual is not quite ready, although the time that it takes to make the decision will vary from child to child.

The psychic system at adolescence is a mixture of strength, weakness, and potential. The ego is stronger than the child's because of experiences and cognitive development. A wealth of ego capacities have now completely matured (i.e., cognition, memory perception, mobility, and so forth). Special talents and abilities may show up. All this creates many new ways for the adolescent to cope with stress. But at the same time that the ego is stronger, adolescent needs and drives are also intensified. The adolescent sex drive and capacity have matured, giving an additional force to deal with. It is important that they be handled constructively. Pubescence makes adolescents biologically equal to their parents. This can have a far-reaching effect, depending on the relationship with the parents and the makeup of the psychic system. It is a basic struggle because the sexual drive and affectual needs are so strong; if the ego is not capable of handling them constructively, negative consequences can result, as we see in the increase in pregnancies among teenagers. In such cases the significance is not so much that the child had intercourse but that she got pregnant in this day of birth control pills and sex education in schools.

Another difficulty inherent in adolescence is the need for independence. This independence is facilitated by turning away in part from parents. Some of the ego strength already gained is reduced as the adolescent turns away from the reliable support of parents. After having internalized into his or her psychic system the love of parents, their experiences, values, and ways of perceiving and thinking, the only way the adolescent feels independent and like an adult is to feel and behave, to varying degrees, the opposite of parents. The length of time the child has spent depending on them and their closeness contribute to this end. As the adolescent turns away from parents, he or she loses a very valuable source of support and attempts to replace them with new people at the same time. This contributes to the adolescent's not knowing who he or she is. It may lead to the adolescent turning inward and becoming quite self-centered. At the same time that this change in ego support is going on, a change in the functioning of conscience is also going on. Recall that the conscience was internalized from the experiences with parents. The child learned right and wrong, good and bad, and moral values from them. When the adolescent turns away from parents, he or she also turns away from conscience. The conscience has also been an internal measure of parental approval and a component of self-esteem. Adolescents experience turning away from this similarly to the way they experience mourning; they may feel that they have lost a loved one. This accounts for the frequent feeling of depression, moodiness, and loneliness. The degree and extent of this depression depend on the degree of hostility previously developed toward the parents (Brenner, 1973). In understanding this, keep in mind that early relationships with parents form the basis of the development of the ego and conscience. During adolescence, memories of these early relationships are reactivated and the adolescent begins to react to them or defend against them. The greater the early hostility, the more difficult it is for the adolescent to deal with the original feelings that are now reactivated. Consequently the turning away from the parents is confused with aggression turned toward the self. The result of the hostility toward the self is depression. Whether it is a customary depression or a neurotic or psychotic depression, an adolescent's acting out or antisocial behavior combines the hostility originally directed toward the parents with other forms of disturbances.

The conscience functioning learned from parents is now temporarily abandoned. As a consequence, not only does the adolescent feel a loss of love, but he or she also feels a reduction in sources of control, evaluation, and prevention. This lets the adolescent engage in unusual or uncharacteristic behavior that ordinarily conscience would prevent. It is common for most adolescents to engage in some semidelinquent or rebellious behavior or behavior that is generally out of character or unexpected. However in Western society it seems that each adolescent must go through this to some degree in order to become relatively independent of parents, to begin to establish identity and become a responsible adult.

The whole adolescent process leads to adulthood and independent functioning. The helplessness of human beings, the lengthy time of dependency, and the resultant affectional bond all make the movement from childhood to adulthood a painful one in spite of the happiness associated with it. The child must work this out in his or her own way, and the decision to move toward adulthood causes ambivalence. Although the adolescent wants to be an adult, he or she also wants to be able to remain a child.

A wide range of adolescent behavior is considered to be average expectable (normal). There is danger, however, when an adolescent's ego is too weak to adequately handle emerging drives, specifically the sex drive. The adolescent can handle this in two harmful ways: (1) early marriage at the expense of prematurely resolidfying the psychic system, or (2) excessive use of repression (Blos, 1962). In getting married prematurely, the adolescent deprives himself or herself of certain dependency gratification and is thrust too quickly into adult responsibilities. The overly repressed adolescent is emotionally shallow, making it difficult for him or her to develop genuine interpersonal relationships and to be able to enjoy pleasures of life.

Even though adolescence is a turbulent phase, most adolescents enter adulthood with a reasonable chance of success. Specifically, the adolescent must emotionally emancipate himself or herself from family so that he or she can establish an identity. This means that the adolescent still loves his or her parents and needs their love but not in the dependent way characteristic of earlier childhood. It means also that he or she takes the wealth of socializing experiences and synthesizes them into a form that represents self, that allows the adolescent to say "I am" rather than "Who am I?" Second, the adolescent must begin to establish a personal identity and reintegrate an adequate functioning psychic system, must prepare for a vocation, and most must prepare for mature heterosexual relationships and to live or associate intimately with a person of the opposite sex.

Adolescence is an age of anxiety for parents as well as for the adolescent. To see a previously dependent child who was malleable and manageable become seemingly independent and rebellious is often painful for the parents. The child's lack of communication and turning away from the family can be quite an awakening for the parents. This awakening occurs on two levels. First, the parents begin to realize that they are growing older and that their child is becoming a young adult. This provokes their feelings about middle age and the speed with which their lives are passing. The greatest anxiety for parents, however, is facing their own unresolved adolescent feelings and conflicts, which are reactivated by their adolescent child. During their own adolescent years they may have been able to set aside their adolescent conflicts and struggles and achieve a certain amount of stability. However, the onset of their child's adolescent development, with all of its struggles and conflicts, reactivates the parents' old conflicts and their own struggles. The parents again need to repress their unresolved conflicts, which is generally manifested in rigid rules and regulations and renewed effort at maintaining control of the adolescent. It is also not unusual for parents to look on their adolescent child as their last chance for achievement and therefore push the child farther than he or she can or wants to go. The reactivation of the parents' adolescent struggles and conflicts can show up in many forms. The important fact is that it influences how the parents relate and react to the adolescent, which in turn creates considerable family upset.

Adolescent and society. The third important factor influencing the adolescent is society. In our society adolescence has been a phase held in abeyance. Unlike other societies, we have no initiation rites or rites of passage, although the driver's license and limited liquor privileges are efforts in that direction. Actually, society itself contributes heavily to adolescent conflict and struggles. For example, the process of sexual maturation is a universal phenomenon; however, the psychological reactions accompanying the physiological changes are influenced by societal expectations. The pressures of this period of transition create strong emotions that the adolescent must cope with in ways that conform to social conditions and expectations, or problems ensue. Although society does not help the adolescent through conflicts and struggles, he or she is still expected to emerge as a healthy and happy adult. The easiest way to cope with such demands and inconsistencies is to do the opposite of what is expected. If sexual inhibition is the problem, then sexual freedom is the solution. However, since sexual freedom is the opposite of sexual inhibition, it really is not a solution but the same coin turned over. At this point sex education in the school is not the answer because it deals with intellectual knowledge rather than emotional reactions.

The lengthy educational process fosters dependency and a patriarchal tradition. The inconsistencies and injustices in our society are also conducive to the adolescent's turning away from society and toward idealism. But real societies do not change easily, and the adolescent must learn to react constructively to the things he or she sees as wrong. To improve conditions, the adolescent must learn to adapt and at the same time to change what can be changed.

Adolescent in crisis. It is generally agreed that adolescence is a time of turbulence. However, we wish to distinguish between adolescence as an expectable phase of upset in which equilibrium is restored, even though with considerable difficulty, and a crisis as defined in this book. We are discussing an adolescent crisis as a problem that is so debilitating that outside intervention is warranted. As a rule an adolescent crisis is a family crisis, and generally the therapist should involve the adolescent's family for the best resolution. The exception, of course, could be some of the usual upset that the adolescent experiences at school, for which he or she goes to the school counselor for help. At the same time, some problems for which adolescents consult school counselors are real crises and should involve the family.

There are three types of adolescent crisis: (1) inability to cope with some developmental task, reflecting intrapsychic conflict or the consequence of adolescence (i.e., sexual problems, peer relationships, academic failure); (2) inability to adjust to or adapt to the rules, expectations, and demands of a social institution (i.e., school or the law); and (3) crisis precipitated by family relationships in which the adolescent attempts to handle the problem by behavior that threatens the functioning of the family, such as breaking a family rule or value by dating an unacceptable person, running away, or attempting suicide. Consider the following examples:

■ Alan, age 15, came to the crisis center on his own because he needed to talk with someone about a problem he was having. It was so personal that he did not want to talk to his parents about it. He had very few friends and no one else he could trust. He said that he was worried about the fact that he had an uncontrollable urge to masturbate and could not stop. He was so worried about it that he could no longer function. He felt depressed and felt that if his mother knew, she would be disappointed in him.

This was a rather benign problem, and Alan responded very well to psychological support, especially reassurance. Cognitive restoration involved relating his urge to masturbate with the degree of his feelings of loneliness. He responded very well and after five sessions had resolved his crisis and begun to make friends. (When adolescents have conflict over masturbation, it is most often the fantasies during the act that cause the conflict rather than the act itself (Blos, 1962).

■ David, age 15, was brought to the crisis center by his mother because he had been expelled from school for fighting. Although David's mother had called the child guidance clinic, he could not be seen there for 5 to 6 weeks. David's mother wanted to get him back into school immediately, but the school officials had said that they would not let David back in school until he had sought professional help. On this basis David's mother thought the situation to be an emergency. David had a history of fighting, and until now his academic performance had been a little above average. During the session David expressed the feeling that his fighting was caused by his peers picking on him and harrassing him. He was especially sorry that he had to miss shop because that was the one class in which he was successful.

In cases like David's (the acting-out adolescent) both the individual and the environment have to be assessed and evaluated quickly. A child who generally has to act out has two basic problems: (1) poor impulse control and judgment and (2) a feeling of being helpless or powerless to significantly influence or control the environment. Successful treatment in such cases requires intervention in both situations.

■ Beverly, 17, was brought to the emergency services of the mental health clinic after she made a suicide attempt by swallowing some aspirins. The act was precipitated by her parents' refusal to let her see her boyfriend, who was 8 years older than she. This relationship had been a source of conflict and trouble for several months. On this particular occasion Beverly was caught after she had sneaked out to see him. Her father slapped her several times, and both parents joined together in forbidding her to ever see him again.

What made this a crisis for Beverly? The answer is that it was a family crisis precipitated by Beverly's desperate effort to solve it in the most expedient way she could think of at the time. What really made it a crisis was that Beverly's behavior threatened the internal functioning of the family. A family with teenagers must be able to adapt to the impending change in family equilibrium. Furthermore, they must be able to tolerate the "empty nest." They must be able to adapt to the change in their own sexuality, which they are made aware of by their teenager's budding sexuality. The questions in Beverly's case are whether her behavior and involvement with this older man represented a serious deficit in her psychic functioning and whether she was trying to resolve some intrapsychic conflicts through this relationship. Adolescence is a time in which the person is still largely a child at the same time that he or she strives toward adulthood and independence. Sometimes adolescents need help in controlling their strong drives in order to constructively accomplish all of the developmental tasks. The family must be the source of help and support. However, if they are too threatened by the adolescent's behavior, they cannot help but make matters worse. At the same time, the adolescent crisis is very often a reflection of a deficit in family functioning or the result of a basic family problem. In cases like Beverly's, family therapy is indicated. After the crisis is resolved, referral for traditional treatment may be necessary.

Treatment of adolescent in crisis. Permission from a parent is generally required to treat adolescents. Adolescents who come for treatment hoping that their parents will not know about it should be informed of this requirement. Most often the treatment of an adolescent in crisis should be family crisis treatment, or it should involve both treatment of the adolescent individually and treatment of the family. In treatment of an adolescent individually and in the family the same procedures are used as discussed in Chapter 5. Treating the adolescent, however, requires a little different perspective. Consideration should be given to the fact that he or she is struggling with a conflict between dependency and independency. This means that the therapist must remain neutral, that is, not overidentify with the adults or with the adolescent. Naturally the therapist should feel very empathic toward the client, but a natural constructive relationship and an understanding of the client's psychic system and functioning should be the therapist's goals. No doubt the adolescent will initially assume that the therapist is on the side of adults, since he is one. However, the therapist cannot deny who he is and should not let the adolescent seduce him into anything other than understanding , accepting, and wanting to help. Being genuinely honest and natural is the best way to establish a constructive relationship with an adolescent.

After the beginning of a constructive relationship is in process, the therapist's intervention should be guided by several goals in working with the adolescent in crisis. The first is to think in terms of reinforcing the adolescent's ego functioning so he or she can more constructively handle problems and conflicts, internal as well as external. This can initially be done through supportive techniques and causal connecting statements. If it appears that the adolescent has not learned and grown from this experience, referral for traditional therapy is indicated. In Beverly's case, did she learn from her crisis experience a way other than suicide to resolve problems? Did she learn about herself so that she can evaluate reality better?

Second, the therapist actively facilitates reality testing. This means that he or she has to help the adolescent appropriately distinguish subjective reality from objective reality, often by pointing out the difference. Adolescents are generally quite receptive to inconsistencies in their own thinking if it is considered in a supporting and understanding relationship.

Third, the therapist should work toward becoming a respected source of support, an alternate ego and conscience for the adolescent. This is done by gaining his or her respect through support, fairness, and neutrality. Finally, the therapist must help the adolescent become responsible for behavior by cognitive restoration. In so doing, the therapist's interpretation of the psychological meaning of the behavior should come after a constructive relationship has been reasonably well established and in the context of the crisis. Extra caution should be used when an adolescent's self-esteem has been seriously damaged. Because the line between average expectable adolescent upset and adolescent pathology is often blurred, careful evaluation of the psychic system should be done.

Middle-age crisis

During young adulthood (21 to 40 years of age) most people function in a relatively stable and satisfactory manner, building over a period of some 20 years mechanisms to facilitate such functioning. Most have a family organization that has offered support and reinforcement. As individuals approach middle age, however, many of these stable conditions begin to change. It is the changes brought on by the human maturational process that make this phase of life potentially crisis producing. The first of these changes that a middle-aged individual must adapt to is the psychological awareness of aging. Signs of aging (balding, the need for bifocals, a tendency toward overweight, a greater propensity to tire, and a longer time to recover) begin to show. Also, contemporaries begin to die, often unexpectedly of heart attacks. Certainly illness is more frequent. This awareness of the aging process causes the individual to become more conscious of self, resulting in a great deal of introspection and self-evaluation. The changes of middle life require adjustments. As we have seen, many middle-aged parents do not want this change. Changes in status or occupation can be another source of crisis. This was reflected in the case of John, who was transferred to Arizona after 24 years in the same city with the same company. The woman whose adult life has been spent raising a family is especially prone to middle-age crisis. In effect she is forced into early retirement. For some women menopause is a critical event, especially for those whose reproductive functions fulfilled multiple purposes. While there are physical discomforts associated with menopause, it is generally believed that they do not per se cause psychological debilitation. Neugarten (1975) did a cross-sectional study of menopause and concluded:

> This is not to say that the menopause is a meaningless phenomenon in the lives of women; nor that biological factors are of no importance in adult personality. Instead these comments are intended to point out: (1) that the menopause is not necessarily the important event in understanding the psychology of middle-aged women that we might have assumed it to be from a biological model or from psychoanalytic theory—not as important, seemingly, as illness, or even as worry over possible illness that might occur in one's husband rather than in oneself; (2) that the timing of the biological event, the climacterium—at least to the extent that we could perceive it—did not produce order in our data; and (3) above all, that psychologists should proceed cautiously in assuming the same intimate relationships between biological and psychological phenomena in adulthood that hold true in childhood.

There have been some reports of menopause in men. If we consider the literal meaning of menopause, that is, the ceasation of child-bearing capacity, there is no male menopause. However, some men may need to compensate for a feeling of sexual decline by either increasing their sexual activities or getting involved with other women. This situation often produces a crisis for the wife or the family more than for the individual, although a crisis can be produced by an individual's conflict over two loves. This was illustrated in the case of Rosemary (see Chapter 2), whose husband Frank resolved his conflict by committing suicide.

In sum, middle age is more a state of mind than a physical change such as adolescence. Again, it is the reaction to the changes of middle age that produces a crisis.

A middle-age crisis can manifest itself in any of the ways that has been discussed thus far, in the individual or the family. Treatment proceeds on the same basis as set forth in Chapter 5.

Old-age crisis

At no other time in the life cycle does the human being have more to adjust to in order to maintain equilibrium than does the aged individual in the United States. First, he or she has to adjust to retirement and the loss of all of the psychic values and benefits of an occupation, that is, status, self-esteem, and feelings of worth, not to mention economic benefits. For many this change is experienced as a loss. For others it is an eagerly awaited event that nevertheless requires a great deal of adjustment. The elderly individual has to adjust to physical changes, including a decrease in strength and an increase in illness. At some point he or she will probably have to adjust to the loss of a love one, leaving him or her feeling alone and lonely. Consider the following case:

■ Mrs. Paulus, a 68-year-old widow, came to the crisis clinic to "get help with her depression." She was neatly dressed and very well groomed. Her posture was good, with no motor retardation. There was no present sign of depression. She stated immediately that she was a great believer in therapy and that it had benefited several friends of hers. She specifically asked for a "compassionate objective friend." She stated that she had never had psychiatric treatment before but now needed help to cope with this "aloneness and loneliness."

For the aged person to adjust and maintain equilibrium, he or she must be able to find a sense of self-worth. The individual may have to deal with a reversal of roles; for example, many elderly people become dependent on their children. Perhaps the aged person's greatest fear is not of death but of becoming dependent on children. All of these conditions tend to make the elderly feel afraid and confused. To counteract these feelings, they must have adequate coping mechanisms. When they do not, a crisis develops. Consider the following case:

■ Mrs. White, a 69-year-old woman, referred herself to the crisis center because she wanted help with her "ups and downs." She stated that she was "exceedingly low" today since she was so worried about her daughter. She thought that she was trying to live her life through her daughter, and she came for help to "stop doing that."

Treatment. Although the basic procedures set forth in Chapter 5 apply to treating the aged, several variations are necessary for most effectivencss. First, it should be recognized that much of the elderly person's behavior is designed to counter the painful feelings of ego loss and impoverishment. Some of these coping mechanisms are constructive, others are not. They must be understood, including which ones are being used and how and the purpose they serve. The elderly person must be helped to counteract these feelings with constructive coping mechanisms. Sometimes intervention in the environment can aid this process also. The major intervention technique with the aged should be psychological support. The focus should be on the individual's reaction to the stress or precipitating events causing the reaction. Third, the therapist should try to stimulate the individual's interest in social activities, especially those that enable the individual to be intellectually active. This may be difficult for the elderly person who is depressed and feels hopeless. Fourth, as a person grows older, relatives and significant others are very important. Environmental support should be assessed and used at every opportunity.

Finally, the aged person should not be treated as a dependent child. The therapist's interaction should be one of respect and acceptance of the individual's capacity.

REFERENCES

Blos, P. *On adolescence: a psychoanalytic interpretation.* New York: The Free Press, 1962.

Brenner, C. *An elementary textbook of psychoanalysis.* New York: International Universities Press, 1955.

Engel, G. L. *Psychological development in health and disease.* Philadelphia: W. B. Saunders, 1962.

Erikson, E. H. Identity and the life cycle. *Psychological Issues, 1959, 1* (1). (Monograph).

Freud, Anna. *The ego and the mechanisms of defense* (Rev. ed.). New York: International University Press, 1966. (Originally published, 1936.)

Goldstein, S., & Giddings, J. Multiple impact therapy: an approach to crisis intervention with families. In G. A. Spector & W. L. Clarborn (Eds.), *Crisis intervention.* New York: Behavioral Publications, 1973.

Neugarten, B. L. Adult personality: toward a psychology of the life cycle. In W. Sze (Ed.), *Human life cycle.* New York: Jason Aronson, 1975.

Olsen, M. *The process of social organization.* New York: Holt, Rinehart and Winston, 1968.

Riskin, J. Methodology for studying family interaction. *Archives of General Psychiatry,* 1963, 8, 343-388.

SUGGESTED READINGS

Ackerman, N. W. *The psychodynamics of family life: diagnosis and treatment of family relationships.* New York: Basic Books, 1958.

Blos, P. *The young adolescent.* New York: The Free Press, 1970.

Butler, R. N., & Lewis, M. I. *Aging and mental health: positive psychosocial approaches* (2nd ed.). St. Louis: C. V. Mosby, 1977.

Freud, A. Adolescence as a developmental disturbance. In W. Sze (Ed.), *Human life cycle.* New York: Jason Aronson, 1975, pp. 245-250. (Reprinted from G. Caplan & S. Lebovicis. (Eds.), *Adolescence: psychosocial perspectives.* New York: Basic Books, 1969.)

Gitelson, M. The emotional problems of elderly persons. *Geriatrics,* 1948, 3(3), 135-150.

Langsley, D. G., & Kapland, D. M. (Eds.). *The treatment of families in crisis.* New York: Grune & Stratton, 1968.

Peck, R. Psychological development in the second half of life. In W. Sze (Ed.), *Human life cycle.* New York: Jason Aronson, 1975.

Satir, V. M. *Conjoint family therapy: a guide to theory and teaching.* Palo Alto, Calif.: Science and Behavior Books, 1964.

Summary and conclusion

This book provides a relatively comprehensive perspective of working with people in crisis, based on the premise that the more knowledge and understanding a therapist has, the more effective he or she can be with skills and individual creativity. Accordingly, considerable focus is given to a functional definition of crisis and the premise of crisis theory. Since the natures of the social environment and the human being make perfect living impossible, states of upset are routine occurrences of everyday living. Hence one of the purposes of the socialization process is to prepare the individual to adapt and cope with states of upset as he or she pursues personal happiness and life goals. It follows therefore that a crisis, as used in this book, is more than just being upset. It is being so overwhelmed with emotions that one is not able to function as effectively as he or she did before the crisis, thereby needing the assistance of another.

Since one cannot fail to function, the crisis therapist must intervene before ineffective functioning becomes a habitual pattern of dysfunctioning, commonly called psychopathology. Since the events that precipitate crises in some people are common problem-solving conditions for others, it is believed that a systematic approach to understanding human behavior will enable the crisis therapist to know why some people develop a crisis and others do not. Consequently, much emphasis is placed on the socialization process and psychic development. During the process of psychic development adaptation patterns and specific forms of coping mechanisms are developed. These are discussed as an integral part of social functioning. To prepare the crisis therapist with the most important medium through which he or she applies knowledge and skills, communication theory and process are presented. This is the bridge between theory and techniques. The techniques of intervention presented are not limited to working with people in crisis but are applicable to all therapeutic intervention. However, the crisis therapist must use them more rapidly and in a shorter period of time. In Chapters 6 and 7 common reactions to crisis conditions are discussed in an effort to expand on the content in Part I. Some special crisis situations are presented, that is, suicidal behavior, homicidal behavior, and rape. The final chapter touches on the family in crisis and on some common life cycle crises, that is, adolescence, middle age, and old age.

It is my hope that the content of this book will contribute to enhancing the knowledge, skill, and effectiveness of those who work with people in crisis. More important, I hope that a comprehensive approach to the individual in crisis will result in more than a "stop for first aid" philosophy that characterizes current crisis theory. Although the temporal limits of crisis theory can be followed, the crisis therapist should devote time and research to learning to do as much as possible to strengthen and resolidify the functioning of the individual in crisis. It is believed that crisis treatment can move beyond the goal of restoring the individual to a precrisis level of functioning.

Bibliography

Ackerman, N. W. *The psychodynamics of family life*. New York: Basic Books, 1958.

Adler, F. *Sisters in crime*. New York: McGraw-Hill, 1975.

Aguilera, D. C., & Messick, J. M. *Crisis intervention: theory and methodology* (3rd ed.). St. Louis: C. V. Mosby, 1978.

Applebaum, R. L., et al. *Fundamental concepts in human communication*. San Francisco: Canfield Press, 1973.

Apsler, R., & Hoople, H. Evaluation of crisis intervention services with anonymour clients. *American Journal of Community Psychology*, 1976, 4(3), 293-302.

Atherton, C. R., Mitchell, S. T., & Biehl Schein, E. Locating points for intervention. *Social Casework*, 1971, 52(3), 131-141.

Atkins, R. W. Psychiatric emergency service. *Archives of General Psychiatry*, August 1967, 17(2), 176-182.

Bach-y-Rita, G., Lion, J. R., Ailment, C. E., & Ervin, F. R., Episodic dyscontrol: a study of 130 violent patients. *American Journal of Psychiatry*, 1971, 127(11), 1473-1478.

Baker, M., Dorzab, J., Winokur, G., & Cadoret, R. J. Depressive disease: classification and clinical characteristics. *Comprehensive Psychiatry*, July 1971, 12(4), 354-365.

Barinbaum, L. Identity crisis in adolescence: the problem of an adopted girl. *Adolescence*, 1974, 9(36), 547-553.

Barman, A. *Helping children face crises*. New York: Public Affairs Committee, Inc., 1976. Special edition, August 1976, pp. 1-24.

Beck, J. E. & Worthen. Precipitating stress, crisis theory and hospitalization in schizophrenia and depression. *Archives of General psychiatry*, 123-29. 1972, 26,

Beers, T. M., Jr., & Foreman, M. E. Intervention patterns in crisis interviews. *Journal of Counseling Psychology*, 1976, 23(2), 87-91.

Belanger, R. R. CPI predictors of clinical effectiveness of volunteers in a suicide and crisis intervention service. I. Factor measures of stability and extraversion. II. A clinical effectiveness scale. *Dissertation Abstracts International*, January 1973, *33*(7B), 3297-3298.

Bellak, L., & Small, L. *Emergency psychotherapy and brief psychotherapy*. New York: Grune & Stratton, 1965.

Bernstein, L., & Bernstein, R. *Interviewing: a guide for health professionals*. New York: Appleton-Century-Crofts, 1974.

Bessell, R. *Interviewing and counseling*. London: B. T. Batsford, 1971.

Bibring, E. The mechanism of depression. In P. Greenacre (Ed.), *Affective disorders: psychoanalytic contributions to their study*. New York: International Universities Press, 1953.

Bieber, I. Homosexual dynamics in psychiatric crisis. *American Journal of Psychiatry*, April 1972, *128*(10), 1268-1272.

Biestek, F. P. *The casework relationship*. Chicago: Loyola University Press, 1957.

Blanck, G., & Blanck, R. *Ego psychology: theory and practice*. New York: Columbia University Press, 1974.

Blaufard, H., & Levine, J. Crisis intervention in an earthquake. *Social Work*, July 1972, *17*, 16-19.

Bloom, B. L. Definitional aspects of the crisis concept. In H. J. Parad (Ed.), *Crisis intervention: selected readings*. New York: Family Service Association of America, 1965, pp. 303-311.

Blos, P. *The young adolescent*. New York: The Free Press, 1970.

Blos, P. *On adolescence: a psychoanalytic interpretation*. New York: The Free Press, 1962.

Bonier, R. J. Research in crisis intervention: methodological problems. *Proceedings of the 76th Annual Convention of the American Psychological Association*, 1968.

Bowerman, C. E., & Elder, G. H., Jr. Variations in adolescent perception of family power structure. *American Sociological Review*, August 1964, 29(4), 551-567.

Brammer, L. M., & Shostrom, E. L. *Therapeutic Psychology*, Englewood Cliffs, N.J.: Prentice-Hall, 1977.

Brenner, C. *An elementary textbook of psychoanalysis*. New York: International Universities Press, 1973.

Brill, N. I. *Working with people: the helping process*. Philadelphia: J. B. Lippincott, 1973.

Brodsky, C. Social psychiatric consequences of job incompetence. *Comprehensive Psychiatry*, November 1971, *12*(6), 526-536.

Brody, S. *Signs of disturbance in the first year of life*. Presented at the 1957 Annual Meeting in a Panel on Child Development Problems (J. A. Rose, Chairman).

Buell, B. Interviews, interviewers and interviewing. *The Family*, May 1925, 6(3), 86-90.

Burgess, A. W., & Holmstrom, L. L. *Rape: victims of crisis*. Bowie, Md.: Robert Y. Brady, 1974.

Butler, R. N. Crises and contributions in later life. *American Journal of Orthopsychiatry,* 1967, *37*(2), 337-338.

Butler, R. N., & Lewis, M. I. *Aging and mental health: positive psychosocial approaches* (2nd ed.). St. Louis: C. V. Mosby, 1973.

Cadoret, R. J., Winokur, G., & Clayton, P. J. Family history studies. VI. Depressive disease types. *Comprehensive Psychiatry,* March 1971, *12*(2), 148-155.

Calhoun, L. G., Selby, J. W., & King, H. E. *Dealing with crisis.* Englewood Cliffs, N.J.: Prentice-Hall, 1976.

Caplan, G. Practical steps for the family physician in the prevention of emotional disorder. *Journal of the American Medical Association,* 1959, *170*(13), 1497-1506.

Caplan, G. Emotional crisis. *Encyclopedia of Mental Health,* 1963, 2, 521-532.

Caplan, G. *Principles of preventive psychiatry.* New York: Basic Books, 1964.

Caplan, G. (Ed.). *Prevention of mental disorders in children.* New York: Basic Books, 1961.

Caplan, G. *An approach to community mental health.* New York: Grune & Stratton, 1961.

Carkhuff, R. R., & Berenson, B. G., *Beyond counseling and therapy* (2nd ed.). Holt, Rinehart and Winston, 1977.

Carnes, E. F., & Robinson, F. P. The role of client talk in the counseling interview. *Educational and Psychological Measurement,* 1948, *8*, 635-644.

Cherry, C. *On human communication.* New York: John Wiley & Sons, 1978.

Cohen, S., & Walder, L. O. An experimental analog derived from crisis theory. *American Journal of Orthopsychiatry,* October 1971, *4*(5), 822-829.

Coleman, J. V. The initial phase of psychotherapy. *Bulletin of the Menninger Clinic,* November 1949, *13*(6), 189-197.

Community mental health and social psychiatry: a reference guide. Cambridge, Mass.: Harvard University Press, 1962.

Cook, L., & Cook, T. D. Evaluating the rhetoric of crisis: a case study of criminal victimization of the elderly. *Social Service Review,* December 1976, *50*(4), 632-645.

Cottle, W. C. Personal characteristics of counselor. *Personnel and Guidance Journal,* April 1953, *31*(7), 445-449.

Cox, J. Drug crisis intervention in America: where it all went. *Journal of Drug Issues,* Fall 1976, *6*(4), 407-410.

Darbonne, A. Crisis: a review of theory, practice and research. In J. Fischer (Ed.). *Interpersonal helping: emerging approaches for social work practice.* Springfield, Ill.: Charles C Thomas, 1973, pp. 237-252.

Davitz, J. R. Fear, anxiety and the perception of others. *Journal of General Psychology, 1959, 61,* 169-173.

DeBurger, J. E. Marital problems, help-seeking, and emotional orientation as revealed in help-request letter. *Journal of Marriage and the Family,* November 1967, *29*(4), 712-721.

Decker, J. B., & Stubblebine, J. Crisis intervention and prevention of psychiatric disability: a follow-up study. *American Journal of Psychiatry,* December 1972, *129*(6), 101-105.

Delworth, U., Rudow, E. H., & Laub, J. *Crisis center/hotline.* Springfield, Ill.: Charles C Thomas, 1972.

Dinoff, M., Finch, A. J., Clements, C. B., & Hodeo, G. L. Testing clinical judgment during crisis. *Psychological Reports,* 1970, 26(1), 181-182.

Dixon, S. L. *Dynamics of human behaviors: an ego psychology perspective.* Unpublished manuscript.

Doob, L. W. A Cyprus workshop: intervention methodology during a continuing crisis. *The Journal of Social Psychology,* February 1976, *98*(first half), 143-144.

Duckworth, G. L. A project in crisis intervention. *Social Casework,* 1967, *48*(4), 227-231. *Educational and Psychological Measurement,* April 1948, 8, 635-644.

Ellis, A. New approaches to psychotherapy techniques. *Journal of Clinical Psychology,* July 1955, *11*(3), 208-260.

Ephrain, N. Using videotapes in crisis intervention. *Social Casework,* June 1975, *56*(6), 357-361.

Erikson, E. H. Identity and the life cycle. *Psychological Issues,* 1959, *1*(1). (Monograph)

Erikson, E. H. *Childhood and society,* New York: W. W. Norton, 1963.

Errera, P., McKee, B., Smith, D. C., & Gruber, R. Length of psychotherapy. *Archives of General Psychiatry,* October 1967, *17*(4), 454-458.

Evans, J. *Living with a man who is dying.* New York: Taplinger Publishing, 1971.

Farberow, N. L. Crisis, disaster and suicide: theory and therapy. In E. S. Shneidman (Ed.), *Essays in self-destruction.* New York: Science House, 1967.

Fast, I. The process of vocational choice as a precipitant of personality change. *Psychotherapy: Theory, Research and Practice,* December 1968, 5(4), 268-271.

Feifel, H., & Ells, J. Patients and therapists assess the same psychotherapy. *Journal of Consulting Psychology,* 1963, 27(4), 310-318.

Fenichel, O. *The psychoanalytic theory of neurosis.* New York: W. W. Norton, 1945.

Fischer, J. (Ed.). *Interpersonal helping: emerging approaches for social work practice.* Springfield, Ill.: Charles C. Thomas, 1973.

Fisher, S. A. *Suicide and crisis intervention.* New York: Springer Publishing, 1973.

Flint, A. A., Jr. Crisis in Marriage: reification or Reality? *American Journal of Orthopsychiatry,* 1968, *38*(3), 560-564.

Forer, B. The therapeutic value of crisis. *Psychological Reports,* August 1963, *13*(1), 275-281.

Fox, S. S., & Scherl, D. J. Crisis intervention with victims of rape. *Social Work,* January 1972, *17,* 37-42.

Freeman, H. L., & Roy, R. G. Some comparative studies of psychiatric emergencies. *Comprehensive Psychiatry,* May 1971, *12*(3), 208-216.

Freud, A. Adolescence as a developmental disturbance. In W. Sze (Ed.), *Human life cycle.* New York: Jason Aronson, 1975, pp. 245-250. (Reprinted from G. Caplan & S. Lebovici (Eds.), *Adolescence: psychosocial perspectives.* New York: Basic Books, 1969.)

Freud, A. *The ego and the mechanisms of defense* (Rev. ed.). New York: International Universities Press, 1966. (Originally published, 1936.)

Freud, S. (1923). *The ego and the id* (Standard ed.). London: Hogarth Press, 1961.

Freud, S. Mourning and melancholia. In *Collected papers.* London: Hogarth Press, 1946, *4,* 152-170.

Freud, S. *The problem of anxiety.* New York: W. W. Norton, 1936.

Fromm-Reichmann, F. *Principles of intensive psychotherapy.* Chicago: University of Chicago Press, 1950.

Galdston, R., & Hughes. M. C. Pediatric hospitalization as crisis intervention. *American Journal of Psychiatry,* 1972, *129*(6), 721-725.

Gattozzi, A. A. Death and bereavement: a cross-ethnic study of attitudes and behavior. *Mental Health Program Reports,* 1972, *6,* 48-65.

Getz, W. L., Altman, D. C, Berleman, W. C, & Allen, D. B. Paraprofessional crisis counseling in emergency room. *Health and Social Work,* May 1977, *2*(2), 57-73.

Getz, W. L., Fujita, B. N., & Allen, D. The use of paraprofessionals in crisis intervention. *American Journal of Community Psychology,* June 1975, *3*(2), 135-144.

Gillman, R. D. Brief psychotherapy: a psychoanalytic view. *The American Journal of Psychiatry,* December 1965, *122*(1), 601-611.

Gitelson, M. The emotional problems of elderly persons. *Geriatrics,* May-June 1948, *3,* 735-750.

Glasser, P. H., & Glasser, L. N. (Eds.). *Families in crisis.* New York: Harper & Row, 1970.

Golan, N. Crisis theory. In F. J. Turner (Ed.), *Social work treatment: interlocking theoretical approaches.* New York: The Free Press, 1974, pp. 420-456.

Golan, N. When is a client in crisis? *Social Casework,* July 1969, *50*(7), 389-394.

Golan, N., & Gruschka, R. Integrating the new immigrant: a model for social work practice in transitional states. *Social Work,* April 1971, *16*(2), 82-87.

Goldberg, S. B. Family tasks and reactions in the crisis of death. *Social Casework,* July 1973, *54*(7), 398-405.

Goldstein, A. P. *Maximizing the initial psychotherapeutic relationship.* Presented at the Ninth Emil A. Gutheil Memorial Conference of the Association for Advancement of Psychotherapy, New York, November 3, 1968, pp. 1-22.

Goldstein, A. P. *Therapist-patient expectations in psychotherapy.* New York: Macmillan, 1962.

Gray, B., Nida, R. A., & Coonfield, T. J. Empathic listening test: an instrument for the selection and training of telephone crisis workers. *Journal of Community Psychology,* April 1976, *4*(2), 199-205.

Hamburg, D. A., & Adams, J. E. A perspective on coping behavior. *Archives of General Psychiatry,* September 1967, *17*, 277-284.

Hammer, E. F. (Ed.). *Use of interpretation in treatment: technique and art.* New York: Grune & Stratton, 1968.

Hankoff, L. D. Adolescence and the crisis of dying. *Adolescence,* Fall 1975, *10*(39), 373-389.

Hartmann, H. *Essays on ego psychology.* New York: International Universities Press, 1964.

Hartmann, H. Ego psychology and the problem of adaptation. *Journal of the American Psychoanalytic Association,* 1958. (Monograph Series, No. 1.)

Hartmann, H. *Notes on the reality principle.* Presented at the Freud Centenary Sessions of the Hampstead Child Therapy Clinic, London, May 4, 1956.

Hellman, D. S., & Blackman, N. Enuresis, fire-setting and cruelty to animals: a triad predictive of adult crime. *American Journal of Psychiatry,* 1966, *122*, 1431.

Henderson, H. E. Helping families in crisis: police and social work intervention. *Social Work,* July 1976, *21*(4), 314-315.

Hertzler, J. O. Crises and dictatorships. *American Sociological Review,* April 1940, 5(2), 157-170.

Horton, P. C. Normality:toward a meaningful construct. *Comprehensive Psychiatry,* January 1971, *12*(1), 54-66.

Hurrich, M. On the concept of reality testing. *International Journal of Psychoanalytics,* 1970, *51*, 299-312.

Jacobson, G. F. Crisis intervention from the viewpoint of the mental health professional. *Pastoral Psychology,* 1970, *21*(203), 21-28.

Jacobson, G. F. Some psychoanalytic considerations regarding crisis therapy. *Psychoanalytic Review,* Winter 1967, *54*(4), 93-98.

Jacobson, G. F. Crisis theory and treatment strategy: some socioculture and psychodynamic considerations. *Journal of Nervous and Mental Disease,* 1965, *141*(2), 209-218.

Jacobson, G. F., Strickler, M., & Morley, W. Generic and individual approaches to crisis intervention. *American Journal of Public Health and the Nation's Health,* February 1968, 58(1), 338-343.

Kadushin, A. *The social work interview.* New York: Columbia University Press, 1972.

Kahn, R. L, & Cannell, C. F. *The dynamics of interviewing.* New York: John Wiley & Sons, 1957.

Kalis, B. L., Harris, M. R., Prestwood, A. R., & Freeman, E. H. Precipitating stress as a focus in psychotherapy. *Archives of General Psychiatry,* September 1961, 5(3), 27-34.

Kaplan, D. M. A concept of acute situational disorder. *Social Work,* April 1962, 7(2), 15-23.

Kennedy, J. F. Maternal reactions to the birth of a defective baby. *Social Casework,* July 1970, 51, 410-416,

Kerns, F. Planned short term treatment: a new service to adolescents. *Social Casework,* June 1970, 51(6), 340-346.

Kin, L. E. The clergyman's use of mental health resources. *Pastoral Psychology,* April 1970, 21(203), 53-56.

Klein, D. C., & Lindemann, E. Preventive intervention in individual and family crisis situations. In Caplan, G. (Ed.), *Prevention of Mental Disorders in Children.* New York: Basic Books, 1961, pp. 283-305.

Kubler-Ross, E. *Death: the final stage of growth.* Englewood Cliffs, N.J.: Prentice-Hall, 1975.

Kubler-Ross, E. *On death and dying.* New York: Macmillan, 1969.

Langsley, D. G., & Kapland, D. M. (Eds.). *The treatment of families in crisis.* New York: Grune & Stratton, 1968.

Laughlin, H. P. *The ego and its defenses.* New York: Appleton-Century-Crofts, 1970.

Laughlin, H. P. *The neuroses.* Reading, Mass.: Butterworths, 1967.

LaVietes, R. L. Crisis intervention for ghetto children. *American Journal of Orthopsychiatry,* October 1974, 44(5), 720-727.

Lester, D. & Brockopp, G. W. *Crisis intervention and counseling by telephone.* Springfield, Ill.: Charles C Thomas, 1973.

Levin, S. Some suggestions for treating the depressed patient. *The Psychoanalytic Quarterly,* 1965, 34, 37-65.

Levy, J. M., & McGee, R. K. Childbirth as crisis: a test of Janis's theory of communication and stress resolution. *Journal of Personality and Social Psychology,* 1975, 31(1), 171-179.

Lewis, A. J. Brief psychotherapy in the hospital setting: techniques and goals. *Psychiatric Quarterly,* 1973, 47(3), 341-352.

Lifschutz, J. E. A brief review of psychoanalytic ego psychology. *Social Casework,* January 1964, 45(1), 3-9.

Lindemann, E. Symptomatology and management of acute grief. In H. J. Parad, (Ed.), *Crisis intervention: selected readings.* New York: Family Service Association of America, 1965, pp. 7-21. (Reprinted from *American Journal of Psychiatry,* September 1944, 101(2), 141-148.)

Lindemann, E. The meaning of crisis in individual and family. *Teacher College Record,* February 1956, *57,* 310.

Linden, L. L., & Breed, W. The demographic epidemiology of suicide. In E. S. Shneidman (Ed.), *Suicidology: Contemporary Developments.* New York: Grune & Stratton, 1976, pp. 70-98.

Lipman-Blumen, J. A crisis framework applied to macro-sociological family changes: marriage, divorce, and occupational trends associated with world war. *Journal of Marriage and the Family,* November 1975, *37*(4), 889-901.

Lowy, F. H., Wintrob, R. M., Borwick, B., Garmaise, G. & King, H. O. A follow-up study of emergency psychiatric patients and their families. *Comprehensive Psychiatry,* January 1971, *12*(1), 36-47.

Luce, G. Why adolescents kill themselves. *Mental Health Program Reports,* 1970, *4,* 53-67.

MacDonald, J. M. Homicidal threats. *American Journal of Psychiatry,* 1967, *124*(4), 475-482.

Mackey, R. A. Crisis theory: its development and relevance to social casework practice. *The Family Coordinator,* July 1968, *17*(3), 165-173.

MacKinnon, R. A., & Michels, R. *The psychiatric interview in clinical practice.* Philadelphia, W. B. Saunders, 1971.

Malecki, J. J. Life history approach to the study of crisis in religious life. *Dissertation Abstracts International,* June 1970, *30,* 12-B-5693.

Maloney, E. The subjective and objective definition of crisis. *Perspective in Psychiatric Care,* 1971, *9,* 257-268.

Mannino, F. V., & Shore, M. F. Family structure, aftercare, and post hospital adjustment. *American Journal of Orthopsychiatry,* January 1974, *4*(1).

Mausner, J. S., & Steppacher, R. C. Suicide in professionals: a study of male and female psychologists. *American Journal of Epidemiology,* November 1973, *98*(6), 436-445.

May, R. *The meaning of anxiety.* New York: Ronald Press, 1950.

McCombie, S. L., Bassuk, E., Saritz, R., & Pell, S. Development of a medical center rape crisis intervention program. *American Journal of Psychiatry,* 1976, *133*(4), 418-421.

McGee, R. K. *Crisis intervention in the community.* Baltimore, Md.: University Park Press, 1974.

McGuire, M. T. The process of short-term insight psychotherapy. II. Content, expectation and structure. *Journal of Nervous and Mental Disorders,* 1965, *41* (2), 219-230.

Meldman, M. J. New medical model for psychiatric diagnosis. *Comprehensive Psychiatry,* January 1971, *12*(1), 82-92.

Mendels, J. *Concepts of depression.* New York: John Wiley & Sons, 1970.

Menninger, K., with Martin, M., & Pruyser, P. *The vital balance: the life process in mental health and illness.* New York: Viking Press, 1963.

Messer, A. A. Mechanisms of family homeostasis. *Comprehensive Psychiatry,* July 1971, *12*(4), 380-388.

Miller, K., & Iscoe, I. The concept of crisis: current status and mental health implications. *Human Organization,* Fall 1963, 22(3), 195-200.

Mirabile, C. S., Houck, J. H., & Glueck, B. C., Jr. Computer prediction of treatment success. *Comprehensive Psychiatry,* January 1971, *12*(1), 48-53.

Moore, J. The child client. *Social Work Today,* October 1976, 8(3), 13-15.

Morley, W. E. Theory of crisis intervention. *Pastoral Psychology,* April 1970, *21*(203), 14-20.

Morley, W. E., Messick, J. M., & Aguilera, D. C. Crisis: paradigms of intervention. *Journal of Psychiatric Nursing,* November-December 1967, 5(6), 531-544.

Morrice, J. K. W. *Crisis intervention: studies in community care,* Elmsford, N.Y.: Pergamon Press, 1976.

Myrick, H. L. Psychological processes in interviewing. *The Family,* March 1926, 7(1), 25-29.

National Institute of Mental Health. *The child's emotions: how physical illness can affect them.* U.S. Department of Health, Education and Welfare, pp. 1-6.

Nebl, N. Essential elements in short-term treatment. *Social Casework,* June 1971, 52(6), 377-381.

Nelson, Z. P., & Mowry, D. D. Contracting in crisis intervention. *Community Mental Health Journal,* 1976, *12*(1), 37-44.

Neugarten, B. L. Adult personality: toward a psychology of the life cycle. In W. Sze (Ed.), *Human life cycle.* New York: Jason Aronson, 1975.

Olsen, M. *The process of social organization.* New York: Holt, Rinehart and Winston, 1968.

Oppenheimer, J. R. Use of crisis intervention in casework with the cancer patient and his family. *Social Work,* April 1967, *12*(2), 44-52.

Parad, H. J. (Ed.). *Crisis intervention: selected readings.* New York: Family Service Association of America, 1965.

Parad, H. J. Brief ego-oriented casework with families in crisis. In H. J. Parad & R. Miller (Eds.), *Ego-oriented casework.* New York: Family Service Association, 1963, pp. 145-164.

Pasewark, R. A., & Albers, D. A. Crisis intervention theory in search of a program. *Social Work,* March 1972, *17*(2), 70-79.

Paul, L. Treatment techniques in a walk-in clinic. *Hospital and Community Psychiatry,* February 1966, *17*(2), 49-51.

Paul, L. Crisis intervention. *Mental Hygiene,* January 1966, 50(1), 141-165.

Paul, T. W., & Turner, A. J. Evaluating the crisis service of a community mental health center. *American Journal of Community Psychology,* 1976, 4(3), 303-308.

Peck, R. Psychological development in the second half of life. In W. Sze (Ed.), *Human life cycle.* New York: Jason Aronson, 1975.

Pincus, A., & Minahan, A. *Social work practice: model and method*. Itasca, Ill.: F. E. Peacock Publishers, 1973.

Porter, R. A. Crisis intervention and social work models. *Community Mental Health Journal*, 1966, *2*(1), 13-26.

Pretzel, P. W. The role of the clergyman in suicide prevention. *Pastoral Psychology*, April 1970, *21*(203), 47-52.

Prichard, E. R., Collard, J., Orcutt, B. A., Kutscher, A. H., Seeland I., & Lefkowitz N. (Eds.), *Social work with the dying patient and the family*. New York: Columbia University Press, 1977.

Rada, R. T. (Ed.). *Clinical aspects of the rapist*. New York: Grune & Stratton, 1978.

Radeoff, L. Sex differences in depression: the effects of occupation and marital status. *Sex Roles*, 1975, *1*(3), 249-265.

Rangell, L. Discussion of the intrapsychic process and its analysis: a recent line of thought and its current implications. *International Journal of Psychoanalysis*, 1970, *51*, 195-209.

Rapoport, L. Crisis intervention as a model of brief treatment. In R. W. Roberts & R. H. Nee (Eds.), *Theories of social casework*. Chicago: University of Chicago Press, 1970, pp. 267-311.

Rapoport, L. The state of crisis: some theoretical considerations. In H. J. Parad (Ed.), *Crisis intervention: selected readings*. New York: Family Service Association of America, 1965, pp. 22-31.

Rapoport, L. Working with families in crisis: an exploration in preventive intervention. *Social Work*, July 1962, 7(3), 48-56.

Rapoport, L. The concept of prevention in social work. *Social Work*, January 1961, *6*, 3-12.

Rappoport, R. Normal crisis, family structure and mental health. *Family Process*, March 1963, 2(1), 68-80.

Raskind, M. A., Alvarez, C., Pietrzyk, M., Westerlund, K., & Herlin, S. Helping the elderly psychiatric patient in crisis. *Geriatrics*, June 1976, *31*(6), 51-56.

Rhine, M. W., & Mayerson, P. Crisis hospitalization within a psychiatric emergency service. *American Journal of Psychiatry*, 1971, *127*(10), 1386-1391.

Roberts, R. W., & Nee, R. H. *Theories of social casework*, Chicago: University of Chicago Press, 1970.

Rogers, C. R. Necessary and sufficient conditions of therapeutic personality change. *Journal of Consulting Psychology*, April 1957, *21*(2), 95-103.

Rosen, V. H. The initial psychiatric interview and the principles of psychotherapy: some recent contributions. In Wolberg, L. R. (Ed.), *The technique of psychotherapy*. New York: Rune & Stratton, 1954, pp. XIV; 869.

Rubinfine, D. Notes on a theory of depression. *The Psychoanalytic Quarterly*, 1968, *37*, 400-417.

Rueveni, U. Network intervention with a family in crisis. *Family Process,* 1975, *14*(2), 193-203.

Rusk, T. N. Opportunity and technique in crisis psychiatry. *Comprehensive Psychiatry,* May 1971, *12*(3), 249-263.

Rusk, T. N., & Gerner, R. H. A study of the process of emergency psychotherapy. *American Journal of Psychiatry,* 1972, *128*(7), 882-886.

Sanchez-Craig, M. B. Cognitive and behavioral coping strategies in the reappraisal of stressful social situations. *Journal of Counseling Psychology,* 1976, *23*(1), 7-12.

Satir, V. M. *Conjoint family therapy.* Palo Alto, Calif.: Science and Behavior Books, 1964.

Saul, L. J. *Psychodynamically based psychotherapy,* New York: Science House, 1972.

Saul, L. J., & Wenar, S. Early influences on development and disorders of personality. *Psychoanalytic Quarterly,* July 1965, *34,* 327-389.

Schachtel, E. G. *Metamorphosis on the development of affect, perception, attention, and memory.* New York: Basic Books, 1959.

Schulberg, H. C., & Shelton, A. The probability of crisis and strategies for preventive intervention. *Archives of General Psychiatry,* May 1968, *18,* 553-559.

Selig, A. L. Crisis theory and family growth. *The Family Coordinator,* July 1976, *25*(3), 291-294.

Shaffer, J. W., Nussbaum, K., & Lewis, S. M. Psychiatric assessment for documentary evidence. *Comprehensive Psychiatry,* November 1971, *12*(6), 564-571.

Shapiro, R. L. The origin of adolescent disturbances in the family: some considerations of theory and implications for therapy. *Family Therapy and Disturbed Families,* Palo Alto, Calif.: Science and Behavior Books, 1967, pp. 221-238.

Shneidman, E. S., & Farberow, N. L. (Eds.). *Clues to suicide.* New York: McGraw-Hill, 1957.

Shoenfeld, L. S., Preston, J., & Adams, R. L. Selection of volunteers for telephone crisis intervention centers. *Psychological Reports,* 1976, *39*(3), 725-726.

Shonee Cavan, R. Unemployment: crisis of the common man. *Marriage and Family Living,* May 1959, *21*(2), 139-146.

Sifneos, P. Crisis psychotherapy. In J. Masserman (Ed.), *Current psychiatric therapies* (Vol. 6). New York: Grune & Stratton, 1966.

Smith, L. L. A review of crisis intervention theory. *Social Casework,* July 1978, *59*(9), 396-405.

Smith, L. L. A general model of crisis intervention. *Clinical social work journal,* 1976, *4*(3), 162-171.

Spaulding, R. C., Edwards, D., & Fichman, S. The effect of psychiatric hospitalization in crisis. *Comprehensive Psychiatry,* 1976, *17*(3), 457-460.

Speers, R. W. *Brief psychotherapy with college women: technique and criteria for selection*. Presented at the 1960 Annual Meeting in a joint session with the Mental Health Section, American College Health Association, pp. 1-11.

Spitz, R. A. *Hospitalism: an inquiry into the genesis of psychiatric conditions in early childhood: the psychoanalytic study of the child*. New York: International Universities Press, 1945, *1*, 53-74.

Steppacher, R. C., & Mausner, J. S. Suicide in male and female physicians. *Journal of the American Medical Association*, April 1974, 228(3), 323-328.

Stricker, G. Implications of research for psychotherapeutic treatment of women. *American Psychologist*, January 1977, 32(1), 14-22.

Strickler, M. Applying crisis theory in a community clinic. *Social Casework*, March 1965, *46*(3), 150-154.

Sullivan, H. S. *The psychiatric interview*. New York: W. W. Norton, 1954.

Susser, M. *Community psychiatry: epidemiologic and social themes*. New York: Random House, 1968.

Sze, W. (Ed.). *Human life cycle*. New York: Jason Aronson, 1975.

Taplin, J. R. Crisis theory: critique and reformulation. *Community Mental Health Journal*, March 1971, 7(1), 13-21.

Trojanowicz, R. C., & Dixon, S. L. *Criminal justice and the community*. Englewood Cliffs, N.J.: Prentice-Hall, 1974.

Truax, C. B. The effective ingredients in psychotherapy: an approach to unraveling the patient-therapist interaction. *Journal of Counseling Psychology*, Fall 1963, *10*(1), 256-263.

Truax, C. B., & Carkhuff, R. R. *Toward effective counseling and psychotherapy*. Chicago: Aldine, 1967.

Verwoerdt, A. Death and the family. *Medical Opinion and Review*, September 1966, *1*(12), 38-43.

Walker, W. J. Neurocirculatory asthenia. In F. C. Massey (Ed.), *Clinical cardiology*. Baltimore: Williams & Wilkins, 1953, pp. 1033-1053.

White, R. W. Ego and reality in psychoanalytic theory. *Psychological Issues*, *3*(whole no. 11), 1963.

Whitlock, G. E. The pastor's use of crisis intervention. *Pastoral Psychology*, April 1970, 21(203), 37-45.

Williams, W. V., Lee, J., & Polak, P. R. Crisis intervention: effects of crisis intervention on family survivors of sudden death situations. *Community Mental Health Journal*, 1976, *12*(2), 128-136.

Wolberg, L. R. *Short-term psychotherapy*. New York: Grune & Stratton, 1965.

Yahraes, H. The rural nurse as a crisis counselor. *Mental Health Program Reports* January 1070, *4*, 281-290.

Yano, B., Alexander, L., & Kuwanoe, C. Crisis intervention: a guide for nurses. *Journal of Rehabilitation*, September-October 1976, 42(5), 23-26.

Index